WHO A
OLD, NEW, AND TIMELESS ANSWERS
FROM CORE TEXTS

*Selected Papers from the Fourteenth Annual Conference
of the Association for Core Texts and Courses
Plymouth, Massachusetts
April 3–6, 2008*

**Edited by
Robert D. Anderson
Molly Brigid Flynn
J. Scott Lee**

University Press of America,® Inc.
Lanham · Boulder · New York · Toronto · Plymouth, UK

Copyright © 2011 by
University Press of America,® Inc.
4501 Forbes Boulevard
Suite 200
Lanham, Maryland 20706
UPA Acquisitions Department (301) 459-3366

Estover Road
Plymouth PL6 7PY
United Kingdom

Library of Congress Control Number: 2010935140
ISBN: 978-0-7618-5371-8 (paperback : alk. paper)
eISBN: 978-0-7618-5372-5

Table of Contents

We the People: A Noble Experiment

The Core and the Core of Persons

Contents

Introduction

When we, the conference organizers, began thinking almost three years ago about the theme for the fourteenth ACTC conference, we knew we wanted something apropos of its location in Plymouth, Massachusetts. Like the pilgrims coming to the New World, we come to liberal education with a firm grasp on principles, an imperfect grasp on our goals and futures, and many uncertainties about how best to proceed. Like the pilgrims' commitment to live true to their creed, our commitment to core texts, courses, and programs is both a minority effort now out of fashion and an old effort stretching back through the millennia. Just as the pilgrims were challenged by an unfamiliar place, so also we as teachers find ourselves and our students challenged by what we are unaccustomed to – whether in the form of perennial wisdom, an intellectual tradition, a cultural heritage, an aesthetic object, or a voice on the margins. Ultimately, we decided on a theme dealing with our full identity as human beings – thinkers, lovers, professionals, family members, citizens, religious believers, global villagers, moderns, post-moderns, and, of course, educators. So, we asked ACTC members to reflect on answers to the question "Who are we?" and, as they always do, they responded with a multitude of insightful and provocative answers from core texts. In fact, they responded with the largest conference to that point.

So, what answers to "Who are we?" are readers in store for? Before getting to the answers by authors, we call attention to the obvious answer that we, as editors, are quite mindful of.

An obvious answer to "Who are we?" is that we are a free association of members able and willing to foster liberal education. This free association is evident in all that ACTC does, from conferences to publications. As a largely volunteer organization, ACTC has no cadre of paid employees to produce these *Selected Papers*. Nor are there publishing elves that can be pressed into service.

Nor can a few editors do alone all that is needed. Instead, the publication of this volume rests on the goodwill and commitment of many others who cherish the genuine good that is found in ACTC. For the seventy submissions to this volume, we thank all their authors, who made the competition for inclusion stiff and agonizingly difficult to adjudicate. For their help in the blind review process, we thank our thirteen readers from six different institutions. They are Peggy Pittas, Lyndall Nairn, Kevin Doyle, Khalil Habib, Mary Mumbach, Fr. Roger Corriveau, Fr. Barry Bercier, Montague Brown, Fr. John Fortin, Joseph Spoerl, Kevin Staley, Max Latona, and Tom Larson. For her yeoman's work in copy-editing this volume, we thank Jean-Marie Kauth. For her generous and gracious help as production editor, we thank Peggy Herron. Finally, for their sage advice on how to gain some speed in the production of this volume, especially in the decision-making on the acceptance of papers, we thank our good friends at Benedictine University who produced the 2006 *Selected Papers*.

While this volume, like all books, progresses linearly from front cover to back, its thematic geometry is better imagined as several concentric circles rather than as a straight line. At the center of this volume – its core – is the section *The Core and the Core of Persons*. In this section we have gathered essays on literary and philosophical accounts of who we are simply as persons, without focusing on the political, communal, historical, or vocational situations that further shape our identities. Enclosing this central section are the second and fourth sections, both of which highlight the person as entwined with other persons and examine who we are in light of communal ties. The first of these two enclosing circles includes essays on the Western experience of democracy, and the second of these two enclosing circles includes essays reflecting on how community informs who we are more generally. Two circles mark the limits of this volume: the first and last sections. In both, authors either explore or display who we are as a result of more external structures. Our historical position in a modern or post-modern, urbanized or disenchanted world is the theme shared by all papers included in the first section. Finally, as addressed by the theme of the fifth section, we at ACTC are educators who model the intellectual life for others by showing them how to read texts carefully and with sophistication.

These five themes, the answers given by our authors to the question of our conference, find their parallels in the pilgrims of Plymouth. Who were they? They were, in their historical moment, moderns forced to leave the old behind; they were democrats; they were individual human persons living in intense communion with others, family and friends. Finally, like ACTC, the pilgrims were determined to face together an unsure future with old but fresh wisdom that springs eternally and from texts that repay every visit.

Those with good memories will recall that Hugh Page did not deliver the included plenary paper in Plymouth. In fact, he delivered it at the 2006 conference in Chicago. With its inclusion here, we have departed from tradition, but we did so with good reason. Hugh Page describes well the plate-spinning act that academics perform as administrators, scholars, and teachers. Because his paper speaks so poignantly to us as academics and to the various in-house threats to the engagement of the mind and heart in liberal learning, we decided to publish a profound reflection on liberal education as profession and as vocation in our volume and to kick off our final section with his contribution.

Readers familiar with ACTC and other volumes of *Selected Papers* will recognize the name and scholarship of Phillip R. Sloan, from the University of Notre Dame. Professor Sloan's last presidential address can be found here in these pages, evincing the same scholarly thought and the same love for liberal arts education using core texts that he exhibited for six years as President of ACTC. The editors of this volume wish to express on behalf of the Board and membership of ACTC their gratitude and respect for the leadership, dedication, ardor, and care that he showed during his term as President.

Our hope is that this volume might have the salutary effect on readers that previous ACTC papers have had on us. Perhaps a paper will entice someone to read or teach a familiar work afresh or a new work for the first time. Perhaps another will produce an admiring exclamation – "I wish I had written that!" – and inspire a contribution to a future conference. Perhaps these papers will give the secret delight that only a good book, read perhaps in a favorite place, can bring. Perhaps they will refuel someone's desire to understand and share understanding with students. Such is our hope.

Robert D. Anderson
Saint Anselm College

Molly Brigid Flynn
Assumption College

J. Scott Lee
Executive Director
Association for Core Texts and Courses

The Contemporary Predicament

Paideia in a Post-Darwinian World: Reconnecting Education and Biology

Phillip R. Sloan
University of Notre Dame

In this, the sixth address I have made from my position as President, I wish to engage us in some more theoretical issues as a way of reflecting on the conference theme of "Who Are We? Old, New, and Timeless Answers From Core Texts." In my previous addresses, I have considered such issues as the role of liberal education in the research university, the challenge of technology, the expansion of our enterprise to an international and even non-western venue, and, just last year, the changes in the idea of education in the period which formed the thought of Thomas Jefferson. The theme this year suggests that we give some consideration to questions of self-identity and how our mission might differ from that of other associations dedicated to general and liberal education. My reflections have been stimulated by reading in manuscript from the important documentary history of the liberal arts, *Voices from the Liberal Arts*, edited and organized by last year's plenary speaker, Professor Bruce Kimball of Ohio State University. This work will be published jointly by ACTC and the University Presses of America, and I have used it with his permission.

I open with a quote from Jean-François Lyotard's *The Post-Modern Condition: A Report on Knowledge*, which was drawn to my attention by my colleague in the Program of Liberal Studies, Felicitas Munzel, in her forthcoming major study of Kant's theory of education. Discussing knowledge in "computerized" societies, he comments:

Our working hypothesis is that the status of knowledge is altered as societies enter what is known as the postindustrial age and cultures enter what is known as the postmodern age.... These technological transformations [created by computerization] can be expected to have a considerable impact on knowledge.... It is reasonable to suppose that the proliferation of information-processing machines is having, and will continue to have, as much of an effect on the circulation of learning as did advancements in human circulation.... The nature of knowledge cannot survive unchanged within this context of general transformation. It can fit into the new channels, and become operational, only if learning is translated into quantities of information. We can predict that anything in the constituted body of knowledge that is not translatable in this way will be abandoned and that the direction of new research will be dictated by the possibility of its eventual results being translatable into computer language.... Along with the hegemony of computers comes a certain logic, and therefore a certain set of prescriptions determining which statements are accepted as 'knowledge' statements.... Knowledge is and will be produced in order to be sold, it is and will be consumed in order to be valorized in a new production: in both cases, the goal is exchange. Knowledge ceases to be an end in itself. It loses its "use-value." (3-5)

Although these lines were originally written in French nearly twenty years ago, the prescience with which Lyotard characterizes the world in which our students are now in fact living – dominated by e-mail, Facebook, YouTube, multi-tasking, Google, and other dimensions of electronic communication – highlights the challenge that we as educators concerned with some traditional conception of liberal education face.

Bruce Kimball's documentary history and his other recent writings describe an emerging "consensus" model in American higher education – what he terms *a Pragmatic model* – with the designation *pragmatic* intended to imply underlying philosophical foundations that are indebted to that specifically American school of philosophy associated with the names of Chauncey Wright, Charles Saunders Pierce, John Dewey, and William James. This analysis is placed within a familiar historical framework which accepts an initial impact of Pragmatism on American philosophy and educational thought, followed by a period of decline and reaction, and then a resurgence of its importance with the development of "neo-Pragmatism" since the 1970s, which has now strongly entered educational theory. This thesis was first put forth in the lengthy essay "Toward Pragmatic Liberal Education" in 1994 by Kimball and commented on by a group of educators. In its wake it generated a considerable literature of response, both supportive and critical. I recommend to those interested in this debate the symposium edited by Robert Orrill under the title *Education and Democracy*.[1] To characterize this "pragmatic" model, in "Naming Pragmatic Liberal Education" Kimball listed, in a subsequent brief restatement of his position, seven defining features which carry in practice a normative character:

first, become multi-cultural; second, elevate general education and integration, rather than specialization; third, promote the commonweal and citizenship; fourth, regard all levels of education as belonging to a common enterprise; fifth, reconceive teaching as stimulating learning and inquiry; sixth, promote the formation of values and the practice of service; seventh, employ assessment. (47)

The wide-ranging controversy that these proposals generated I will not attempt to summarize except on one point.[2] This point concerns Kimball's claim that this collection of properties is built upon a more fundamental philosophical position. Critics have denied that there is any such definable unifying position in American liberal education, or they have argued that other unifying theoretical positions could work as well – e.g., post-modernism. But I am willing to grant for the sake of this argument Kimball's strong claim here as a descriptive truth and to see what implications it has for our conception of core text education.

As Kimball would define the "pragmatic" foundation, it is used by him to differentiate it from the underlying projects of the two main traditions he characterized in his well-known work on the history of liberal education, the first, the tradition of education that emphasized "oratory" skills and that in the hands of the Romans gave rise to the classical *humanitas* education, devoted particularly to developing the skills of the trivium and the study of classics, and the second, the "philosophical" tradition, owing more to Greek sources, that pursued systematic inquiry into theoretical knowledge, logic, science and philosophy, and that sought synthesis and the attainment of theoretical ends.[3] Kimball's argument is that a more recent "pragmatic" model has come to supplant particularly the oratory tradition, whereas the philosophical tradition has given us the tradition of the research university.

Several of the seven characteristics Kimball uses to define "pragmatic" liberal education are, I am sure, familiar to most everyone in the audience. If your experience is like my own, I am hearing more and more about the need for assessment, for student-centered learning, for the need to expand our vision to include diverse cultural traditions and life experiences; we are asked to offer greater justification of the practicality of liberal arts degrees; questions are raised about the necessity of reading classical authors as a central component of liberal education. But those not familiar with Kimball's discussions have likely not seen a formal label placed on this conjunction of characteristics as defining a natural kind built upon a specific philosophical position.[4]

Drawing upon Kimball's characterization of pragmatic liberal education and on some of the documents that he cites in support of this claim in his documentary history, one can make some more general philosophical points regarding this approach to liberal education. It emphasizes experiment over stability; inquiry into deeper metaphysical issues is eschewed in favor of an approach that seeks workability and consensus formation; it is a communally-oriented form of education rather than private, and leads, in Pierce's sense, over time to a "fixation of belief" through trial and error process rather than to the discovery of some transcendental truth; it does not begin from deeper foundations in episte-mology and metaphysics as founding assumptions upon which an educational theory is constructed, as we might find in Kant, for example; instead it begins from the interaction of the individual and environment; in the writings of John Dewey in particular, it was also oriented to satisfying the needs of the American democratic experience of post Civil-War America. But does it give any place to the study of the classic authors, to the works of the past, or to dead languages? Here the answer is much more ambiguous.

In our American educational history, we have collapsed together in varying blends aspects of the collegiate liberal arts tradition derived from a variety of sources – British, Scottish, Jesuit, and Protestant Reformist – with that of the German university that largely entered after the Civil War, and we still retain ideals of a broadly-based "collegiate" educational experience typically con-ducted in the first two years of undergraduate education, on which is built the disciplinary major that might lead to graduate or professional school for its completion. Our core programs exist somewhere in this mix of traditions. But the challenges many of our programs may feel either from aspects of what Kim-ball has defined as an emerging "pragmatic" consensus, or from the pressure of the graduate school and the research ideal, lead to some considerations I wish to explore in the rest of this paper.

To organize these reflections, I am going to take an unusual approach and tackle this issue by pursuing the relation of education to our biological being. This is not a new approach. Certainly there has been a long tradition that we can trace from Aristotle onward in which education and the formation of the human being is considered to have some intimate relation to our existence as rational animals, who are dependent on our biological being for the realization of human capacities, with the presumption that there is some internal *telos* in a human de-velopment toward knowledge. We find this reiterated in such early modern edu-cational theorists as Rousseau and in modern genetic epistemologists such as Jean Piaget. Connection of education and biology was a fundamental interest for John Dewey as we will explore below, and it is an important consideration of more recent educational theorists who identify themselves as pragmatist or neo-pragmatist.[5]

But a divorce of the biological from issues of most concern to rational hu-man existence is also well entrenched in modern thought and for understandable reasons. The notion of the "naturalistic fallacy" – the illegitimate inference from statements of empirical fact to propositions of value – is as old as Hume and was raised to new prominence by G.E. Moore in his critique of evolutionary ethics in 1905. It took another direction in the divorce of cultural from biological ap-proaches to anthropology emphasized by George Boas. It maintains its force in the critique by many philosophers of strong sociobiology.

Challenge to this sundering of the biological and the human has also come recently from individuals who are not known to be enamored with the naturalis-tic program to biologize all things human and who could not be considered ad-herents to philosophical pragmatism. In his *Dependent Rational Animals,* the neo-Aristotelian Alasdair MacIntyre's Carus Lectures for 1997, a series, I note, that began in 1925 with John Dewey's *Experience and Nature* lectures, MacIntyre decided he had himself been in error in his earlier *After Virtue* of 1981 in thinking that questions of ethics and moral purpose could be divorced from issues of our fundamental biology. As he argues in *Dependent Rational Animals:*

> [N]o account of goods, rules and virtues that are definitive of our moral life can be adequate that does not explain – or at least point us towards an explanation – how that form of life is possible for beings who are biologically constituted as we are, by providing us with an account of our development towards and into that form of life. (Preface x)

But if he is correct, as I think he is, that we cannot develop a coherent moral life, or a satisfactory educational theory, without some attention to the biological nature of who we are and who we educate, the crucial issue seems to be a determination of *what* that biology is. And we know we get a different answer from Aristotle and MacIntyre than we might get from Richard Dawkins, Francis Crick, and Stephen Pinker.

I will pursue this issue by asking us to begin with one of the great core authors whose writings appear in many of our programs, Charles Darwin. Next year marks the 200th anniversary of Darwin's birth and the 150th of the publication of the *Origin of Species*. There will be international symposia, plays, displays, exhibits, publications, and public discussions that will center on Darwin and his impact. The importance of Darwin for issues that range far beyond technical scientific questions of biological science is unquestioned. In a recent *New York Times* column, David Brooks spoke of how we are in fact living in an "Age of Darwin." This was a surprising statement to me when I first encountered Brooks's article, but I can see why he made this argument. To a surprising degree, Darwin and the collection of theories and analyses his work has spawned seem to be on the resurgence. Unlike most works of the history of science, his writings remain relevant to contemporary biological inquiry in ways represented by no other figure of nineteenth century science.[6] And I am sure we are all familiar with the continuous flow of works today that offer evolutionary explanations of social life, altruism, love, sexuality, ethics, religion, gender relations, art, and music.

If Kimball is correct in characterizing American liberal education as settling on a "Pragmatist" consensus, Darwinism is of some definite interest in understanding something about the conceptual underpinnings of this movement. Several important studies have discussed the importance of Darwin's works for the reflections of the Cambridge, Massachusetts, metaphysical circle that included Wright, Pierce, and William James.[7] I will pick up a little later layer in the Pragmatist movement and look at John Dewey, who had the greatest impact in developing a "pragmatic" theory of liberal education.

In his address at Columbia University in 1909, "The Influence of Darwinism on Philosophy," delivered as his contribution to a commemorative series of lectures celebrating the 50th anniversary of the publication of the *Origin of Species*, Dewey articulated his own views of how Darwin had changed the fundamentals of western philosophy. Among other points, he makes two fundamental claims: first, Darwin has undermined the notion of the essentialism implied in classical notions of species and substantial forms, and he has undermined the assumption of some kind of unchanging realities behind appearances. Second, since the conception of a fixity of kinds and natures was tied to some notion of teleological purposiveness, the new natural philosophy instituted by Darwin undermined traditional notions of natural teleology, and made "chance," rather than purpose or design, the new foundation of natural philosophy. This implies, for Dewey, a "new logic," one that is concerned with the concrete, the practical:

> What does our touchstone [in chance as a causal principle of nature] indicate as to the bearing of Darwinian ideas upon philosophy? In the first place, the new logic outlaws, flanks, dismisses – what you will – one type of problem and substitutes for it another type. Philosophy forswears inquiry after absolute origins and absolute finalities in order to explore specific values and the specific conditions that generate them.

> Philosophy must in time become a method of locating and interpreting the more serious of the conflicts that occur in life, and a method of projecting ways for dealing with them: a method of moral and political diagnosis and prognosis. (9, 11)

Dewey attributes to Darwin a conceptual revolution as profound as what he sees instituted by Copernicus. There are reasons to conclude that he took this seriously, and that his well-known promotion of educational reform and the concept of "progressive" education reflect some of this conclusion.

Calls for a new basis for liberal education, and even a reconceptualization of what it meant were not, of course, new with Dewey. The reform of the Harvard curriculum under the forty-year presidency (1869-1909) of Charles W. Eliot already had created an extensive reform movement that had made the notion of liberal arts education something very different than it had functioned traditionally, introducing a heavy study of the sciences, modern culture, and history, dropping the emphasis on the study of classical languages, removing mandatory attendance requirements, and introducing a free elective principle along with the introduction of teaching from the standpoint of scholarly expertise as a component of the undergraduate college experience.[8]

What Dewey did was provide some philosophical rationale for these reconceptualizations, and there is sufficient evidence that this rationale at least in part rested on his interpretation of the importance of Darwin for contemporary culture. If Darwin has undermined the foundations upon which education is conceived as a disciplined "training of the mind" to fulfill a divinely-ordained teleological end of the human being, as James McCosh, the President of Princeton, argued in his critique of Eliot in 1885,[9] liberal education must find its rationale from other sources. Darwin provided one of these.

A particular interpretation of Darwin, one strongly influenced by what has been defined as American neo-Lamarckian interpretations, seems to have played a formative role in Dewey's interpretation of Darwin's impact. This neo-Lamarckian reading of Darwin placed the emphasis on such issues as the inheritance of acquired characters and the internal dynamism of the living being as interacting with its environment. It was optimistic about history in that it assumed the model of embryological development as a model of evolutionary change.[10] This "soft" American Darwinism is an optimistic Darwinism that embraced notions of progress and improvement through adaptation. We can get the flavor of this in a comment from Dewey's *Art as Experience* of 1934:

> If life continues and if in continuing it expands, there is an overcoming of factors of opposition and conflict; there is a transformation of them into differentiated aspects of a higher powered and more significant life. The marvel of organic, of vital, adaptation through expansion (instead of by contraction and passive accommodation) actually takes place. Here in germ are balance and harmony attained through rhythm. Equilibrium comes about not mechanically and inertly but out of, and because of, tension.... Order is not imposed from without but is made out of the relations of harmonious interactions that energies bear to one another. Because it is active...order itself develops. It comes to include within its balanced movement a greater variety of changes. (14-15)

I will illustrate the practical consequences of this kind of implicit "soft" Darwinism with the report of the conference on Liberal Education at Rollins College in Florida, which under the presidency of Hamilton Holt became known as a new progressive college with an experimental curriculum. A conference held in January of 1931, chaired by Dewey himself, developed a document on these ideals. This document is found in Bruce Kimball's documentary history.[11] Although the Rollins conference issued in a consensus group report, rather than in a treatise specifically by Dewey himself, the proposals that emerged from that conference seem to capture many of his views. The Report emphasizes that the function of the liberal arts college is to "achieve the values and significance of life, individual and social." This is expanded in terms of a definition of eight general purposes of liberal education:

> 1. A realizing sense of the controlling importance of continuity in the human quest and the integration of personal aims with that quest.
> 2. An increasing understanding and control of the physical world, and the achievement and maintenance of a favorable physical environment.
> 3. An increasing understanding of the nature of man in his human relations, and the realization of social harmony.

4. An increasing knowledge and control of the biological nature of man and of eugenic processes.

5. A search for the nature and significance of meanings, ends, and values in human experience, through inquiry and through personal emotional experience of such values.

6. Helping the individual to find his appropriate life-work and stimulating him toward mastery therein.

7. Helping to realize the importance of the intelligent use of leisure, including the lifelong development through education of new interests and capacities as these emerge, and the fostering of interest in nature and the various fine arts and handicrafts.

8. The development of wholesome physical and mental habits, the development of ideals, the education of the will and of the emotions as well as of the intellect, the harmonizing of the elements of personality, both innate and acquired, and the stimulation and increase of creative powers. (2, 494-95)

If we consider these eight proposals as a practical expression of the ideals of an early version of "pragmatic" liberal education, we can see both the impact of a kind of Darwinian naturalism, captured in the curious item 4, which speaks of the need to gain control over human nature, with an appeal to eugenics as the means, echoing the kind of "progressive" eugenics of the 1920s.[12] But these eight proposals also retain many of the goals of the prior liberal arts tradition. This Rollins College statement still embodies a notion of liberal education as transmitting value; it is concerned with character formation; and it is oriented toward communal responsibility. Such goals are certainly not alien to many of the classical ideals of the liberal arts tradition. What is different is the lack of appeal to some inherent teleological end or purpose in human beings that grounds these ideals.

Nothing in these Rollins College proposals would lead to an emphasis on core curricula or the reading of classic texts as an end in itself.[13] The split over this issue separated the Deweyans from those concerned with more traditional conceptions of liberal education and defined some of the great curricular battle lines of the 1930s. Robert Maynard Hutchins's *Higher Education in America* of 1936 represented one response to this challenge and served to define his alternative – the emphasis on required curricula, the reading of a canon of great books, and the cultivation of a philosophical program of education based on rational foundations in Aristotle and Aquinas that came to define the Hutchins-era college program at the University of Chicago.[14]

If I am correct in characterizing the Darwinian naturalism beneath Dewey's thought as based on a neo-Lamarckian reading of Darwin, with this supplying some deep foundation for the kind of liberal educational program that emerges from his writings, two important developments since Dewey need to be considered if we are to seek some deeper tie between education and biology. The first is the replacement of the assumptions of classical Darwinian and the neo-Lamarckian interpretations of Darwinism of the 1920s with the rigorous mathematical interpretations developed by theoretical population genetics in the 1930s that has given us the shape of modern consensus neo-Darwinian theory, the Modern Synthesis associated with the names of Theodosius Dobzhansky, R. A. Fisher, Sewall Wright, Ernst Mayr, George Gaylord Simpson, and many other architects of modern evolutionary theory.[15] Two subordinate points in this theoretical development as they might bear on some of the issues of relevance to the education of the human being are the following: first, this established natural selection as a fundamental position, and this involved a much stronger denial of teleological directionalism that makes even the notion of "progressive development" in the sense used by Dewey suspect. Independent of the popularizations of people like Richard Dawkins, who have simply tried to make a natural philosophy out of this principle, there is a much more fundamental appeal to the concept of "chance" in modern evolutionary theory than was evident before the 1930s.[16]

Second, the synthesis of the 1930s drew genetics into evolutionary theory in a way it had never been before. Evolution must now rest on a sophisticated Mendelian theory of inheritance. The incorporation of genetics and natural selection theory in the Modern Synthesis has given us a picture of evolution as working on the selection of deterministic genes in populations rather than on real organisms in nature. If these two principles define what we now mean by a "Darwinian" foundation, it is difficult to draw from it the kind of plastic, probing educational theory we find in Dewey.[17] Natural selectionism is now much more fundamental to contemporary efforts to extend Darwinism to the explanation of all matters of human existence in contemporary evolutionary naturalism.[18]

To this shift in underlying science has been added the consequences of one other important scientific development since the 1930s. This is the development of the profoundly reductionist theory of life that has come from the theoretical work of the functional and molecular sciences. We can date this conveniently from the "molecular" revolution associated with the names of Watson and Crick in the 1950s, although it extends considerably beyond the work of these two iconic early molecular biologists. Again, such developments might seem technical issues within the sciences, except we know that the resultant "molecularization" of life has not stopped at the doors of the research laboratory. In the words of molecular biologist Francis Crick who helped create the "molecular" revolution of the 1950s,

> The ultimate aim of the modern movement in biology is in fact to explain *all* biology in terms of physics and chemistry. Thus eventually one may hope to have the whole of biology "explained" in terms of the level below it, and so on right down to the atomic level. (*Of Molecules and Men*, 10, 14)

It is my argument that the intersection of the views expressed by Crick here with the general naturalism of the "hard" Darwinism of the Modern Synthesis presents us with a new set of problems in reconnecting our human and social interests with biology. We are confronted with a growing discourse employing genetic determinism and "bottom up" explanations of life that seems to many to be an implication of the success of molecular biology. This is combined with the project of a stronger form of evolutionary naturalism based on anti-teleological natural selectionism. The deliverances from some authorities of the life sciences – Crick, Jacques Monod, Dawkins, E. O. Wilson, Michael Gazzaniga, and Stephen Pinker – and support for them from philosophers like Daniel Dennett, Alexander Rosenberg, and the Churchlands offer us a relentlessly reductive view of the human being that seems to allow little grounds for the development of an educational theory based on the study of texts of the tradition and required curricula of the kind I suspect many of us would embrace or even of the optimistic educational theory that we might derive from Dewey's pragmatic alternative.[19]

Must we therefore assert, as a defense of a humanistic liberal education, that a radical disjunction must still be made between nature and human interests, between is and ought, and between thought and body? Are empirical issues of this kind simply irrelevant to questions of education?

As I set out earlier in the talk, I do not believe this is the case, and I believe education cannot escape making some assumptions about the individual being educated or making some contact with human nature. The recognition of the importance of this is certainly one of the important insights of Dewey. But I will acknowledge that I think there is a basis for richer defense of an education that is closer to the Hutchinsonian than the Deweyan alternative, if we are to refer back to these dividing lines of the 30s.

To develop this claim I want to turn to some issues in theoretical biology, and then move to some comments on how these might bear on a conception of liberal education that seeks to recover and restate some of the classical goals of humanistic education I have discussed above.

The theoretical issues I will address concern the growing attention to the notion of systems and systems approaches in theoretical biology as a way to move beyond the reductionism of molecular biology, biophysics, and strong natural selectionism. The notion of organisms as hierarchical systems of coordinated relations, rather than as collections of matter or individualized parts, is, of course nothing new, and such appeals can be traced back into the eighteenth century where we first see the language of "organism" introduced by such important authors as Immanuel Kant. More recently, we can refer to the substantial development of these views in the interwar years in relation to notions of "holism," "organicism," and "general systems" by developmental biologists, gestalt psychologists, and physiologists who sought ways to resolve the theoretical dispute between mechanists and vitalists at the time.[20]

But after several decades of marginalization, new attention to these issues has been forced on to the table by the failure of reductive methodologies to solve the empirical problems of developmental biology, gene regulation, organized metabolism, ecosystem analysis, and even evolutionary development itself solely by appeals to traditional material and efficient causation. Introduction into contemporary biological theory of concepts like "organism," "organization," and "system," are now widely encountered in current biology.[21] This necessarily brings with it some attention to notions of formal and final causes, of function and teleological directedness in organic systems, even if these are often discussed under other names.

Exploring this diverse literature involves us in technical issues in the philosophy and practice of the life sciences that quickly get complicated in ways that would be counterproductive to follow in this talk. I wish only to extract one fundamental point from these developments. This is to argue that there are strong reasons, emerging within our life sciences themselves, which are requiring new attention to notions of organism, function, system, and directional development in biology.[22] We are not, in other words, simply trapped within the framework of reductionist interpretations of organic life that eventually slide over into interpretations about human existence as well, interpretations that leave us either attempting to work out solutions within a horizon defined by genetic determinism, molecular biology, and strong sociobiology, or else with the radical dissociation of ethical and educational goals from our biological and species life, splitting these apart by appeal to the force of the naturalistic fallacy. Finding some more intimate relation between these two poles of our existence was certainly a goal of Dewey's. But it was also that of the older tradition of Aristotle, Aquinas, and Hutchins.

More recent efforts to restore a practical connection between biology and knowledge of relevance can be seen in the cognitive development theory of Jean Piaget, and the moral development theory built upon Piaget's linkage of biology and cognitive development by the late Lawrence Kohlberg of Harvard.[23] Piaget in particular approached the questions of human development through his well-known stages with a commitment to systems biology and to the hierarchical and directional development that derived much of its empirical foundations from his own early training as a systematic and developmental biologist.

Kohlberg then developed on these foundations a stage-theory of moral development, claimed to be cross-cultural, that led to a moral maturation in the recognition of ethical universals, such as the demand for justice. There are substantial debates over Kohlberg's theory that I acknowledge, and I have criticisms of my own. But the important issue is that through the notions of organism, system, and developmental direction there are educational implications that follow that are plausible educational goals.

Piaget's linkage of biology and epistemological development might be seen as incongruent with the life science of the 1960s when he formulated its principles in such works as *Biology and Knowledge* (1967). But with the renewed interest in systems biology and attendant issues in current life science, his arguments take on new interest, and with this some deeper empirical warrant for the kind of developmentalist educational theory that we find in Kohlberg.

My central point here is that there are reasons to reconnect again our notion of what it is to be human, even in a post-Darwinian world, with the notion of purpose, both in our fundamental conception of life, and then in the concept of human purposiveness itself. In doing this, we also have made a point of contact with the educational vision not only of the optimistic Darwinism of Dewey and Piaget, but also with those of tradition who sought to form the noble human person by classical *paideia* which drew deeply on the writings of tradition.

At the conclusion of his 1909 address, Dewey commented that the Darwinian insight was "the greatest dissolvent in contemporary thought of old questions, the greatest precipitant of new methods, new intentions, new problems" (12). But there are suggestions that the scientific foundations on which some of this dissolution has been based may itself be undergoing a quiet revolution. This may give us new ways of thinking about an education that seeks the good, the true and the beautiful that is also congruent with who we are as humans in a post-Darwinian world, with some of our best companions on this journey the writings of a long tradition of philosophers, humanists, scientists, mathematicians, masters of prose and poetry, and theologians, all of whom have attempted in various ways to penetrate to the core of human existence. We may even have as companions some important theorists within contemporary life science.

Notes

1 See also Paris and Kimball, "Liberal Education: An Overlapping Pragmatic Consensus" (to be reprinted in Kimball's *Voices from the Liberal Arts* and used with permission of the author) and Kimball, "Naming Pragmatic Liberal Education," 47.

2 See contributions by Ryan, Harris, and Freedland.

3 I will not attempt to assess here the criticisms of his classification. Both his narrative of the recent tradition and his selection of texts ignore many of the refinements and developments that occurred in the "philosophical" tradition, especially in the Germanies. The forthcoming work by my colleague, Felicitas Munzel, on Kant's theory of pedagogy introduces a much broader conception of some of these issues.

4 American Pragmatism as a philosophical project encompasses a broad spectrum of positions, and its founding representatives held differing positions on several important philosophical issues. I will not attempt to sort out these differences in this essay. Kimball has summarized many of them in his "Toward Pragmatic Liberal Education," sections 3-4.

5 For examples, see "Toward Pragmatic Liberal Education," section 7.

6 Recently, for example, we have seen the reissuing of two collections of Darwin's primary texts, one edited by Nobel Prize winning molecular biologist James D. Watson, and the other by Harvard entomologist and founder of modern sociobiology E. O. Wilson.

7 Philip Wiener's *Evolution and the Founders of Pragmatism* has explored these roots primarily with a focus on Chauncey Wright, C.S. Pierce, and others in the Cambridge circle of the 1860s and 70s.

8 I am drawing here on Eliot's "Many New Methods of Giving Instruction" and on documents from the Eliot-McCosh debate of 1885 and 1886 also as given in Kimball, *Voices from the Liberal Arts*, 2, 269-83.

9 "Education is essentially the training of the mind – as the [Latin] word *educare* denotes – the drawing forth of the faculties which God has given us. This it should especially be in a university – in a *Studium Generale*, as it used to be called. The powers of mind are numerous and varied: the senses, the memory, the fancy, judgment, reasoning, conscience, the feelings, the will, the mathematical, the metaphysical, the mechanical, the poetical, the prosaic (quite as useful as any); and all these should be cultivated, the studies necessary to do so should be provided, and the student required so far to attend to them, that the young man by exercise may know what powers he has and the mental frame be fully developed" (McCosh, qtd. in Kimball 272-73).

10 For an overview of American neo-Lamarckianism, see Bowler, *The Eclipse of Darwinism*, chapters. 6-7. As Bowler summarizes the main defining feature: "The truly distinguishing feature of the American School [was] its vision of evolution advancing step-by-step along a regular pattern of development mirrored by the embryological growth of the individual organism" (119). The relation of Darwin to the foundations of Dewey's thought has not been explored extensively. The recent article by Christopher Perricone "The Influence of Darwinism on John Dewey's Philosophy of Art" reviews some of the literature.

11 In *The Curriculum for the Liberal Arts College, Being the Report of the Curriculum Conference Held at Rollins College*, Winter Park, FL: Rollins College, 1931. See also remarks on the College history at <http://www.rollins. edu/aboutrollins/heritage.shtml>.

12 See Ludmerer, *Genetics and American Society*.

13 It does not, however, exclude this. For example, the concept of the "Great Books" seminar, central to the education in my own Program of Liberal Studies and others committed to this model of education, took its origin from the democratic, open-discussion model first initiated by the John Erskine General Honors seminars at Columbia University in 1917 in Dewey's era, in which model, to the shock of disciplinary experts ever since, the aim was to read a classic text per week, typically in translation, in an open discussion with the teacher as a fellow-discussant. The discussion allowed even undergraduates to comment upon and to critique major works of the tradition without reading extensive scholarly apparatus. There is something deeply Deweyan in this model of education, even if it is not justified on explicitly pragmatist grounds. On the context of the Erskine seminars, see Bell, 13-14.

14 See Ehrlich, 225-262.

15 For some overview, see my "Evolution" and contained references.

16 This new element was imported by R.A. Fischer into early population genetics and from the statistical mechanics of Ludwig Boltzmann. See my "Evolution."

17 There is some defense of such a view in E. Mayr, "Biology, Pragmatism, and Liberal Education," 287-97. Mayr is not, however, a strong "genic" selectionist and is generally favorable to Dewey's enterprise as a result.

18 For a recent review, see A. Rosenberg, "Darwinism in Moral Philosophy and Social Theory": "[Darwinian] naturalists look to the theory of natural selection as a primary resource in coming to solve philosophical problems raised by human affairs in particular" (310).

19 Obviously, I would take issue with Perricone's efforts in "The Influence of Darwinism on John Dewey's Philosophy of Art" to assimilate Dawkins, Dennett, and Pinker to a Deweyan position, although they could be related to the new Darwinian naturalism embraced by some versions of neo-Pragmatism.

20 These developments were critiqued by the strong empiricism of the Vienna Circle and the unity of science movement, and they have had little discussion in Anglo-American philosophical circles as a consequence. The growth and success of biophysics and molecular biology since World War II also has served to marginalize institutionally the work of developmental and organismic biologists who continued to advance these views – here I might cite names like Conrad Waddington, Joseph Needham, J.S. Haldane, and Ludwig von Bertalanffy as examples – in favor of the strong reductionism of molecular biology. I am exploring these issues in my current research.

21 For example, a search in Harvard's card catalogue under the topic "systems biology" brings up 670 titles of books and monographs published since 1960, and 220 of these have been published since 2000. Little exploration of systems theory has been made in the technical philosophy of biology, but see Boogerd, Bruggeman, Hofmeyr, and Westerhoff, *Systems Biology: Philosophical Foundations*.

22 A useful discussion of the theoretical issues involved is found in the joint paper by a cell biologist (Maureen Condic) and a philosopher Samuel Condic) "Defining Organisms by Organization." Some extension of these issues to ethical implications can be seen in the paper by William Hurlbut "Framing the Future: Embryonic Stem Cells, Ethics, and the Emergent Era of Developmental Biology."

23 I am drawing on L. Kohlberg, *The Meaning and Measurement of Moral Development*, especially chapter 1.

Works Cited

Bell, Daniel. *The Reforming of General Education: The Columbia College Experience in its National Setting*. New York: Columbia UP, 1966.

Bowler, Peter J. *The Eclipse of Darwinism*. Baltimore: Johns Hopkins UP, 1983.

Brooks, David. "Age of Darwin." *New York Times* April 15, 2007. <http://select.nytimes.com/2007/04/15/opinion/15brooks.html?r=1&scp=1 &sq=brooks+age+of+darwin&st=nyt&oref=slogin>> Accessed 5 March 2008.

Condic, Maureen and Samuel Condic. "Defining Organisms by Organization." *National Catholic Bioethics Quarterly* 5.2 (2005): 331-53.

Crick, Francis. *Of Molecules and Men.* Seattle: U Washington P, 1966.

The Curriculum for the Liberal Arts College, Being the Report of the Curriculum Conference Held at Rollins College. Winter Park, FL: Rollins College, 1931: 8-14. In Kimball, *Voices from the Liberal Arts*, 2, 490–505.

Dewey, John. *Art as Experience.* New York: Minton, Balch & Co, 1934.

---. "The Influence of Darwinism on Philosophy." In *The Influence of Darwin on Philosophy and Other Essays in Contemporary Thought.* Ed. L.A. Hickman. Carbondale: S Illinois UP, 2007. 5-12.

Ehrlich, Thomas. "Dewey vs. Hutchins: The Next Round." In *Education and Democracy: Re-imagining Liberal Learning in America Education.* Ed. Robert Orrill. New York: College Entrance Examination Board, 1997. 225-62.

Eliot, Charles W. "Many New Methods of Giving Instruction." *Annual Reports of the President and Treasurer of Harvard College 1879-80.* Cambridge: Harvard UP, 1880: 12-19. In Kimball, *Voices from the Liberal Arts*, 2, 245–50.

Freedland, Richard. "Pragmatism Won't Save Us But It Can Help." In *The Condition of American Liberal Education: Pragmatism and a Changing Tradition.* Ed. Robert Orrill. New York: College Entrance Examination Board, 1995. 158-62.

Harris, Ellen. "Prognostication and Doubt." In *The Condition of American Liberal Education: Pragmatism and a Changing Tradition.* Ed. Robert Orrill. New York: College Entrance Examination Board, 1995. 253-58.

Hurlbut, William. "Framing the Future: Embryonic Stem Cells, Ethics, and the Emergent Era of Developmental Biology." *Pediatric Research* 59 (2006): 4-12.

Kimball, Bruce A. "Naming Pragmatic Liberal Education." In *Education and Democracy: Re-imagining Liberal Learning in America Education.* Ed. Robert Orrill. New York: College Entrance Examination Board, 1997. 45-68.

---. "Toward Pragmatic Liberal Education." In *The Condition of American Liberal Education: Pragmatism and a Changing Tradition.* Ed. Robert Orrill. New York: College Entrance Examination Board, 1995. 3-122.

---, ed. *Voices from the Liberal Arts.* 2 vols. Forthcoming from UP of America. A shortened version of this manuscript is also forthcoming from UP of America in 2010 under the title *The Liberal Arts Tradition: A Documentary History.*

Kohlberg, Lawrence. *The Meaning and Measurement of Moral Development.* Worcester: Clark UP, 1981.

Ludmerer, Kenneth. *Genetics and American Society*. Baltimore: Johns Hopkins UP, 1972.

Lyotard, Jean-François. *The Postmodern Condition: A Report on Knowledge*. Trans. Geoff Bennington and Brian Massumi. Minneapolis: U Minnesota P, 1989.

MacIntyre, Alasdair. *Dependent Rational Animals: Why Human Beings Need the Virtues*. Chicago: Open Court, 1999.

Mayr, Ernst. "Biology, Pragmatism, and Liberal Education." In *Education and Democracy: Re-imagining Liberal Learning in America Education*. Ed. Robert Orrill. New York: College Entrance Examination Board, 1997. 287-97.

McCosh, James. *The New Departure in College Education, Being a Reply to President Eliot's Defense of It*. New York: Scribner, 1885. In Kimball, *Voices from the Liberal Arts*, 2, 272-73.

Orrill, Robert, ed. *The Condition of American Liberal Education: Pragmatism and a Changing Tradition*. New York: College Entrance Examination Board, 1995.

---, ed. *Education and Democracy: Re-imagining Liberal Learning in America Education*. New York: College Entrance Examination Board, 1997.

Paris, David C. and Bruce A. Kimball. "Liberal Education: An Overlapping Pragmatic Consensus." *Journal of Curriculum Studies* 32 (2000): 145-158.

Perricone, Christopher. "The Influence of Darwinism on John Dewey's Philosophy of Art." *Journal of Speculative Philosophy* 20 (2006): 20-41.

Rosenberg, Alexander. "Darwinism in Moral Philosophy and Social Theory." In *The Cambridge Companion to Darwin*. Ed. M.J.S. Hodge and G. Radick. Cambridge: Cambridge UP, 2003. 310-32.

Ryan, Alan. "No Consensus in Sight." In *The Condition of American Liberal Education: Pragmatism and a Changing Tradition*. Ed. Robert Orrill. New York: College Entrance Examination Board, 1995. 244-49.

Sloan, Phillip R. "Evolution." In the *Stanford On-line Encyclopedia of Philosophy*. http://plato.stanford.edu/entries/evolution/

Systems Biology: Philosophical Foundations. Ed. Fred Boogerd, Frank Bruggeman, Jan-Hendrik Hofmeyr, and Hans Westerhoff. Amsterdam: Elsevier, 2007.

Wiener, Philip. *Evolution and the Founders of Pragmatism*. New York: Harper, 1965. (First published in 1949.)

The Great "Civilized" Conversation: A Case in Point

William Theodore de Bary
Columbia University

Those familiar with the early history of the movement at Columbia identified with John Erskine's Honors Course and "The Classics of the Western World," known later in Chicago and St. John's as "the Great Books Program," will recall how its early advocates, including among others Mark Van Doren and Stringfellow Barr, referred to the dialogue among the great writers and thinkers as "The Great Conversation." They thought of it as the great minds speaking to each other over the centuries about the perennial issues of human life and society. Contrary to those who misperceived the process as one of handing down fixed, eternal truths, for them it was a vital process of re-engaging with questions that had continued human relevance age after age. One could not afford to ignore what had been said about those issues earlier because civilization depended on building upon the lessons of the past. Thus tradition, like civilization, continued to grow. It was cumulating and cumulative, not fixed.

Not all of the issues engaged in this conversation had to do with civilization and society – some religious issues might go beyond that – but sustaining the conversation itself required a civilized life, a willingness to show a decent respect for what others have learned or thought for themselves and what others have valued or held dear. Indeed, it was an appreciation for human life as it has been lived.

In the earlier phases of this movement, the conversation was largely within the Western tradition and was closely tied to the question of how classics, originally expressed in the classical languages of the West, especially Latin and Greek, could still survive in the modern vernacular as part of a classical education. But it was easily assumed that translation into the vernacular was possible because of a continuity of both language and culture into the later period. Such continuity in cultural values overrode historical change. As we shall see, this was largely (but not entirely) true of the major Asian traditions as well. They too had longstanding traditions of a Great Conversation as later writers spoke to and reappropriated their own classics and thus engaged with the great minds of the past.

It was not, however, a matter simply of conserving received tradition. It was, as the word *conversation* suggests, the present speaking to the past in its own voice, actively repossessing and renewing the classics in modern terms that spoke to contemporary concerns as well. In other words, these traditions had within themselves the capacity for reexamination and self-renewal.

In modern times, this meant reflecting on the classics in a way that responded to the new cultural situation in which modern writers found themselves. By the eighteenth century at least, Western writers recognized that Asian traditions had classic thinkers who spoke to the same issues and concerns, though perhaps in somewhat different terms. Thus, Enlightenment thinkers began to speak to the thinkers of classical China as well as to Western classics, and the New England Transcendentalists spoke also to philosophers of ancient India. Benjamin Franklin, at the founding of the American Philosophical Society, dedicated it to the study of Chinese philosophy as well as Western. All this had an effect on early twentieth-century writers like W.B. Yeats, Ezra Pound, T.S. Eliot, and many others too numerous to mention. But as of the twentieth century, though the most creative minds were already extending the Great Conversation to Asia, it had as yet little effect on Western education at the base level. Asian classics did not become part of the Great Books program. They were not among Mortimer Adler's 100 Great Books; nor did his 100 Great Ideas include any Asian concepts.

Another limitation on the inclusion of Asian classics in the Great Conversation as conducted in the modern West was the tendency to focus the conversation on the classic writers of the Asian traditions but not as part of a continuing conversation over time that matured well beyond ancient times. Thus, Ezra Pound thought he could directly engage with the Confucian classics and even translate them himself with minimal sinological expertise. Sometimes he succeeded brilliantly in intuiting and appropriating them for his own poetic purposes, but this fell short of explaining what the *Analects* or *Great Learning* had meant to later Chinese, Japanese, and Korean civilizations. In other words, it was more of an extension of Pound's own culture, his own exploratory venture into the past and his idealizing of Confucianism, than a substantial engagement with Chinese culture or civilization in its mature forms.

The time has come, however, for us to extend the conversation to twenty-first-century education in ways that do justice to Asian classics, not just as museum pieces but also as part of the historical process to be factored into an emerging world civilization. Given the domination of education today by economic and technological forces – the same forces that drive world business – this will not be an easy thing to do. Indeed the preservation of any humanities education at all is problematic now anywhere in the world. I have written elsewhere about the crisis in East Asian education as modern universities have found it difficult to sustain the reading of even their own classics in the undergraduate curriculum. But the reasons for it are the same as those that militate against any classical education at all, even in the West. For the most part, Chinese or Japanese classics are read only by a few students majoring in Classics departments. Meanwhile, most students want to concentrate on economics, science and technology, and for these English is the relevant language. Thus the problem for Asian education is little different from that in the West: how to sustain any place at all for the humanities in the curriculum. It is a global problem and raises the question everywhere whether traditional humanistic learning can be sustained as part of a new global culture, which would otherwise be dominated simply by the market and technology.

The most recent challenge to the core curriculum as centered on the great landmarks of human history and thought has come from those who believe that priority should be given to theory – especially to different epistemological and hermeneutic theories. But as the German scholar Karl-Heinz Pohl at Trier University has recently pointed out, most of the theories advanced in the recent culture wars

> are matters of fashion and *Zeitgeist*, fluctuating *à la mode*.... Their universal application...must be questioned because they have all been creations of the modern Western mind.... Thus if one focuses on the most up-to-date Western themes, China and the other Asian countries will always lag behind, trying to catch up with the hot themes of yesterday, not of today; ...what now appears to be *haute culture* ends up being *haute couture*, a question of style fluctuating *à la mode*. (1-3)

Whatever you call the works themselves – classics, great books, or major texts – these are works that have stood the test of time, as most theories have not. They have challenged generation after generation and have survived repeated contestation. They speak to each other in a continuing dialogue in which great minds and great writers recognize and speak to each other over the ages.

By their very durability and substantiality they have established themselves as hard artifacts of human history. Everyone who has *taught* them, so to speak, knows that it is the works themselves that teach us. They are bigger than anything we can say about them, and that is why teachers often say "the books teach themselves." They are that great.

But the books cannot do this unless you have people ready to set up the programs and keep them going – that is, the collegial bodies that take responsibility for education, as academic organizations only sometimes do for a defined curriculum aimed at educating the whole person.

Let me illustrate the point by citing a traditional ritual that is followed every year at Columbia's commencement – the administration of the Hippocratic Oath to the new Doctors of Medicine. This takes place annually after most of the deans have introduced the graduating classes of their schools. The deans' congratulations of their students has increasingly become a raucous circus, as each dean tries to outdo the other in boisterous cheerleading that would be appropriate at a sporting event, but unfortunately at Columbia occurs only rarely at our athletic field. But after the Dean's presentation of the Medical School graduates, he administers to them the Hippocratic Oath. Suddenly all the hoopla comes to an end. Instead of the deans' ballyhoo of their graduates and the students' noisy hijinks in response – the Business graduates waving their dollar bills and the journalists their newspapers – everyone falls silent, while the Dean of Medicine asks the new doctors solemnly to swear that they will practice their profession only for the good of their patients and will keep inviolate everything they learn that should be privy only to the patient.

Everyone understands that this is serious business, and if one stops to think about it at all, one realizes that any profession should be practiced with the kind of dedication and humane respect the Hippocratic Oath implies – true even for the natural scientists who might seem to be the most focused on the physical or material aspects of existence.

Now if we proceed to even a second or third thought about the matter, it may occur to us that this ancient rite endures from the remote past in the same way as the classic texts one reads and ponders in a core curriculum. Like the Greek and Latin classics, the Oath comes down from a "dead white boy." It could be dismissed just as easily by those who advance a specious multiculturalism to denigrate the so-called Western canon. The fact is, however, that no Asian tradition I know of would not assent to the same values as the Hippocratic Oath.

The deconstructionists could find as much to question about the attribution to Hippocrates as some do about the attribution of the *Iliad* and *Odyssey* to Homer. The post-modernists could problematize and contextualize it – to use their favored jargon. They could problematize it into utter meaningless, but even the advocates of high-flown and overblown theory have to fall silent in the face of truths so plain and homespun that no one can fail to be directly, personally moved by the simple human truths the Oath conveys. Suddenly, all present remember what Commencement is all about, that it renews the commitment to learning and public service at the founding of King's College. We are in the personal presence of enduring truths. It is not a question of hermeneutics or epistemological subtlety, but whether or not we personally are prepared to live by these truths and give them new meaning in our own time. From my own experience as a teacher at Columbia for fifty-five years, I can say that the *Analects* and *Mencius* speak to my students just as personally as does the oath of Hippocrates.

A new stage in bringing East and West together on issues of commonality and diversity has been the planning of workshops and colloquia for the stage beyond the introductory Humanities and Civilization courses, whether Western or

Asian, at which the products of the several traditions could be brought together in colloquia on key issues bridging East and West.

The significance of this project is that it can provide a model for integrated undergraduate education that focuses on common human values and issues while also recognizing cultural differences. Without the articulation of such common values, undergraduate education is exposed to political demands for courses based instead on diversity alone – on a multiculturalism defined only in terms of minority representation, which, with little concern for intellectual commonalities or shared human and community values, threatens the Balkanization of the curriculum and fosters a radical extremism that is divisive rather than pro-active in the service of common goals. The consequence of not moving forward toward such common goals will be for young people to be increasingly attracted to simplistic and separatist fundamentalisms – ideologies that narrow the vision and offer a specious identity to those who lack perspective on themselves and their place in a larger world.

In *Confucian Tradition and Global Education,* I cited the difficulties that New Asia College, supposedly a bridgehead of Confucian culture into the modern world, was experiencing in trying to sustain the study of the Confucian classics. Let me now cite a similar case nearer home (even though today it is a question what one still can call *home,* educationally speaking). It comes from a publication you may know of, *Inside Academe,* which speaks for an organization dedicated to upholding academic standards and traditional values in American education. In its Summer 2007 issue, *Inside Academe* had an article entitled "Where's the Bard?" reporting on a new survey, headlined as "The Vanishing Shakespeare," of more than 70 universities, which reported that only 15 among them require their English majors to take a course on Shakespeare. Instead, it says, "English majors are being offered an astonishing array of courses on popular culture, children's literature, sociology and politics...."

The article goes on to cite a long list of American publications from *USA Today* to *The New Republic* that regarded these survey results as significant. I doubt that many of us familiar with college education in the U.S. will consider this news. But for those concerned with how traditional humanistic learning stands in today's curriculum, the real significance of the report lies in its narrow focus on what is happening in English departments, to English majors – an academic vested interest – similar to what is happening to their counterpart departments in East Asia, i.e., the erosion in the study of their own classics, as upwardly mobile students choose to study the going language of English as the lingua franca of the twenty-first century. What adds to the irony in this case is that, before this, educated East Asians in the nineteenth and twentieth centuries had already come to admire Shakespeare as a world classic.

For traditionalists of almost any stripe, it would be a matter of concern that Shakespeare was being put on the shelf, unstudied, in any English department, but the reason for it is something antecedent to the state of the English major. If there is no place for the humanities in a globalized market for education, then even English majors will turn away from so great a figure as Shakespeare to whatever finds favor in the current media or marketplace.

My point is that mere conservatism – holding to an old line that has long since been overrun – will not avail today unless we can establish a place for lo-cal tradition in a global humanism that has something to say about what values might direct and control a runaway market economy and technology. Put in such global terms, the magnitude of the problem may seem overwhelming. How can one deal with the problem locally except in the larger context of global educa-tion? But how can one get a handle on something so massive and complex as global education? If we have to think globally (as the saying goes), how can we act locally to work our way toward that goal? The answer, it seems to me, is that even if we have to deal within the limits of what is practicable in our local situa-tion, we can begin the process of sharing our goals and experiences on a wider scale, so that the resources of the larger scholarly and educational community can be brought to bear upon, and be availed of, on behalf of beneficial, incre-mental change.

One way to get at this is to share our views on what has been considered *classic* in the major mature traditions of the civilized world and on how these can best be incorporated into our pooled educational resources – to put it simply, to make these resources available in a form that can be adapted to local systems. Thereby one might hope to establish some kind of working consensus in the same way that the United Nations established a consensus on human rights in its Universal Declaration of 1948. The Universal Declaration did not effectively become law, but it did set an international standard that few could disagree with and almost all states formally ratified, however much or little they actually com-plied with it. Activists, always a minority, at least had a standard they could in-voke in working toward its implementation. Fortunately, the English text of the Declaration had the benefit of multicultural consultation and was less culture-bound than would otherwise have been the case. Something like that should be done to establish *Classics for an Emerging World*.

Let us compare our situation to that in American education a century ago. No sooner had President Eliot of Harvard set up his Five Foot Shelf of Classics than he went over to a system of free electives, which meant that students were free to ignore the Five Foot Shelf. Columbia responded by making its *Classics of the Western World* a required Humanities course (a core course for all under-graduates). The Chicago version of this was dubbed *General Education*, with the idea of its being intended for students in general, young or old, elite or popu-lar (as the Columbia program itself had been). But *generality* was its undoing when general education at Harvard succumbed to diverse academic interests and disciplines – to *ways of knowing* (among other methodologies) that could lead anywhere. The core of the classics earlier had been *ways of living*, i.e., what *the good life* could mean in human terms, but this was premised on what it meant to be human. *Ways of knowing* was one aspect of this, but only one. Without a core of central human concerns, *ways of knowing* could lead to a diffuse unbounded-ness, out on the so-called *cutting edge* of knowledge.

The elective character of even general education at Harvard was congenial to the free market that has dominated almost all aspects of cultural life in the past century, and it has benefited from the affluence – the great range of choices – that free enterprise has afforded the better classes, based on the pervasive assumption of unlimited growth and expansion. Education in the twenty-first century, however, without the luxuries of a bubble prosperity, will find itself constrained to make choices within much stricter limits. Choices are still there to be made, but just as the economy will have to live with much less exploitation of natural and human resources, society will have to make harder choices – giving up some of the freedom our affluence has afforded in order to preserve other values judged more essential. Education will have to do the same – make judgments as to what is most essential. Without closing the door on intellectual growth, we will have to prepare people to make qualitative judgments as to what is most conducive in the longer run to *the good life* and what human goods are sustainable.

If we no longer have a full range of free electives but still must make choices, how can we make ourselves sufficiently self-aware and well-informed to make those choices wisely? Wisdom is clearly necessary, not just information and technical expertise. And if we look to the past for this maturity of judgment, in the twenty-first century we can no longer look just to our own past but must hope to share the mature experience of others.

To do this, I do not believe we need agreement at the start on how to define a *classic*. In fact, it is important not to theorize about this until we have taken into account what representatives of the major world traditions have considered classic, whatever the terms or genres of expression they propose. From this base of reference arrived at inductively, not deductively from our own premises, we might also ask, to what extent have certain classics, sprung from one tradition, come to be recognized by others, as many Chinese classics came to be accepted by other East Asian traditions, insofar as, for example, the classic literature of Korea and Japan incorporated Chinese classics into their own canon. In the same way, one can ask, given the influence of Buddhism in East Asia, to what extent did Buddhist sutras or other forms of Buddhist literature (e.g., the Chinese *Journey to the West* [*Xiyu ji*]) become classics for the Japanese and Koreans? Since in the nineteenth and twentieth centuries Western classics in philosophy, religion, and literature often became widely recognized in East Asia as classic (e.g., Shakespeare and Dostoevsky), this convergence of classics in modern reading lists should also be taken into account.

In this process, we shall be taking as classic what has survived into modern times, and this survival itself has an important claim on our consideration. These are works that have lasted, and their enduring character is what compels our attention: they are artifacts of human civilization, hard facts of historical survival that cannot be ignored. What else cannot be ignored, however, is that they are the products of history. They take the form history has given them, and as received later, many can no longer be taken simply as representing the original text that generated the classic tradition.

Let me conclude by reporting on recent developments that augur well for Columbia's leading role in the extension of our core curriculum to a wider range of world education. I refer to a conference held here in January that brought together:

1. Leaders of our own core program
2. Leaders in the national preservation of core texts in the Association for Core Texts and Courses
3. Leaders in new efforts being made to establish core programs in East Asia.[2]

Both of the latter two groups had tended to follow the much-publicized models of general education at Chicago and Harvard. The unhappy experience of those who did so and the more recent publicity surrounding the failure of the Harvard model and unsuccessful attempts to fix it at Harvard, have created a new awareness of what Columbia has done better.

The second factor is the implosion of the educational system in China based since the days of Mao on a Stalinist/Maoist version of Marxism and, after its collapse, on the headlong pursuit of Western science and technology. We now witness a new eagerness to provide a plan for the humanities in Chinese education.

In the current situation, the natural desire to reclaim their own classics as part of their own Chinese identity converges on the need to reengage with the outside world and find a place in the curriculum for other world classics to supplement or replace Marxist works.

When we planned our January conference on *Classics for an Emerging World*, we were well aware of these trends and extended invitations broadly to the groups just mentioned. As things turned out, the response was beyond all of our expectations, and the enthusiasm was overwhelming for extending the discussion further in additional conferences both here and in the Far East. For this purpose, an international committee of correspondence is being formed to plan such meetings here and abroad, coordinating our efforts with those of others both nationally and internationally. In the meantime, we are publishing the proceedings of our January conference in both English and Chinese under the title *Classics for an Emerging World*.

Let me know if you want to get on the mailing list of corresponding members. If enough of you are interested, we may even form an alumni division. After all, lifelong learning was encouraged as part of the original core at Columbia, so there is no reason why alumni should not be included, even in a movement of these global proportions.

Notes

1 The conference was titled Classics for an Emerging World and held January 19-20, 2008.

Works Cited

de Bary, Wm. Theodore. *Confucian Tradition and Global Education.* Hong Kong: Chinese UP, 2007.

Pohl, Karl-Heinz. "Reflections on Avant-Garde Theory in a Chinese-Western Cross-Cultural Context – Or an Amateur Attempt in Metatheory." *Newsletter for the Study of East Asian Civilizations. Taipei: National Taiwan University* 3 (April 2004): 2-15.

The Vanishing Shakespeare. A Report by the American Council of Trustees and Alumni. April 2007. <<https://www.goacta.org/publications/downloads/VanishingShakespeare.pdf>>.

"Where's the Bard?" *Inside Academe* 12.4 (Summer 2007): 1-2.

Who We Were, Are, and Will Be, Seen Through a Darwinian Lens

Debra Everett-Lane
Columbia University

For many texts, there is little question about their validity as part of a humanities course. That is not the case with the works of Charles Darwin, though, at least based on my own experience. Within my primary discipline of history, science tends to be treated as something separate, a topic relegated to the isolated field of history of science rather than incorporated into general historical discussions. And scientific texts are often treated in a similar way with respect to the humanities. Thus, Darwin is set aside as a scientist, whose focus on biology, biogeography, geology, and even anthropology has little philosophical or cultural bearing on our understanding of human nature and our experience in the world.

So, today I will make my own case for his great relevance to how we think about ourselves by using *Origin of Species* and *Descent of Man* to look at the past, present, and future. I will begin with "who we were." I would like to explore this in two ways, the first of which is in terms of who we thought we were before Darwin's theory came along.

Before Darwin, the most prevalent belief was that species were stable, based both on the Judeo-Christian tradition and on the evidence of empirical observation, since we do not generally see new species form before our eyes. Everything had already been created; nothing new would arise. Beyond this, there was the belief that species had been created as part of a divine plan and so had been created with purpose and perfection. Humans were without question part of this divine plan as well, also created with purpose and perfection (though we had fallen and become imperfect since Eden). We were perhaps related to other species through a great chain of being or perhaps an entirely separate act of creation, but, again without question, humans were at the top of the hierarchy: humans were made in God's own image and given stewardship over the rest of nature. This conviction of our specialness and superiority colored our view of our place in the world, of our right to use and control nature as we saw fit. It led to the assurance that we were (or had the potential to be) God-like. What imperfections we had due to desire, ignorance, or sin had the potential to be resolved, at least to some degree, through conscious effort, whether based in faith or rationality.

This image of our origins, nature, and role in the world was radically challenged by Darwin, which leads me to my second understanding of "who we were" – what Darwin tells us about our past. He fiercely attacked those who advocated a literal Scriptural understanding of our origins, arguing instead for the evolution of the human species from related species over an immensely long period of time. Our appearance on the earth was not the result of purposeful special creation, but the result of the trial-and-error of natural selection. We were not separate from other species but were part of the endless branching of the tree of life. We share physical similarities to other species to the extent that, as we have since discovered, we share 99% of our DNA with chimpanzees, 98% of our DNA with fruit flies, and 40% of our DNA with yeast. We share emotions, the power of reasoning, and language with animals. Darwin even argues in *Descent of Man* that those attributes that we think of as distinctly human, the concepts of religion and morality, could have evolved from the capacity for rational speculation and from social instincts. In sum, Darwin says, "we must acknowledge...that man with all his noble qualities, with his god-like intellect which has penetrated into the movements and constitution of the solar system – with all these exalted powers – Man still bears in his bodily frame the indelible stamp of his lowly origin" (561).

So, we were not separate. We were not even superior to other species because Darwin's theory redefines perfection not as an ideal form at the top of a hierarchy, but instead as simple survivability. Man and cockroach are therefore equally perfect, the cockroach perhaps more perfect since as a species it is 100 times older than we are. According to Darwin's theory, humanity was no longer special or ideal, no longer imbued with purpose and superiority. Freud would later claim that, with this retelling of our past, Darwin had dealt humanity a great narcissistic wound, that he had permanently knocked man off of his pedestal.

And yet, there is a doubleness to Darwin. Even though his theory clearly implies that humanity is related to and little different from other species, Darwin reveals a reluctance to abandon an anthropocentric view. He sees humanity simultaneously as only one branch of the all-encompassing tree of life and also as the pinnacle of that tree: "Man may be excused for feeling some pride at having risen, though not through his own exertions, to the very summit of the organic scale; and the fact of his having thus risen, instead of his having been aboriginally placed there, may give him hope for a still higher destiny in the distant future" (561). Even if man was not created with purpose, he nonetheless seemed the fulfillment of purpose.

This leads us to "who we are." Who are we today in the context of Darwin's theory? This is the question of nature versus nurture writ large: how much of who we are comes from our DNA and evolutionary ancestry, and how much comes from the influence of culture and society? But one of the most challenging ways for students to look at the question of "who we are" is to frame it in terms of free will. If much of our behavior can be explained by biology, by hormones, by instinct, what kind of control over ourselves are we left with? This is an immensely important question to ask considering that many earlier authors that students will have read absolutely rely upon a notion of free will, the idea that we can deliberately choose to reject (or at least mitigate) appetites and bad conduct, that we can choose to conform to reason and virtue. Is it still possible to rely on an idea of free will after Darwin?

Take morality as an example. In *Descent of Man*, Darwin explains how a moral sense could evolve through natural selection as a result of three developments. First, social instincts would not only lead an organism to be cooperative in a way that aids community survival, but would also lead the organism to take pleasure from the community, resulting in sympathy. Second, highly developed mental faculties would allow for reflection on (and therefore judgment of) past actions and motives. Third, language would enable expression of common opinion about what constitutes good conduct. So, morality for Darwin is a combination of sympathy, rationality, and common opinion, not unlike theorists of moral sentiment like David Hume and Adam Smith. Morality is natural. Morality aids community survival: an appealing conception.

And yet, the idea of a moral instinct is also troublesome. For Hume, when sympathy does not go far enough, as with our detachment from a stranger in a far-off land, rationality and general standards step in to guide us. But does this happen in the same way for Darwin's moral instinct? What if the survival benefits of our sympathy do *not* extend to those outside of our community and instinct can *not* always be trumped by rationality? What if we are trying to push our morality beyond its natural limits?

Beyond this, there is also the problem of relativism. The idea of a common moral instinct might suggest that morality is absolute. And yet, this possibility is undercut by Darwin's assertion that the specific manifestation of a moral sense is very much relative to the species. Thus, his speculation on the morality of bees:

> In the same manner as various animals have some sense of beauty, though they admire widely different objects, so they might have a sense of right and wrong, though led by it to follow widely different lines of conduct. If, for instance, to take an extreme case, men were reared under precisely the same conditions as hive-bees, there can hardly be a doubt that our unmarried females would, like the worker-bees, think it a sacred duty to kill their brothers, and mothers would

strive to kill their fertile daughters; and no one would think of interfering. (526)

Clearly, this is not the morality of humans, which leaves open the possibility that at least as a single species we might share a single form of morality. But maybe it does not. Maybe morality is as relative to groups within species as to species as a whole. For example, today many scholars – from disciplines as disparate as sociobiology, evolutionary psychology, and anthropology, to name a few – argue that we are born with a universal moral grammar, composed of five main elements: the notions of fairness, community loyalty, authority, purity, and avoidance of harm to others (Pinker). Yet despite a common moral grammar, we speak different moral languages because the ranking that we give to these different elements is cultural. I may give greater weight to fairness and avoidance of harm, and you may give greater weight to community loyalty and respect for authority. As a result, we develop moralities that conflict. Where does this leave us? Can we deliberately modify our moral ranking so that we can reach a universal standard? Would that undercut Darwin's initial assertion that morality develops in part to benefit the specific community in which it arises? Above all, the main question here is to what extent we can control and change our behavior – a question that is of unending interest to students.

So, we come to the future: what does evolutionary theory tell us about who we will be or who we can be, not just as individuals but as a species? Here again there is a doubleness due to the question of whether humanity is still embedded in natural processes or whether we have somehow escaped them. Are we still governed by natural selection? Do we now select ourselves? And if we select ourselves, by what criteria? Darwin himself ponders these questions in *Descent of Man*, when he says that:

> Man scans with scrupulous care the character and pedigree of his horses, cattle, and dogs before he matches them; but when he comes to his own marriage he rarely, or never, takes any such care…yet he might by selection do something not only for the bodily constitution and frame of his offspring, but for their intellectual and moral qualities. Both sexes ought to refrain from marriage if they are in any marked degree inferior in body or mind; but such hopes are Utopian and will never be even partially realized until the laws of inheritance are thoroughly known. All do good service who aid toward this end. (559)

And we can add to Darwin's hypothesis our own increasing attempts to select our progeny through the use of genetics. Are these attempts to ensure a fitter humanity a fulfillment of natural selection? Or are they a rejection of natural selection, due to the assumption that we can do a better job ourselves at determining and increasing the best traits?

Also, consider how we apply the concept of the natural struggle for existence to human society. Do we understand this concept in the narrow sense of the struggle between individuals, leading us to advocate (or at least allow) a competition of all-against-all? Do we understand it in the wide sense of the struggle of a species as a whole, leading us to favor internal harmony as we struggle with a united front against environmental challenges? Do we reject the concept of a struggle for existence altogether on the grounds that different rules now apply to humans? Exploring whether struggle in society is natural or not and inevitable or not is a means to speculation about what kind of society we think we will or should be.

Finally, beyond the question of who we will be, there is the question of whether we will even continue to be at all. For Darwin, the fluctuation of environments, the spontaneity of variation, and the absence of a preordained plan means that there is no possibility of predicting which species will survive. As he says in *Origin of Species*:

> Looking to the future, we can predict that the groups of organic beings which are now large and triumphant...will for a long period continue to increase. But which groups will ultimately prevail, no man can predict; for we well know that many groups, formerly most extensively developed, have now become extinct. Looking still more remotely to the future, we may predict that...of the species living at any one period, extremely few will transmit descendants to a remote futurity. (174)

This is a remarkably destabilizing thought. We might optimistically define ourselves as one of those groups that is currently "large and triumphant," assuming that we will continue to increase for a long period yet to come, but that is no guarantee of permanence. In the Christian tradition, the concept of Judgment Day signals the end of our corporal existence, but with the implication that there will be an end to corporal existence in general and that we ourselves will continue in a spiritual existence. In the Darwinian tradition, there is the greatest probability that there will come an end to our species and that it will be complete. But for the rest of nature, life will go on. According to the title of the recent book by Alan Weisman, there will be the world without us. Does this realization lead us to humility, to despair, or to a spirit of *carpe diem*? How does the awareness of our own impermanence impact our choices for the future?

To conclude, Darwin offers myriad avenues for exploring who we were, are, and will be that both challenge our oldest assumptions and inform our contemporary debates. And though I have raised far more questions than I have answered, that is what good discussion is all about.

Works Cited

Darwin, Charles. *The Descent of Man.* In *On the Origin of Species by Means of Natural Selection.* Ed. Joseph Carroll Peterborough. Canada: Broadview, 2003.

Pinker, Steven. "The Moral Instinct." *New York Times Magazine* 13 January 2008.
Weisman, Alan. *The World Without Us*. New York: Thomas Dunne, 2007.

Georg Simmel's "The Metropolis and Mental Life": An Anchor for the First-Year Core

Kathleen A. Kelly
Phyllis Anina Moriarty
Babson College

As a core text for a first-year foundation course exploring the question "Who are we?" Georg Simmel's essay "The Metropolis and Mental Life" (1903) can be especially illuminating. Although written over a century ago, Simmel's description of the forces at work in the metropolis offers students insights into their own immediate college experiences. As a result of this personal connection, students are more ready to inquire into the historical forces that contributed to the conditions of modernity, and to empathize with the experiences of their contemporaries around the globe responding to similar forces in circumstances very different from their own. In short, Simmel's essay can become the center of a rich cluster of core and contemporary texts. To illustrate, we identify Simmel's key concepts and then apply them to Fritz Lang's *Metropolis*, Ngugi wa Thiong'o's "Minutes of Glory," and Gabriel Axel's *Babette's Feast*.

In his essay, Simmel explains the powerful forces of modernity that at once enable the individual's quest for independence and distinction and at the same time threaten it. Simmel's essay focuses immediately on the beleaguered individual: "The deepest problems of modern life derive from the claim of the individual to preserve the autonomy and individuality of his existence in the face of overwhelming social forces, of historical heritage, of external culture, and of the technique of life," forces he captures in the term "objective culture" (409). At the heart of his explanation is the contrast between the development of the individual in the small town or traditional community and the metropolis. In rural and traditional communities the small circle affords the individual a comforting, habitual rhythm of life that allows for "deeply felt and emotional relationships" (410). For the development of individuality, however, it allows only a narrow field with well-monitored boundaries: "the smaller the circle which forms our milieu is, and the more restricted those relations to others are which dissolve the boundaries of the individual, the more anxiously the circle guards the achievements, the conduct of life, and the outlook of the individual..." (417).

In contrast to deeply felt emotional relations, the metropolis develops intellect, and is characterized by impersonal time, rapid change, and an overstimulation of the senses. These, in turn, promote three characteristic defenses: a reductively calculating mind with a reliance on money as the measure of all things, a blasé attitude, and a social reserve or antipathy. If the individual develops these protective defenses, however, the metropolis frees him from the narrow expectations of the small circle: "in the thickest crowd of the big city...the bodily proximity and narrowness of space makes the mental distance [and hence the freedom from surveillance] only the more visible" (418).

This mental distance, this freedom from the guardians of the small circle, permits the development of individuality, an individuality the metropolis not only allows but also requires. For in order to succeed in the urban market, the individual must develop a high degree of specialization and must stimulate within fellow metropolitans ever newer and more particular desires to attract them to buy: "the seller must always seek to call forth new and differentiated needs to the lured customer" (420). Thus while the individuation that the metropolis encourages could mean a unique and fulfilling self-development, the great danger is that individuation will be for its own sake, meaningless, without spiritual value, and eccentric merely in order to attract attention and recognition. In Simmel's terms, there may be a striving to be "audible" at the expense of "spirituality, delicacy, and idealism" (422).

Because he focuses particularly on the mental life of the striving individual, rather than on more classical sociological questions (Levine 102), Simmel's concepts can readily be applied to the conditions of the first-year student. Students new to college can feel uprooted from the relatively small circle of their families and high schools as they are transplanted into the larger circle of a university, where they are challenged to establish their identity in the face of a much larger or more competitive and select crowd. They may feel a new sense of freedom and autonomy, but may also feel overwhelmed and anonymous, and have a strong need to be recognized, even if that means through exaggerated or extreme behavior. Students may arrive with a calculating attitude, seeing college primarily as a ticket to a well-paying job, and at the same time, they may be eager to examine the crude equation of money with happiness.

Simmel's concepts help explain the sense of personal emancipation, autonomy, and inducements to self-distinction students may feel as they move from the small to the large circle, but also the dangers that can be corollaries to these freedoms: a feeling of being overwhelmed by social forces, the development of a blasé attitude, a calculating mentality, a reserve toward others, or a striving to be "audible" at the expense of cultivating more fulfilling interests and activities. Simmel ends his essay without taking a position as to whether the metropolitan will become tragically shallow, speciously individuated, and necessarily overwhelmed by objective culture, or whether he or she will become the uniquely blessed recipient of the metropolis' gifts of freedom, autonomy, and opportunity: "it is not our task," he tells us in closing, "either to accuse or to pardon, but only to understand" (424). It is just as possible, however, to see that Simmel's account actually constitutes a powerful challenge: if we continually struggle to resist being overwhelmed by objective culture, we may take advantage of all that the metropolis offers for developing a unique and fulfilling subjectivity.

In defining this challenge, Simmel's essay looks backward and forward, and thus it can help draw together and reinforce themes emphasized in commonly used core texts. For example, in his discussion of the small circle, Simmel cites the fifth-century Athenian's vexed sense of freedom and constraint, as well as the emergent freedoms of medieval towns. He also sees the metropolis as the inheritor and entanglement of two historical ways of defining the subjective ideal: the eighteenth century's belief that freedom from outmoded traditional inequalities would "permit the noble substance common to all to come to the fore" and Romanticism's desire to develop the individual's "qualitative uniqueness and irreplaceability" (423). Simmel thus can reinforce the relevance that core texts related to these historical struggles have for the contemporary metropolitan.

Simmel also helps illuminate contemporary texts, and since traditional texts will be familiar options for foundation core courses, here we demonstrate using three works that postdate Simmel's essay. We have chosen works that, though radically different in form, style, and place of origin, are readily accessible to first-year students: the film *Metropolis* directed by the early twentieth-century German director Fritz Lang; a short story, "Minutes of Glory," by the contemporary Nigerian writer Ngugi wa Thiong'o; and Danish director Gabriel Axel's 1988 film based on Isak Dinesen's short story, *Babette's Feast*. Lang's film offers a powerful visual representation of the struggle between the metropolis's objective and subjective cultures, Thiong'o depicts the crushing effect objective culture can have on a single individual, and Axel's film offers a paradoxical vision of small circle and metropolitan values brought together through the power of art.

Set in 2026, Fritz Lang's *Metropolis* offers a futuristic vision of a vast metropolis where for the majority no individuation is even possible, where objective culture has destroyed autonomy. Fueled by huge engines in the bowels of the earth and kept going by masses of workers hardly distinguishable from cogs in the huge machines they operate, the metropolis is literally governed by clocks. Every ten hours the screech of a whistle punctuates the change of shift. Workers enter and exit the machine rooms in phalanxes of six abreast, each wearing identical caps and coveralls. Walking in lockstep with bowed heads, identified by numbers not names, one is indistinguishable from another.

In stark contrast, Joh Fredersen manages the city from high above the streets atop a new Tower of Babel, his office resembling a cross between the floor of a stock exchange and a military command center. He embodies Simmel's metropolitan man, governed by intellect, absorbed by endless calculation, and far removed from the emotional relationships that Simmel posits in small town life. The manager's blasé attitude shields him from observing the fear of his office flunkies and renders him indifferent to the "blood" with which his workers "lubricate" the pulsing machines essential to the functioning of the metropolis. Fredersen is the "head," and the laborers are the "hands" of the city.

Fredersen and the other fathers, "for whom every revolution of a machine wheel meant gold," have created a pleasure garden for their sons. However, the attraction of the luscious plants, seductive women, and exotic birds cannot distract Fredersen's son, Freder, from the magnetism of the saintly Maria, who suddenly appears in the middle of this ersatz paradise. Maria personifies idealism, purity, and spirituality, the very qualities at risk in the metropolis. Meanwhile, Maria's alter-ego, a robot created by the mad scientist Rotwang, personifies what freedom without communal values might lead to: irrationality, corruption, and destruction. The drama of *Metropolis* turns around which Maria will lead the workers to revolution. In the end, Freder as savior reconciles the workers and capitalists, and the film concludes with the same epigram with which it began: "The Mediator between head and hands must be the heart." Inspired by Maria, Freder has saved the city by restoring a spiritual subjectivity – the "heart" of a society.

Whereas Lang uses an epic canvas to depict the dystopia of a futuristic metropolis split into two warring cultures, Thiong'o's "Minutes of Glory" focuses more narrowly, on the struggles with objective culture experienced by a single Kenyan woman. Beatrice left her parents' farm to find work in the city, and when the story begins she is working in a beer hall and occasionally taking in men clients. Although not particularly bad looking, she is not popular with the customers – "a hard-up customer's last resort" (557) – perhaps because she "had a horror of soliciting lovers or directly bartering her body for hard cash. What she wanted was decent work and a man or several men who cared for her. Perhaps she took that need for a man, for a home, for a child with her to bed. Perhaps it was this genuine need that scared off men who wanted other things from barmaids" (559-560).

She is especially envious of Nyagūthū, a glamorous, popular, and yet completely blasé barmaid, and eventually Beatrice decides to prove to herself and to the others that she, too, can be glamorous. She robs a client, spends the cash on high heels, earrings, stockings, and dresses, and develops a "slight glint in her eyes that made men's eyes turn to her. This thrilled her" (565). She then returns to the bar where she committed her crime, enjoying the stares of the girls who can hardly recognize her and acting blasé toward the men who flock to dance with her. The police eventually arrive to arrest her, and as she is taken to the door, knowing that her few "minutes of glory" are over, "she turned her head and spat" (566). Ironically, Nyagūthū, the glamorous girl who was the object of Beatrice's envy, weeps at Beatrice's transformation and arrest. Far from feeling herself superior to Beatrice, Nyagūthū had said of her: "But you, you seemed above all this – somehow you had something inside you that I did not have" (565). Illustrated here is the profound disruption of moving from an agrarian village into the capitalist metropolis. Beatrice is freed from the expectations of her small circle, but the forces of the objective culture that turn her into a commodity crush her. With no understanding of how she is being shaped by these forces, she has no wherewithal to counter the objective culture by developing a subjective strength of her own.[1]

Babette's Feast illustrates a more successful struggle to develop within the same breast the emotional depths and communal unity characteristic of the small circle and the autonomy and individual distinction accessible to the metropolitan. Two sisters in remote Jutland, Martine and Philippa, refuse their suitors' invitations to follow them to the metropolis to build a life of fame and distinction. Instead, the sisters devote themselves to ministering to the small congregation established by their minister father. When Babette, a beleaguered metropolitan, is washed up on their shores as a result of a civil war in Paris, the sisters rescue her, and in return, Babette becomes their willing servant.

Unbeknownst to the sisters, Babette brings a personal distinction from the metropolis: she is a world-class chef. Out of their rural scarcity, Babette skillfully coaxes modest and tasteful pleasures and gradually becomes an essential member of their small community. When, after many years in her new life, Babette suddenly wins the lottery, instead of using the money to return to the metropolis, she spends the entire sum preparing a single, astounding feast to help the community honor their deceased minister. The result of this abundant feast in the midst of the pinched community is a liberation from old grudges, sins, and sorrows, and a renewed spirit of generosity and forgiveness.

Fortuitously, Martine's former suitor and now a famous general in the metropolis, comes to the dinner with a secret challenge to himself. This night he will decide his lifelong debate: in giving up his pursuit of Martine and her ascetic and spiritual life, had he, despite his subsequent worldly accomplishments, in fact merely wasted his life in vain pursuits? Much to his astonishment, Babette's surpassingly abundant feast in this poorest of villages enables him to realize the paradox of spiritual wholeness he had thought unattainable: "Everything we have chosen has been granted to us. And everything we rejected has also been granted to us." Babette, whose artistry enables this realization, had cultivated and excelled at the individuation required by the metropolis, but here she came to know the emotional depth and community of the small circle. Through her generosity and her art, she has brought her guests to the insight that for a whole life, both sets of values must be appreciated and celebrated.

Taken together, these three texts suggest the broad applicability and analytical power of Simmel's classic essay. Whether the emphasis is on the power of the metropolis to overwhelm or to liberate, the essay clarifies the ongoing struggle required to create a life that pursues self-development and distinction together with communal and spiritual values.

Note

1 Included in the same anthology of short stories (Halpern), Haruki Murakami's "The Elephant Vanishes" also and delightfully illustrates Simmel's concepts. In the mode of magical realism, it represents the struggle of a Tokyo salesman to comprehend and share the vision of spiritual balance and harmony he experiences while observing the eponymous elephant.

Works Cited

Babette's Feast, dir. Gabriel Axel. Perf. Stéphane Audran, Birgitte Federspiel. 1988. DVD. MGM, 2001.

Halpern, Daniel, ed. *The Art of the Story: An International Anthology of Contemporary Short Stories.* New York: Penguin, 1999.

Levine, David N. "Simmel as Educator: On Individuality and Modern Culture." *Theory, Culture & Society* 8 (1991): 99-117.

Metropolis, dir. Fritz Lang. 1927. Restored authorized edition. DVD. Kino International, 2002.

Murakami, Haruki. "The Elephant Vanishes." Trans. Jay Rubin. In Halpern, Daniel, ed. *The Art of the Story: An International Anthology of Contemporary Short Stories.* New York: Penguin, 1999: 453-465.

Thiong'o, Ngugi wa. "Minutes of Glory." In Halpern, Daniel, ed. *The Art of the Story: An International Anthology of Contemporary Short Stories.* New York: Penguin, 1999: 557-566.

Simmel, Georg. "The Metropolis and Mental Life." *The Sociology of Georg Simmel.* Trans. Kurt Wolff. Glencoe, IL: Free Press, 1950: 409-424.

The Woman in the Dunes as a Core Text: Abe Kōbō's Search for a New Modern Identity

Peter Rothstein
Juniata College

> Writing a novel is very different from thinking something through logically. Whereas now we operate under new social relationships, our inner selves still cling to the older values. Thus there is a conflict between the self who seeks a new social relationship and the self who tries to maintain the older form. Regardless of what one wants, one still must face the new relationship, although the older self rejects it. I suppose that this has been a common literary theme forever. Whether man will survive or not is also an eternal subject, though more pronounced in our time. I think that a characteristic of modern literature is this unpleasantness regarding human existence, which has been superimposed on a desire for new human relationships. That is to say, there is an uneasiness as to whether the quest for new relationships is meaningful or whether human relationships are worth seeking at all. They might simply disappear altogether. – *Abe Kōbō* (Hardin 454-55)

The theme of this conference poses the question "Who are we?" and addresses the place of core texts in helping students to ask and answer that question in their experience of higher education. Embedded in the question are issues such as what might be the basis for forming an identity, how and when such an identity is formed, and what the role of a liberal arts education is in helping students either find or reform their identities. Such questions do not lead to easy answers, and part of the task of a higher education is to help students to acknowledge the complexity of the question as well as to help them shape an answer using as resources thoughts and texts left behind by others grappling with those same questions. Of course, implicit in considering the role of core texts in helping students think through these issues is the question of just what a core text is anyway. It struck me that the experiences that I have had teaching a core course at a small liberal arts college would prove germane to this discussion.

The course in question is "Interdisciplinary Colloquium: Modern Knowledge and the Self," a course which investigates the development of the modern and transition to postmodern via themes of dominant discourses of knowledge, conceptions of identity and the idea of a self as an autonomous individual. We do this in a broad manner and use a combination of general introductions to theory, philosophy, novels, and various primary sources. In choosing the texts for the course, the faculty members involved have been concerned with finding documents that I think fit within the boundaries of what make up core texts – texts that ponder questions of the nature and mechanics of knowledge, bases for social structures and relations, and conceptions of identity. The range of readings is wide, from authors fundamental to the formation of a modern (and perhaps western) identity, such as Descartes, Condorcet, Newton, and Smith, to others who raise questions about that modern formation, such as Baudrillard, Bordo, DeLillo, the Dalai Lama, and Abe Kōbō, among others. We encourage the students to actively engage with these sources via journals, discussions, and group projects, as well as by using standard lectures.

Central to the structure of the course is a look at the modern from outside of Europe and the United States, and as a historian of Japan, this is where I come into the course. The Japanese experience of modernity (if one can really try to claim that there was a singular Japanese experience) is something that was quite different from that of western nations, and the rapid and orchestrated nature of the modernization of Japan helps to put some of the basic tensions and questions that are at the heart of the modern experience into focus. The question of modernity and also postmodernity is something that has been hotly debated in Japan since people in Japan began the project of modernization, and in some circles the question is still debated whether one can claim that Japan was ever modernized because modernity can be seen as a culturally bound phenomenon.

At the crux of the question of modernity are concepts of an autonomous self in relation to society and the central place of a scientific, or, as some describe it, a material-realist understanding of the world. These two concepts form the core of the novel *The Woman in the Dunes*, written by Abe Kōbō in 1961-2, a text that we use in some senses as a hinge to swing the course from a focus on a modern worldview to that of a postmodern one.

To discuss this novel (especially as an historian), it is helpful to give a brief background to the world in which Abe was writing and to the brief and tumultuous experience that people in Japan had with modernity in the roughly ninety-four years before Abe published this work.

For about two hundred and fifty years prior to 1868, what we now call Japan had been officially isolated from the rest of the world and was maintained in a state somewhat analogous to European feudalism. It was essentially un-mechanized and agrarian. In 1868, in what really amounted to a revolution, a new government largely made up of people who had studied the development of Europe and the United States took power and began a process of rapid industri-alization and social and cultural modernization. Aside from the rapid physical modernization, by which within the space of roughly forty years Japan became a significant world power with relatively well developed infrastructure and a for-midable military, the government and prominent intellectuals pushed a program of "Civilization and Enlightenment," which sought to inculcate a rational, mod-ern mindset in the populace. By the turn of the twentieth century there was nearly universal participation in the new compulsory education system, which placed a heavy emphasis on mathematics and physical sciences, and the path to success was ostensibly to excel in studies and climb up a meritocratic ladder as an enlightened individual. On the cultural front, a generation of novelists strove to find and develop the meaning of a modern individual through the investiga-tion of a self that could be explored and exhibited in the art form of the novel.

Of course, just as had become clear in Europe and the United States, the conflicts inherent in modern conceptions of society and individuals had begun to manifest, and tensions bubbled up. For every one individual who could move up though society via their rational, autonomous agency and become materially and socially successful, there were thousands who had flocked to the cities, only marginally and functionally educated, to become more like automatons than autonomous individuals. The government of Japan, which initially began its program of modernization so as not to become colonized by western powers, had become a colonial power itself and became committed to an idea of a Dar-winist competition of survival of the fittest nation, which led to the conflagration of the Pacific War.

It was in this period of the flowering of Japan's modernization, the 1920s, that Abe was born. In a new nation in which schoolchildren were inculcated with a national identity said to stretch back 2600 years to the first Emperor, Abe grew up in the de facto colony of Manchuria, never quite feeling like he had a true national identity. He had distrust for a sense of belonging to a nation, a sense of belonging that is a core part of a modern identity, and that distrust is something that appears again and again in his work. Abe sat through school be-ing taught that as a Japanese he should have a deep affinity for his native moun-tains and seashore, all the while being raised in the vast Manchurian plains, and he never felt quite right when visiting Japan. He watched the mistreatment of ethnic Chinese (who were considered "brothers" in the rhetoric of the Japanese Empire) by his Japanese-Manchurian compatriots and questioned by what ac-count such treatment made sense. At the end of the war, he experienced first-hand the utter collapse of the society in Manchuria and witnessed Japanese sol-diers turning on their Japanese civilian kin (Keene 72-73; Shields 27-35).

Many intellectuals in Japan considered the war a failure of rationality or, rather, a result of following supposedly rational structures of nation and state that used the fruits of science to devastating results. Abe, too, tried to consider ways that humans could relate and form groups that were somehow more genuine or meaningful than political units such as nations. In the decade following the war, he was attracted to the ideals of the Japanese Communist Party (JCP) and felt that in communism there was some hope for transcending national identities and at the same time forming new social communities that solved some of the fundamental modern tensions between individuals and societies. However, with the ill-fated Hungarian revolution of 1956, he became disenchanted with communism, and his vocal opposition later got him expelled from the JCP (Motoyama 320-21). He was also concerned with working out the problems of social relations in cities, which had swelled in population with the first wave of modernization in Japan and were again swelling in the postwar re-industrialization. Abe was attempting in his literature to portray the disorientations resulting from this rapid urbanization as well as trying to work out new ways for people to connect within it. In Abe's words, the city was a foreboding presence, but it could not be ignored. "I think that the city is associated with nightmare because we have not yet found a way of adequately expressing the city, of putting it into words," and his driving force was "to find the city's own words in order to challenge the illusion of the city's disease of loneliness" (Pollack 134). His work abounds with characters who are lost in cities, who disappear in the course of court proceedings, whose physical selves are replaced by name cards or objects such as suitcases, or who turn into sticks or empty cocoons while searching for their place in an urban society. (For examples of this, see the following: Abe Kōbō, *Suna No Onna;* Abe Kōbō, *Beyond the Curve;* Abe Kōbō and Keene; Iles; Mitsutani; Richter; and Yamamoto.)

The Woman in the Dunes is a work that is full of these questions of individual identity, social relations, the possibility for reconciling individuals and societies, and the place of rational or scientific thought in establishing or maintaining one's identity. In the story, there is a man who we learn peripherally is a schoolteacher and who is on a quest to find a unique insect so that he can have his name immortalized alongside a new species of bug, thereby giving his life meaning. His approach to the task is described by Abe in a manner that renders it nearly absurdly rational, and in seeking this new insect, the man ends up being tricked into confinement in a sand pit in a seaside village, a place that exists solely because a few households ceaselessly shovel sand from the bottom of the pits in which their houses lie. The entire action of the novel centers on this man's attempts to leave the hole, and the novel ends asymptotically with the man having the means but no longer the will to escape to his former urban existence.

The main characters in the novel, the man and the woman whose house the man is thrown into, are never labeled anything other than "the man" or "the woman." While we know the man's name, Niki Junpei, it is only from official forms that we are shown by the author, which attest to his identity and proclaim his status as missing and finally as declared officially dead. Throughout the novel, the man appeals to his status as a "registered resident" (59) and to the fact that he pays his taxes as evidence that he should not be put into this situation, and he hangs onto these artifacts of the social order as a hope that the forces of the urban society of which he was a part will come and rescue him. No help ever does come, however, and in an episode in which he is attempting to escape the village and falls into quicksand, it is the villagers that have cruelly entrapped him and that exist by virtue of his slave labor who heed his cries for help. In numerous places throughout the novel, the meaninglessness of the man's life as a teacher who participates in an "illusory education" (98) is made clear and implicitly compared to what the reader might see as the meaninglessness of continually shoveling sand out of the bottom of a sandpit, an existence which the man in the end seemingly finds meaningful.

Abe gives us two sides of individual existence that are perhaps nearly equivalently meaningless, in the hole and outside of the hole, and he gives us two views of social organizations, the absurd sand village as well as urban society, that really allow very little apparent place for individual meaning or autonomy. The single place that seems to yield meaning in the novel is the interaction between the man and the woman, yet it is often cruel and inhumane. In the end, it yields a fleeting physical union that produces what is most likely a fatal extrauterine pregnancy that probably leaves the man in the hole alone – free to leave but unwilling to. However flawed it may be, the interface between humans that is shaped by their needs, desires, actions, and inactions, a place stripped of national, cultural, and orderly social trappings, is where Abe focuses the search for meaning of his novels and plays.

The question, of course, is: with this as a core text how do students react? Keyed in beforehand to the ideas of the modern conception of autonomous individuals, post-war doubts about perhaps irrational adherence to rational, scientific thought, and the social and economic forces that weigh in on the individual-social balance, students tend to do well in finding those elements in the novel. One thing that often surprises me is that students very often want to interpret the novel as a cry for the loss of some indigenous pre-modern Japanese identity. I suspect that this is due to the very element of cultural and national identification that made Abe queasy, something that is very much part of what students often uncritically consider the core of their identity. In working with that very misreading of the text, I have found that consciously considering elements of their own identities is a useful tool for helping students. In a broader sense, Abe's seemingly absurd plot, setting, and characters consistently get the students thinking about their own identities, their location within social structures, and the space for individual agency therein.

Works Cited

Hardin, Nancy. "An Interview with Abe Kobo." *Contemporary Literature* 15.4 (1974): 439-56.

Iles, Timothy. *Abe Kōbō: An Exploration of His Prose, Drama and Theatre.* Florence, Italy: European Press Academic Publishing, 2000.

Keene, Donald. *Five Modern Japanese Novelists.* New York: Columbia UP, 2003.

Kōbō, Abe. *Beyond the Curve.* Tokyo: Kodansha International, 1991.

---. *Suna No Onna.* Tokyo: Shinchōsha, 1962.

---. *The Woman in the Dunes.* New York: Vintage Books, 1991.

Kōbō, Abe and Donald Keene. *Three Plays.* Modern Asian Literature Series. New York: Columbia UP, 1993.

Mitsutani, Margaret. "Abe Kōbō's Early Short Fiction." *Japan Quarterly* 38.3 (1991): 347-49.

Motoyama, Mutsuko. "The Literature and Politics of Abe Kōbō: Farewell to Communism in *Suna No Onna.*" *Monumenta Nipponica* 50.3 (1995): 305-23.

Pollack, David. *Reading against Culture: Ideology and Narrative in the Japanese Novel.* Ithaca: Cornell UP, 1992.

Richter, Frederick. "A Comparative Approach to Abe Kōbō's S. Karuma-Shi No Hanzai." *The Journal of the Association of Teachers of Japanese* 9.2/3 (1974): 1-13.

Shields, Nancy K. *Fake Fish: The Theater of Kobo Abe.* New York: Weatherhill, 1996.

Yamamoto, Fumiko. "Metamorphosis in Abe Kobo's Works." *The Journal of the Association of Teachers of Japanese* 15.2 (1980): 170-94.

Descartes and the Existentialists: The Continuing Fruitfulness of the *Cogito*

James Woelfel
University of Kansas

Our conference theme is the question "Who are we?" and the role that classic texts can play in shedding light on the question for us today. In the field of philosophy there is no better example of such a text than Descartes's *Meditations on First Philosophy*, and specifically the First and Second Meditations, which famously enunciate the *Cogito ergo sum* – the certitude the individual consciousness has of its own existence – as the absolute foundation of knowledge. With the *cogito* Descartes initiates the modern philosophical preoccupation with the nature of consciousness and its relationship to the world and to the problem of personal identity or selfhood. The Cartesian *cogito* is furthermore an excellent example of one of the things that makes classic texts classic. Two of the major philosophers of the twentieth century, Edmund Husserl and Jean-Paul Sartre, explicitly returned to it, creatively reinterpreted it, and made it the foundation of two dramatically new approaches to philosophy.

In my paper I want to present, in ridiculously brief compass, Husserl's and Sartre's innovative use of the Cartesian *cogito*. My title, "Descartes and the Existentialists," refers to the fact that, contrary to his own intentions and despite his objections, the lasting influence of Husserl's pioneering work in phenomenology was as a methodology for some of the existentialists – notably Sartre, Maurice Merleau-Ponty, Simone de Beauvoir, and the American existentialist and Sartre translator Hazel Barnes.

For the most part I want to let Husserl and Sartre speak for themselves – not an easy assignment, since each wrote a lot on his use of the *cogito* and much of it is somewhat difficult reading – and I will try to clarify and interpret as we go. Precisely for clarity's sake, my Husserl text will be a 1931 lecture, "Phenomenology and Anthropology," which is a sort of summary of his ideas during the most "radical" phase of his philosophical development, as expressed much more fully in his book *Cartesian Meditations*. It was during the same period, in 1933-34, that Sartre studied in Berlin and was philosophically transformed by studying Husserl's phenomenology. Sartre will be represented here by his 1937 critique of Husserl, *The Transcendence of the Ego*, which lays the foundation for *Being and Nothingness*.

In "Phenomenology and Anthropology," Husserl makes unmistakably clear Descartes's unique importance and his own indebtedness. "All modern philosophy," he says, "originates in the *Cartesian Meditations*.... Accepting only what is evident to me, I, as an autonomous ego, must pursue to its ultimate grounds what others, following the tradition, regard as scientifically grounded. These ultimate grounds must be immediately and apodictically evident" (281-282). With Descartes's *Meditations*, Husserl asserts, "No longer is the world naively presupposed as self-evidently existing and self-evidently given in experience: self-evidence becomes a problem" (280). Employing the method of a radical skepticism in the First and Second Meditations, Descartes opened up the modern inquiry into the *transcendental* nature of consciousness: the immediately apprehended existence of consciousness itself as the absolute, *a priori* foundation or matrix of all knowledge.

Like all sympathetic interpreters of Descartes, Husserl distinguishes between what is of lasting validity in the *cogito* and the errors of Descartes's own conclusions. Referring to the *Meditations*, he says, "We shall be guided only by their form and by the resolute scientific radicalism which pervades them, while disregarding the content which is vitiated, in many respects, by unnoticed prejudices" (281). By general consensus Descartes's big mistake, reflecting the lingering influence in his thought of the prevailing Scholasticism, was to interpret the *cogito* to mean the existence of the individual consciousness as a "thinking substance" and from there to go on to argue for the existence of God as the guarantor of the reality of the world and the general reliability of our senses and reason.

Pursuing Descartes's method of doubt that led to the *cogito*, Husserl interpreted its status and meaning differently, as revealing the existence of a *transcendental ego* or subjectivity:

> Let the existence of the world be questionable for me now because it
> is not yet grounded, let it be subject to the epoché [the "bracketing"
> of the questions of the existence of the world and the nature of its
> contents]; I who question and practice the epoché, I exist nonetheless.
> I am conscious of my existence and can grasp it immediately and
> apodictically.... As this apodictic [or transcendental] ego, therefore, I

am prior to the existence of the world because I exist as this ego
whether or not the world's existence can be accepted and accounted
for.... As...[a transcendental] ego I am not this man in the existing
world, but the ego who doubts the existence of the world, as well as
its being thus-and-so.... The world still appears as it appeared formerly; the life in and of the world is not interrupted: the world is now
a bracketed "world," a mere phenomenon; it is the flow of experience
and consciousness, in general.... (283)

Husserl's career-long ambition, following directly in Descartes's footsteps,
was to establish philosophy as the fundamental science and the ground of all the
others: "Philosophy, genuine science," he writes, "aims at absolute, ultimately
valid truths which transcend all relativity" (279). This is the work of the transcendental ego, which is the level at which philosophical reflection properly
functions. True philosophy is phenomenology, the "systematic study of concrete
transcendental subjectivity." "The question is," Husserl continues,

how this subjectivity confers meaning and validity upon a world objective in itself. My own self, the essential structures of my entire
sphere of consciousness together with the structures of actual and
potential meanings, and the conferring of validity, must all be made
the themes of an eidetic science [i.e., a science of the *eide*, the "es-
sences" or essential structures of consciousness in its relations with
its objects] by me, the ego. (287)

Central to Husserl's influential contributions to phenomenological analysis was
the *eidos* of *intentionality*: consciousness is always consciousness *of* something,
whether physical phenomena, other people, ideas, or inner states.

Sartre constructed his own philosophical method, which he called an "existential phenomenology" or "phenomenological ontology," squarely on Husserl's
work while rejecting, with striking originality, Husserl's belief that what the
cogito discloses is a transcendental ego. It is hardly an exaggeration to say that
his departure from Husserl would become the distinctive linchpin of Sartre's
whole philosophical outlook. Like Heidegger, Husserl's other famous student,
Sartre rejected Husserl's whole project of making phenomenology a pure
Gründewissenschaft founded on the transcendental ego. Heidegger and Sartre
took from phenomenology a method of analyzing general characteristics of
"lived" human experience that would be an illuminating hermeneutic and not an
exact science, an enterprise of thoroughly concrete reflecting selves and not of
selves as transcendental egos. I hasten to add here that unlike Sartre, Heidegger,
whose lifelong philosophical pursuit was to recover the primordial meaning of
"being," considered the whole post-Cartesian effort to ground philosophy in
consciousness or subjectivity to be a fundamental mistake. The foundation of the
existential analytic in *Being and Time* is the human self's "everyday Be-
ing-in-the-world," a realm of social practices and relations to the physical world
out of which ideas of consciousness and its objects emerge as reflective distinc-

tions. In this absolutely crucial respect, Sartre always remained much closer to Husserl. Heidegger also significantly influenced him, but he clearly interpreted Heidegger in terms of his own Cartesian starting-point and analysis of consciousness.

In his famous 1945 lecture "Existentialism is a Humanism," defending existentialism against its critics, Sartre asserted his Cartesian starting-point:

> As our point of departure there can be no other truth than this: *I think therefore I am*. This is the absolute truth of consciousness confronting itself. Any theory that considers man outside of this moment of self-awareness is, at the outset, a theory that suppresses the truth, for outside of this Cartesian cogito, all objects are merely probable, and a doctrine of probabilities not rooted in any truth crumbles into nothing... in order for any truth to exist, there must first be an absolute truth. (40)

As is well known, this was a popular lecture, given without notes, to a general audience. It is a brilliant talk and remains a classic existentialist text, but it contains necessary simplifications and occasional factual errors. Sartre's statement aligning himself fully with the Cartesian *cogito* is one of the former. The "full story," with all the needed philosophical elaboration and clarification, appears in *The Transcendence of the Ego* and *Being and Nothingness*.

Scarcely three years after Sartre was introduced to Husserl's thought, he wrote *The Transcendence of the Ego*, a stunningly bold critique of Husserl and proposal for a new approach to phenomenology. Sartre begins by praising Husserl's work but immediately raises a question:

> We readily acknowledge the existence of a constituting consciousness. We find admirable all of Husserl's descriptions in which he shows transcendental consciousness constituting the world by imprisoning itself in empirical consciousness. Like Husserl, we are persuaded that our psychic and psycho-physical *me* is a transcendent object which must fall before the epoché. But we raise the following questions: is not this psychic and psycho-physical *me* enough? Need one double it with a transcendental *I*, a structure of absolute consciousness? (36)

Sartre goes on to argue that the consciousness that is immediate, intuitive awareness of phenomena is "'pre-personal,' without an I." Husserl's mistake is to identify this transcendental consciousness as an "I"-consciousness, a transcendental *ego*:

> The phenomenological conception of consciousness renders the unifying and individualizing role of the *I* totally useless. It is consciousness, on the contrary, which makes possible the unity and the personality of my *I*. The transcendental *I*, therefore, has no *raison d'etre*.... (40)

This "pre-personal" consciousness is by its very nature reflexive or self-aware: "the type of existence of consciousness is to be conscious of itself...consciousness is purely and simply consciousness of being conscious of...[an] object" (40). Sartre calls this primary form of consciousness "unreflected" consciousness. In *Being and Nothingness* he will call it the "pre-reflective cogito" and contrast it with the "reflective" or "Cartesian" cogito, which constitutes the "I." The "I" and the "me" belong among the objects of consciousness, not to consciousness itself, which is nothing but a translucent (self-) awareness that makes the world present and constructs its meanings. This analysis would issue in Sartre's whole discussion of consciousness as "Being-for-itself": a freedom or spontaneity within the density of the world ("Being-in-itself") that is undetermined by anything else while at the same time being "nothing" other than this activity of awareness. As consciousness, I am "not" any of the things I am conscious of, including my thoughts and feelings and myself as a self or "I." I freely and continually construct and reconstruct both my world and myself through my choices and actions and am entirely responsible for my life.

Clearly, the need for brevity has led me to gallop breathlessly through the implications of Sartre's dramatic revision of Husserlian phenomenology. Let me conclude all-too-quickly by expressing my (unelaborated) belief that these two great "Cartesians" – the master of phenomenology and his deviant student – like Descartes himself, have provocatively illuminated and thereby only deepened the mystery of human subjectivity.

Works Cited

Husserl, Edmund. *Cartesian Meditations: An Introduction to Phenomenology.* Trans. Dorion Cairins. The Hague: Martinus Nijhoff, 1960.

---. "Phenomenology and Anthropology." Trans. Richard G. Schmitt. In Charles Guignon and Derk Pereboom, eds. *Existentialism: Basic Writings.* Indianapolis: Hackett, 2001. Reprinted from *Philosophy and Phenomenological Research* 2 (1941): 1-14.

Sartre, Jean Paul. *The Transcendence of the Ego: An Existentialist Theory of Consciousness.* Ed. Forrest Williams. Trans. Robert Kirkpatrick. New York: Farrar, Straus, and Giroux, 1957.

---. *Existentialism is a Humanism.* Ed. John Kulka. Trans. Carol Macomber. New Haven & London: Yale UP, 2007.

We the People: A Noble Experiment

Dark Night of Our Souls' Democratic Vistas

Rev. Theophus "Thee" Smith
Emory University

Who are we? We are a nation of people who started out in the eighteenth century on a "noble experiment"[1] in democratic self-governance. But our experiment has faltered often enough for us to query yet again, "Who are we?" In particular, at the end of the present decade we have accumulated some of the most intractable issues of a superpower in the twenty-first century. In response, the following essay resonates with that classic text of sixteenth-century western spirituality, *Dark Night of the Soul.*

The choice here of a *dark night* metaphor to address questions of national and cultural identity is a phenomenological choice. For the most noble and praiseworthy endeavors in human experience also feature phenomena of intractable *darkness.* Defined here in more general, non-theological terms, spiritual darkness involves the absence or eclipse of visionary intelligence, a loss or purgation of enlightenment regarding one's spiritual integrity, and cascading consequences for both cognitive and affective experience. Related phenomena include, most significantly, inability to experience the power of one's cherished or hallowed ideals, and thus a loss of confidence in their reality and efficacy. In theological terms, as articulated in the *Dark Night* treatise by St. John of the Cross, the key phenomena involve a sense of the "eclipse of God" and "aridity" in one's affective experience of divine things.

In that connection, it is a phenomenological task to ascertain the sources of such negation. What is negating the power and reality of ideals that were formerly most vivid and compelling? The tradition of dark night spirituality poses alternative sources of such negation: (a) the noble source of attempting one's ideals and then appropriately, in due course, graduating to the state of experiencing their negation as a precondition and deeper preparation for their attainment. An alternative source is (b) the ignoble, more commonplace failure of not sufficiently attempting to sustain those ideals in a genuine or concerted way.

Dark Night of the Soul is a classic text in part because it provides in a definitive way and with enduring impact on the tradition of western spirituality a phenomenological description of the distinction between those two opposite conditions of our common psychological and moral experience. "Since these aridities might frequently proceed," wrote John of the Cross, "not from the night and purgation of the sensual desires aforementioned, but from sins and imperfections, or from weakness and lukewarmness, or from some bad humour or indisposition of the body, I shall here set down certain signs by which it may be known if such aridity proceeds from the aforementioned purgation, or if it arises from any of the aforementioned sins. For the making of this distinction I find that there are three principal signs…" (I.9.1).

In that regard, the present epoch in our U.S. experience offers an excellent opportunity to explore dark night phenomena as a heuristic (or *search engine*) for repristinating or reclaiming the democratic ideals of the nation. We will not, in that connection, enact a very different pastime of the nation: the American Jeremiad. The term *jeremiad* bears the name of the Hebrew prophet Jeremiah for his characteristic lamenting of his nation's gross moral and spiritual failures. As a genre of sermons and exhortations, jeremiads became popular among New England Puritans in the colonial period and are still alive and well today. Here, however, we will not follow the jeremiadic model of cataloguing or analyzing the nation's grosser sins and betrayals of its ideals as a rhetorical strategy for reaffirming or reinstating those ideals.[2]

Instead, we will deploy the sixteenth-century Spanish classic of *Dark Night of the Soul* in heuristic consonance with a fourteenth-century English classic of western mysticism, that of Dame Julian of Norwich (d. 1413). In her spirituality of divine generosity, *Revelations of Divine Love*, Julian hypothesized that failed idealism is not always, not necessarily, or not altogether a moral or spiritual failing. Rather, through divine grace it may be more profoundly construed as an unintended "fall." Metaphorically, it is like falling into a pit or abyss of negation while honorably endeavoring to attain one's ideals, rather than a thoroughgoing failing through willful, intentional, or culpable denial of those ideals.[3]

Again, this essay invokes such classic texts to answer the query "Who are we?" By following these texts' description of failed enlightenment in the pursuit of nobility and virtue, we will attempt a heuristic (again, a cognitive *search engine*) for renewing or reclaiming the nation's identity as constituted by its ideals. However, since our search for identity is fundamentally an American quest, we will, in concert with our Spanish and English sources, correlate the classical features of dark night spirituality with two texts that are also compelling classics of American self-definition: (1) the poet Walt Whitman's monograph, "Democratic

Vistas" (1871) and (2) *The Souls of Black Folk* by the African American scholar-activist W.E.B. DuBois (1903).

To anticipate the correlation of these works with a dark night schema, consider this more concise, proverbial instance from the celebrated oratory of the Rev. Dr. Martin Luther King, Jr.:

> I refuse to accept the view that mankind is so tragically bound to the starless midnight of racism and war that the bright daybreak of peace and brotherhood can never become a reality. (1964 Nobel Prize Acceptance Speech)

This quotation is felicitous because it combines a *dark night* and a *coming light* schema to correlate issues of war and racism with our democratic ideals as a nation and our prospects as a world leader, prospects that keenly interest many of us today. While reviewing similar themes in the works by Whitman and DuBois, we will keep the scope of this essay to only a brief exposition. At best, we can outline in treatise format the final sections of Whitman's expansive "Democratic Vistas" (498-499). Likewise, in the case of DuBois's *Souls*, we must limit our view to a single chapter, albeit a key chapter, "Of Our Spiritual Strivings" (44-47).

In the closing paragraphs of his "Democratic Vistas," Whitman, in a prophetic or prescient way, plays upon our selected themes of darkness and light, imperfection and contingency:

> [T]he problem of the future of America is in certain respects as dark as it is vast. Pride, competition, segregation, vicious willfulness, and license beyond example, brood already upon us. Unwieldy and immense, who shall hold in behemoth? Who bridle leviathan? Flaunt it as we choose, athwart and over the roads of our progress loom huge uncertainty, and dreadful, threatening gloom. It is useless to deny it.... Even today, amid these whirls, incredible flippancy, and blind fury of parties, infidelity, entire lack of first-class captains and leaders, added to the plentiful meanness and vulgarity of the ostensible masses − that problem, the labor question, beginning to open like a yawning gulf, rapidly widening every year − what prospect have we? We sail a dangerous sea of seething currents, cross and undercurrents, vortices − all so dark, untried − and whither shall we turn? It seems as if the Almighty had spread before this nation charts of imperial destinies, dazzling as the sun, yet with many a deep intestine difficulty, and human aggregate of cankerous imperfection, − saying, lo!...You said in your soul, I will be empire of empires, overshadowing all else, past and present, putting the history of old-world dynasties, conquests behind me, as of no account − making a new history, a history of democracy, making old history a dwarf − I alone inaugurating largeness, culminating time. (124-6)

Surely Whitman's rendering here is intentional in exposing national hubris. But it is a hubris that he himself shares, as evidenced elsewhere throughout his "Democratic Vistas." In this same passage, however, he allows for a type of judgment on that hubris that is not divine wrath but rather an immanent justice involving an integral, organic historical process:

> But behold the cost, and already specimens of the cost. Thought you greatness was to ripen for you like a pear? If you would have greatness, know that you must conquer it through ages, centuries – must pay for it with a proportionate price. *For you too, as for all lands, the struggle, the traitor, the wily person in office, scrofulous wealth, the surfeit of prosperity, the demonism of greed, the hell of passion, the decay of faith, the long postponement, the fossil-like lethargy, the ceaseless need of revolutions, prophets, thunderstorms, deaths, births, new projections and invigorations of ideas and men.* (126, emphasis mine)

Thus, the voice of "the Almighty" is implicit in the nation's dark night experience, as though the God of historical process were saying "for you too comes my Dark Night before my Coming Light."

Now precisely here we may turn to an entirely different text to hear a convergent voice and discern a similar processual reality. This time the dark night theme is sounded by W.E.B. DuBois in his *The Souls of Black Folk*, published in 1903 just after the turn of the twentieth century and written in the context of the succeeding generation (40 years) since Lincoln's 1863 Emancipation Proclamation:

> Away back in the days of bondage they thought to see in one divine event the end of all doubt and disappointment; few men ever worshipped Freedom with half such unquestioning faith as did the American Negro for two centuries. To him, so far as he thought and dreamed, slavery was indeed the sum of all villainies, the cause of all sorrow, the root of all prejudice; Emancipation was the key to a promised land of sweeter beauty than ever stretched before the eyes of wearied Israelites. In song and exhortation swelled one refrain – Liberty; in his tears and curses the God he implored had Freedom in his right hand. At last it came, – suddenly, fearfully, like a dream. With one wild carnival of blood and passion came the message in his own plaintive cadences: – "Shout, O children! / Shout, you're free! / For God has bought your liberty!"
>
> Years have passed away since then, – ten, twenty, forty; forty years of national life, forty years of renewal and development, and yet the swarthy spectre sits in its accustomed seat at the Nation's feast. In vain do we cry to this our vastest social problem: "Take any shape but that, and my firm nerves Shall never tremble!"

> The Nation has not yet found peace from its sins; the freedman has
> not yet found in freedom his promised land. Whatever of good may
> have come in these years of change, the shadow of a deep disap-
> pointment rests upon the Negro people – a disappointment all the
> more bitter because the unattained ideal was unbounded save by the
> simple ignorance of a lowly people. (6-8)

Despite this disappointment, however, DuBois also envisioned a light at the end
of his people's dark night. For him it was not a divine light but a longed-for union of black and white Americans expressed in humanist ideals such as:

> the ideal of human brotherhood, gained through the unifying ideal of
> Race; the ideal of fostering and developing the traits and talents of
> the Negro, not in opposition to or contempt for other races, but rather
> in large conformity to the greater ideals of the American Republic, in
> order that some day on American soil two world-races may give each
> to each those characteristics both so sadly lack. (13)

In this connection DuBois announces an ideal collaboration between his "two
world races" as the "end" of black America's "spiritual striving...to be a co-
worker in the kingdom of culture, to escape both death and isolation, to husband
and use his best powers and his latent genius...."

Thus, we see in DuBois's *Souls* a juxtaposition of the presence of darkness
with the dispelling of darkness: breaking the spell of that "swarthy spectre sitting in its accustomed seat at the Nation's feast." The counter-spell proposed is a
union of two cultures – a civic-political union of black America with the larger
democratic culture. Such a long awaited and long deferred union would effectively resolve, DuBois conjectured, the agony of black Americans' "double-
consciousness." Implicitly, it would also transform double-consciousness into an
asset for the nation, a basis for black Americans' role as "co-workers in the
kingdom of culture," to use DuBois's felicitous phrase, rather than the continuation of the phenomena of "twoness...[two] warring ideals in one dark
body...being torn asunder."

Here we pose the following tripartite query: how can (1) DuBois's quest for
unity between black and white cultures in his *Souls* converge with (2) Whitman's quest to escape the dark side of the nation's democratic vistas via (3) the
wisdom of John of the Cross as expounded in the *Dark Night*? Is such a convergence of three texts in their contexts coherent?

Dark Night of the Soul is an exemplary religious poem accompanied by the
theological and ethical commentary of the poet himself: the Spanish mystic and
doctor of the church, St. John of the Cross (1542-1591). But the author gave us
more than an exposition of dark night phenomena. He also prescribed practices
that enable the experience to run its full course and thereby achieve its optimal
end, its *telos* of divine illumination. On this view, the sublime magnitude of such
an outcome lies far beyond the conventional reduction of the term *dark night of
the soul* to mean only a series of negative experiences.

Even in cases where a theological focus is evident, conventional references to the *dark night* envision most of all its negative aspects. A singular example is the 2007 disclosure of Mother Teresa's experience of spiritual darkness enduring into the last years of her life. The collection of her letters is subtitled suggestively *Come Be My Light*. The absence of such "light" constitutes the conventional use of the term *dark night* to refer chiefly to the negation or "eclipse of God" in one's lived experience. In his definitive exposition, however, John of the Cross never envisioned such negation as an enduring, final outcome but instead anticipated the "coming light" for those who receive effective spiritual direction.[4]

Thus, an altogether opposite prospect awaits the practitioner who exchanges an activist spirituality for a deeper reliance on transcendent agency in one's inner experience. A breakthrough into spiritual illumination occurs for which the dark night is actually the penumbra, the antecedent or precursor. As John of the Cross never tires of repeating, it is precisely because the coming light is so luminous that it short-circuits, annihilates, or darkens the senses of the practitioner. What is experienced as an "eclipse of God" is actually an eclipse of our faculties for apprehending God, so overwhelming is the magnitude of the divine luminosity. He says:

> There is a question which at once arises here –namely...why does God, in this night, darken the desires and faculties with respect to these good things likewise, in such a way that the soul can no more taste of them or busy itself with them than with these other things, and indeed in some ways can do so less? The answer is that...although these faculties be given the desire and interest in things supernatural and Divine, they could not receive them save after a base and a natural manner, exactly in their own fashion. For, as the philosopher says, whatsoever is received comes to him that receives it after the manner of the recipient.... Therefore, O spiritual soul...consider it a great happiness, since God is freeing thee from thyself and taking the matter from thy hands. For with those hands, howsoever well they may serve thee, thou wouldst never labour so effectively, so perfectly and so securely...as now, when God takes thy hand and guides thee in the darkness, as though thou wert blind, to an end and by a way which thou knowest not. Nor couldst thou ever hope to travel with the aid of thine own eyes and feet, howsoever good thou be as a walker. (II.16.4 & 7)

Note well: there is a paradoxical *telos* to which this dark night leads according to John of the Cross. The dark night is not an end-in-itself, but rather through that night one is led "to an end and by a way which thou knowest not" (cf. that other spiritual classic, *The Cloud of Unknowing*). In that connection, we should amend the term *dark night* to include its ideal *telos*. The expression *dark night-coming light* gives a more complete description of the full experience (II.24.2).

Unfortunately, the mystical doctor warns, too many souls fail to experience that end point or goal because the dark night itself is so forbidding that they lapse into despair or regress to more self-directed, activist, and ego-driven forms of the spiritual life. He says:

> These souls turn back at such a time if there is none who understands them; they abandon the road or lose courage; or, at the least, they are hindered from going farther by the great trouble which they take in advancing along the road...But this trouble that they are taking is quite useless, for God is now leading them by another road...very different from the first.... (II.10.2)

The heuristic question of national identity in our time follows directly from the aforementioned danger: how can we avoid "turning back" from the process of dark night illumination that is our destiny? How can we collectively, instead, stay the course and allow ourselves to be led "to an end and by a way which thou knowest not?" In addressing that question, we will also be correlating our trialogue of classic texts and asking: How can we retrieve and advance

> 1. DuBois's quest to escape the darkness of "death and isolation" through cultural cooperation between black and white Americans?
> 2. Whitman's quest to escape hubris as the dark side of the nation's democratic vistas?
> 3. St. John's wisdom of cooperation with dark night spirituality versus an activist foreclosure of the process and thus forfeiture of its "coming light" or *telos*?

The correlation proposed here envisions a transition from the *dark night* of our *democratic vistas* to the *coming light* of diverse and collective *souls-in-solidarity*. That emergent solidarity includes, yet exceeds, DuBois's apologetic for "the souls of black folk" in his 1903 manifesto, in which he sought cultural solidarity between black and white "souls" in the American context. An emergent solidarity would also include, and yet exceed, Whitman's efforts to encompass the multifaceted "soul of America" in his magnum opus *Leaves of Grass* (1881). Those efforts he nonetheless and even inevitably qualified with his acknowledgment of the "plentiful meanness and vulgarity of the ostensible masses – [and] that problem, the labor question, beginning to open like a yawning gulf, rapidly widening every year" ("Democratic Vistas" 498).

An emergent solidarity of souls in the American context would require, beyond both DuBois's and Whitman's visionary acumen, practices of solidarity that we are finally beginning to fathom since the late twentieth century. Such practices are both *purgative* and *contemplative*, to retrieve the classical language of John of the Cross, or *psychodynamic* and *subjective*, in the language of the contemporary critical theorist that follows Erica Sherover-Marcuse (d. 1988). For when John of the Cross evokes the reliability of being led "to an end and by a way which thou knowest not," his discourse is homologous to the following description by Sherover-Marcuse of "the *emergence* of a self-in-solidarity" with others.

> [E]mancipatory *intent*...cannot guarantee that its own activity in the service of liberation will be free from domination...cannot escape its embeddedness in the historical context of domination. There is no external vantage-point...[no] immunity to the influences of the oppressive society.... Indeed the positing of such an ideal...reveals a basic misconception about the dynamics of oppression.... [For there is] a permanent risk of being "contaminated" with the toxins of domination. The danger of the degeneration...is a permanent danger, intrinsic to the very nature of oppression....
>
> An emancipatory subjective practice would thus have to struggle continuously against its own reification, against the incremental sedimentation of liberatory processes into fossilized procedures, against the distortions of domination which ingress into all attempts at liberation. It could do so only if its own praxis nourished and encouraged in individuals a critical intelligence and a sense of self-worth *in the context of a developing solidarity*....
>
> Therefore an emancipatory practice of subjectivity must posit as its goal not the immediate realization of "the (given) self," but the *emergence* of a "self-in-solidarity." One measure of the effectiveness of such a practice would be the extent to which it assisted and enabled people to act in co-operation with each other in achieving the communal goals of liberation. (141-42)

Emergent solidarity is the "democratic vista and the breakthrough illumination" to which all our dark night experiences as a nation and a people combine to usher us. What is required to realize and experience the "coming light" of that solidarity is the will to stay the course and cooperate with its trajectory. We can do so through practices that both purge the inevitable toxins and correct the cumulative excesses of our democratic ideals. But key to identifying and understanding those toxins and excesses is our invaluable resource of each other and of those myriad *others* who are otherwise excluded and marginalized by our democratic ideals.

As we contemplate such solidarity with so many marginalized others, the impact on our collective soul as a nation and a people may seem forbidding. The prospect of so many others may seem itself to augur a dark night of culture. Precisely here our democratic ideal of confidence in the declaration "'we the people" awaits testing in an ever widening circuit – a testing of our identity not as an already achieved democracy, but as a still emerging democracy. Listen to John of the Cross's description of the coming light:

> On a dark night, Kindled in love with yearnings – oh, happy chance! –
> I went forth without being observed, My house being now at rest.

In darkness and secure, By the secret ladder, disguised – oh, happy chance! –
In darkness and in concealment, My house being now at rest.

In the happy night, In secret, when none saw me,
Nor I beheld aught, Without light or guide, save that which burned in my heart.

This light guided me More surely than the light of noonday
To the place where he (well I knew who!) was awaiting me –
A place where none appeared.

Oh, night that guided me, Oh, night more lovely than the dawn,
Oh, night that joined Beloved with lover, Lover transformed in the Beloved!

Upon my flowery breast, Kept wholly for himself alone,
There he stayed sleeping, and I caressed him,
And the fanning of the cedars made a breeze.

The breeze blew from the turret As I parted his locks;
With his gentle hand he wounded my neck
And caused all my senses to be suspended.

I remained, lost in oblivion; My face I reclined on the Beloved.
All ceased and I abandoned myself, Leaving my cares forgotten among the lilies. (Prologue)

Notes

1 As an expression of U.S. idealism the phrase *noble experiment* is understandably attributed to the founding fathers, e.g., the third President of the U.S., Thomas Jefferson (1743-1826) or the sixteenth president, Abraham Lincoln (1809-1865). In fact, the phrase was popularized by 31st U.S. president Herbert Hoover (1874-1964) to refer to the constitutional Prohibition on the use and abuse of alcohol as a controlled substance in the decade of the 1920s (1920-33). This particular noble experiment, however, failed to realize the temperance visions of its advocates and even worsened the impact of organized crime in civic life by criminalizing the production, sale, and distribution of a consumer staple. Moreover, Prohibition was fueled not only by a large constituency of women nobly seeking to correct the moral character, family impact, and social ills of men acting out chronic alcohol abuse. It has also been viewed critically as a reform movement of nativist white Protestants confronting early twentieth-century urban problems associated with immigration.

2 Cf. Sacvan Bercovitch, *The American Jeremiad* and David Howard-Pitney, *The African American Jeremiad: Appeals for Justice in America.* Consider

also the more recent case of the African American jeremiad in the case, ironically, of the Rev. Jeremiah Wright's rhetorical alternation of the conventional phrase *God bless America* with the epithet *God damn America*. By contrast, consider as an example of a non-jeremiadic criticism of U.S. national history and foreign policies Harold Pinter's 2005 Nobel Prize Acceptance Speech, "Art, Truth and Politics."

3 "And I looked carefully to see any blame or fault in [the fallen servant], or if his lord should lay any blame upon him, and truly there was none to be seen. For the only reason he fell was because of his goodwill and his great desire – and he was still as eager and good at heart after he fell as he was when he stood before his lord, ready to do his bidding" (101).

4 "While this crisis is assured to be temporary in nature, it may be extended. The dark night of Saint Paul of the Cross in the eighteenth century lasted forty-five years, from which he ultimately recovered. Mother Teresa of Calcutta, according to letters released in 2007, "may be the most extensive such case on record," lasting from 1948 almost up until her death in 1997, with only brief interludes of relief between. Franciscan Friar Father Benedict Groeschel, a friend of Mother Teresa for a large part of her life, claims that "the darkness left" towards the end of her life.

Works Cited

Bercovitch, Sacvan. *The American Jeremiad*. Madison: U Wisconsin P, 1978.

DuBois, W.E.B. "Of Our Spiritual Strivings." *The Souls of Black Folk*. New York: New American Library, 1969.

Groeschel, Benedict. "Mother Theresa." <<http://en.wikipedia.org/wiki/Dark_night_of_the_soul>>. Accessed 4 April 2008.

Howard-Pitney, David. *The African American Jeremiad: Appeals for Justice in America*. Philadelphia: Temple UP, 1990.

St. John of the Cross. *Dark Night of the Soul*. <<http://www.ccel.org/ccel/john_cross/dark_night.vii.ix.html>> Accessed 20 May 2008.

Julian of Norwich. *Revelations of Divine Love*. In *All Shall Be Well: Daily Readings from Julian of Norwich*. Ed. Sheila Upjohn. New York: Morehouse, 1992.

Mother Teresa and Brian Kolodiejchuk. *Mother Teresa: Come Be My Light*. New York: Doubleday, 2007.

Sherover-Marcuse, Erica. *Emancipation and Consciousness: Dogmatic and Dialectical Perspectives in the Early Marx*. Oxford: Basil Blackwell, 1986.

Whitman, Walt. "Democratic Vistas." In *Complete Poetry and Selected Prose by Walt Whitman*. Ed. James E. Miller, Jr. Boston: Houghton Mifflin, 1959. <<http://xroads.virginia.edu/~Hyper/Whitman/vistas/vistas.html>> Accessed 20 May 2008.

Old Maps, New Worlds:
A Case of Culture and Core

Anne Leavitt
Vancouver Island University

Just as a heads up, I should say that this paper begins with an enigma and ends with a conundrum. Here is the enigma:

> You gotta be careful if you don't know where you're going, because
> you might not get there.

For some reason, when Scott Lee called me last summer inviting me to address the ACTC, these words of the great Yogi Berra ran through my head. This might have had something to do with the fact that it was a gloriously hot day, that I had just finished mowing the lawn, and that I was on my second cold beer, reposing comfortably in my hammock on the back porch. I find that odd things spring to consciousness at such moments. It also might have had something to do with the conference theme that Scott gave me only *after* I had agreed to speak.

Scott said that, while the theme of the conference was still a work in progress, it would have something to do with the question of who we are, and that it would reference Alexis de Tocqueville's claim that, as in the case of individuals, so in the case of nations, our early, familial origins are more formative of our virtues and vices than what happens to us after we reach maturity and enter the world on our own. Why Yogi Berra would have spoken to me at that moment, I have no idea.

But it might have something to do with the fact that I am a Canadian of a certain age and a long North American lineage who has lived through certain debates in my own country for probably far too long. Indeed, the question of "Who we are?" is a question that seems to define Canada and has done so from its earliest proto-incarnations, although no Canadian has ever provided an answer that has ever completely satisfied almost anyone but himself. We have never been able to collectively answer the question as to who we are; indeed, if there is anything that defines us, it appears to be our periodic obsessive quest for an answer. Canada, that is, can well be described as a nation that has never been sure of where it is going and so has had to be very careful to make sure it did not miss the chance to get there. As the old joke goes, the tragedy of Canada is that it could have had British culture, French cooking, and American technology, but instead it got American culture, British cooking, and French technology. Not knowing where we were going, we may well have missed the chance to get there.

Or maybe not. But what I did know when Scott asked me to speak on the conference theme was that it would be a challenge for me to think of anything to say. For those of you who know me, this is not a position I am used to occupying. But how to speak of we who attend the ACTC as a collective *we* given our differing national and regional origins and directions, our differing disciplinary backgrounds, and the differing educational missions of our respective programs and institutions? Are we a *we*? Should we be trying to be a *we*? Do we have a shared sense of where we are going and, if we do not, should we be careful not to miss the chance to get there? My uncertainty as to how to approach these and other such questions mapped my inability to sit down and write this paper for far too many months.

Part of my conundrum had to do with de Tocqueville himself and his being linked to the conference theme. Having read him with students in both the US and in Canada, I will tell you that it is a whole different ball game to talk about de Tocqueville's *Democracy in America* in an American classroom than in a Canadian one. And there is one very obvious and simple reason for this. To read *Democracy in America* with American students is to invite them to read a book that, at first blush, appears to be very much about themselves. To read the same text with Canadian students, including immigrants to Canada, is to read a book that, at first blush, appears to be very much about other people. Could the reasons why a core-text program in the United States might put *Democracy in America* on it syllabus ever really be the same reasons why it might show up on a similar list in Canada?

When you put de Tocqueville's *Democracy in America* before Canadian students, and not many people do, their reactions are quite interesting. I should first say that one tends to have to excerpt it quite a bit if one wants to get anywhere. All those details in Book I about the early colonies and the evolving American system of government tend to leave most of them cold. A good many of the cultural references are not part of their lexicon, and some of them will tell you, quite candidly, that there are better books on American history and politics that are far more up to date, including any number of films and books by Michael Moore. De Tocqueville the historian does not immediately grab them.

And, if truth be told, they find the Puritans, and all that Cotton Mather stuff, downright freaky.

There are, of course, deep-seated and long-embedded cultural reasons for these reactions, even if Canadian students are not entirely aware of what those reasons are. For not just in recent years, but from the earliest days, the populations that became the political entity called Canada have always had mixed feelings about their cousins to the south. One major reason for this is that the populations that first became the political entity called Canada are the very populations that fell off the map that Americans have drawn for themselves from the earliest days of their nationhood. And the reason they fell off the map is that, for the most part, they chose to.

In order to explain what I mean by this, I am going to spend a few minutes doing something no Canadian should ever do, especially if there are other Canadians in the room. I am going to take us on a romp through some key moments in Canadian history. The danger here is not only that my fellow Canadians are likely to dismiss my story as pure invention but also that, in trying to stay on the safe ground of what we might actually agree upon, my story risks becoming boring in the extreme.[1] I will do my best to prevent that from happening. But the fact that I am trained in philosophy and am not an historian should serve as a warning that some inventiveness on my part is probably inevitable. In any event, I would like to start with Samuel de Champlain's justly famous 1632 map of New France, a map at which he worked constantly for twenty-four years after founding what is now Quebec City in 1608, 400 years ago. On it are many places that you know, including Plymouth, Massachusetts, where the Pilgrims came in 1620. It is a very old map of what was then a relatively new place for the French who, ignoring any sovereign claims the original inhabitants might have had, mapped and claimed it first for themselves before even more hordes of English-speaking people came to map and claim even more bits of it for themselves.

Now one of the things Yogi Berra could have said was, "You gotta be careful if you don't know where you're going, so get yourself a good map," but, of course, he would not have. Champlain's problem was that he could not have. Until he drew this one up, there just were not any complete maps of most of the places he found himself. The interesting thing, though, is that, despite managing to produce this one, Champlain never really did figure out where he was going. For most of his life, he believed, like Jacques Cartier who was there before him in the 1530s, that if he just pushed a little further west, he would find the open water he needed to get to China. As great an explorer as he was, he did not really know where he was going, which turned out not to be China at all, but where he ended up was stuck in a very new world, farther from China than he ever imagined he could be.[2]

The first point I would like to make is that Champlain, while making a beautiful new map of a place very new to his countrymen, was still located in a very old world, a world preoccupied with finding a better and quicker trade route to the spices of the east. For him, the new world that he mapped so well was primarily a throughway for the old; it was the world one had to get through for the old world to reach the east. As much as he took meaning from his adventures, found for himself a place among the native populations he encountered, and built some settlements that have persisted for 400 years, he was not really interested in establishing a new world so much as he was in extending the old. The new world he encountered was simply in the way.[3] His attitude was in stark contrast to the Puritans who arrived a few years after he did, having deliberately left their old world precisely to get where they got and to start something very new in that very same place.

As we all know, Champlain's map, so definitive in his day, did not remain so. While neither France nor England took a huge interest in their North American populations in the early days, as they grew and began to turn a profit, conflict between the French and the English in North America was inevitable. The upshot, if I may be allowed to leap over more than 100 years of history in a single sentence, was the fall of Quebec in 1759. The French population, long known as *Canadians*, was soundly defeated, not only by fresh troops sent from Britain but by several hundred colonial conscripts and regulars. Needless to say, these defeated Canadians, who were very much tied to the old world of Catholic France and who had been where they were for a over a hundred years, were none too keen to find themselves conquered by Britain and her local colonial population. Britain herself eventually realized that she could not rule over the Canadians with an iron fist, and so, like the other colonies, her new acquisition was allowed its own assembly with its right to pass laws, as well as the democratic franchise. The Quebec Act of 1774 reinstated French civil law in the colony, recognized the Catholic Church, and granted the inhabitants the right to their own language. For the Canadians, defeat clearly smarted, but things could have been worse.[4]

The maps of British North America in those days show it triumphantly ascendant on the continent by 1763.[5] Champlain's New France has vanished. But, as we all know, the supremacy of the British did not last, and the maps changed again.[6] A little over ten years after the fall of Quebec, the famous thirteen colonies rebelled and the rest, as some say, is history. However, one of the things that is remembered in Canada is that not all the residents of the thirteen colonies were as excited about shrugging off the imperious and tyrannical yoke of Britain and forming a new country. More than 70,000 people, representing 3% of the American population, who were loyal to the British monarchy (though not necessarily happy with crazy King George) and who could afford to, fled the new American regime, taking up residence largely in what is now Ontario but some also in what are now Quebec and the Atlantic provinces. Those 70,000 or so Loyalists were matched almost equally by the 60,000 French-speaking Canadians living predominantly in the newly British, old New France.

British North America thus changed dramatically in these remarkable, short years. While she had grown considerably with the conquest of New France, within a little more than a decade, her colonial population was reduced to two almost equally divided groups of French and English speakers, each with its own equally divided traditions and loyalties. Aside from sharing the relatively democratic forms of colonial government bequeathed by the British, the only other thing the two populations shared in common was that they were no longer included within the borders of the newly emergent map of the United States.

What was initially a marriage of happenstance, however, became much more when the United States attacked British North America in 1812.[7] Not only if they had lost that war but also more important, without that war, the colonies of British North America might never have united into what, fifty-five years later, became the Dominion of Canada. And that is because, for British North Americans, the war made a few things very clear. The first was that the French and English populations, regardless of their differences, needed each other to protect themselves from their ever-expanding neighbor to the south. And they equally needed the protection of the British across the water. For both populations, the issue was not simply the need to secure their livelihoods in the geographic spaces they occupied. The issue was also a need to secure their ways of life, ways of life very much tied to older worlds, worlds that the Americans had explicitly rejected. While their old worlds were not the same, both populations could read the same maps. Mutual defense of the shared border against their neighbour to the south was essential for the survival of each.[8]

I will bring my story to a close by observing that it was yet another American war, the Civil War, that helped unite the British North American colonies into the political entity of Canada in 1867. While there had long been economic reasons for union, partly because no one knew where a highly militarized, reunified, and westward expanding America might look next, within two years of the Civil War's end, Britain's North American colonies[9] had hammered out a deal, the British North America Act, and the Dominion of Canada was born.[10] Still tied to Great Britain, it was a federation of a few provinces populated by two peoples with different religions, loyalties, languages, and histories, who had no clear and shared vision for the future save economic prosperity and the mutual preservation of their differing old world values from the Americans to the south. It says much about the animating spirit of the newly created Canada that the British North America Act was set to preserve, not "life, liberty, and the pursuit of happiness" but "peace, order, and good government."[11] By this time, both of the founding peoples of Canada firmly shared with each other and with the Americans a commitment to representative government and democracy, but, of course, that did not mean they all trusted each other. But, if there was one thing that the French and English populations of the new Dominion agreed on, despite living on a continent that bore the name, they were definitely not Americans.

However much Canada has changed in the intervening 141 years, and it has changed a great deal, a number of its early features are clearly recognizable today. While its commitment to democracy and democratic institutions makes it easy for it to appreciate and to identify with its cousins to the south, the steps taken along its very different path to nationhood lead it to see itself as very much other. Canada was not born in an act of self-conscious and shared rebellion against an old world in the name of individual liberty. Rather, it emerged slowly as the result of numerous compromises between two dominant cultural groups with strong attachments to their own older worlds, brought closer together by shared fear and rejection of the very Americans with whom they also identify.

All this brings me to why reading *Democracy in America* with Canadian students can be so much fun: because, if there is one thing all Canadian students are certain of, it is that they are definitely not Americans. While they may not have a collectively shared story which tells them who they are in any positive sense (though French-speaking Canadians of French descent, recent immigrants, and people of First Nations descent tend to share one among themselves), whatever it is that all Canadians are, they are certain that they are not Americans.[13] This is despite the fact, of course, that they listen to American music, watch American TV, play American video games, live surrounded by American consumer products, and follow American sports. In the relevant sense, and for them the relevant sense is the political sense, they may be many things, but they are not Americans. Politically, they will point out, Canada is far more egalitarian and considerate of its citizens, as evidenced by universal health care and the support of poorer provinces by richer ones; it is less hierarchical, as evidenced by economic and tax policies that keep a limit on the gap between rich and poor; it is more peaceful and law-abiding, as evidenced by gun controls and low crime rates; it is more tolerant of differences, as evidenced by its attitudes towards new immigrants and gays; unlike the United States, it does not mix religion and politics; and it is not hubristically patriotic.

Now, as you can see from the way I have formulated this list, it is clear to Canadian students that not only are they not Americans, they are better than Americans. They identify what they believe is distinctly their own, as opposed to what they share with America, as what makes them distinctly good. Their identification of their own with what is good is not, of course, uniquely Canadian. It seems to be pretty universal. But what is interesting is that young Canadians, in particular, are convinced that such identification of one's own with what is good is actually a uniquely American characteristic, and it disturbs them. One of their great sources of moral and national self-satisfaction is the belief that one of the things that makes Canadians better than Americans is that Canadians are not preoccupied with demonstrating to everyone that they are morally and politically better than everyone else. The result is indeed an odd piece of national character. While vast numbers of Canadians believe they are better than Americans, what particularly convinces them that they are better is that they feel it would be improper to tell anyone else that they are, except each other, who, of course, already know and so do not really need to be told. They do not fly Canadian flags off their porches on Canada Day as that would be, well, too American.

Reading *Democracy in America* with Canadian students is therefore an interesting experience. While their initial interest, to the extent that they have one, is to learn about the other against whom they so clearly define themselves, the text has the capacity to invite them to a most disconcerting encounter with themselves. This does not tend to happen for most Canadian students as they read Book I, a book where de Tocqueville the historian maps the origins of the early colonies and the emergence of the American system of government. The connection between democratic inclinations and the Puritan flavour of Protestantism that sowed the seeds of the American regime is certainly interesting to many insofar as most modern Canadians have trouble understanding how religion and democratic politics can mix. One of the conditions for the establishment of the Canadian democracy, after all, was to much more thoroughly separate the two, given the lack of a religiously homogenous population from the beginning.[12] The connection between Protestantism and democracy in America is therefore illuminating and goes some way to explaining, for Canadian students, the persistence of that connection into the twenty-first century, even though they continue to find it somewhat alienating. And, of course, while some find de Tocqueville's mapping of the evolution of American institutions interesting, they already know that their own institutions trace a related, though historically different path, more directly back to the parliamentary traditions and institutions of Great Britain. While the early part of de Tocqueville's work can deepen their understanding of some aspects of the American regime, they see nothing in this historical account that would suggest that America is fundamentally other than they tend to think it is. Its founding people, history, and institutions are different than theirs, albeit both countries are democratic, but they already knew that before they picked up de Tocqueville.

It is as de Tocqueville begins to drop his mantle as historian and begins to map the contemporary culture and social psychology of Americans that Canadians begin to have a chance to see themselves. This, of course, begins towards the end of Book I, in chapter XV, where de Tocqueville gives his brilliant analysis of the tyranny of the majority in the United States. It is, by the way, one of the very few places where de Tocqueville refers to the war of 1812. He offers as an example of the tyranny of the majority a large mob disturbance that followed the publication in Baltimore of a newspaper editorial opposed to the war, a war that was immensely popular at the time. One of the editors of the paper was killed, the others were left for dead, and the guilty parties, though brought to trial, were acquitted by jury (261).

While Canadian students may be tempted to see the prevalence of the tyranny of the majority in the nature of the American regime, particularly in light of events over the past five years, de Tocqueville does not easily let them off the hook. It does not take much, after all, to see that his analysis demonstrates quite nicely that the tyranny of the majority is a potential threat to all democracies and how, in the name of the majority, liberty of thought, speech, action, and association can be effectively curtailed if not destroyed. If Canadian students were alarmed, not only at the overwhelming American support for the war with Iraq, but also at how the level of support was responsible for the suppression of dissenting American voices, de Tocqueville invites them to consider whether the overwhelming Canadian opposition to the war did not have the same effect on some of their fellow Canadians.

For me, a Canadian teacher of core texts to Canadian students for many years, the brilliance of de Tocqueville is most evident in his analysis of American democracy not simply as a set of political institutions with a particularized history but also as a set of prevalent social psychological phenomena characteristic of North American culture. That analysis begins with his account of the tyranny of the majority as a political phenomenon logically arising in any society that defers to the majority, as opposed to any minority, individual, or the gods, as authoritative. But de Tocqueville does not stop there. He goes on to connect the threat of this particular form of tyranny with a uniquely modern psychology that is, I believe, not only fundamental to Americans and Canadians, but something we moderns may be no more able to escape than our own skins.

In his chapter "On the Philosophical Method of the Americans," de Tocqueville notes that "America is...one of the countries where the precepts of Descartes are the least studied and are best applied" (II.3). By this, of course, he is referring to the propensity of Americans, each being equal to any of the others and deferring to no other authority, "to fix the standards of their judgement in themselves alone." He notes, of course, that this way of thinking did not arise in America. He traces its antecedents to Bacon and Descartes who, in science and philosophy, "abolished received formulas, destroyed the empire of tradition, and overthrew the authority of the schools" as well as to Luther and Voltaire who extended its application to religion and politics.[13] By the eighteenth century, de Tocqueville avers, this way of thinking had become the "standard of intelligence" and, while not universally common throughout the ranks of society, had nonetheless been adopted throughout Europe (II.5). Only in America, though, where democracy was thoroughly embraced and all appeal to authority outside that invested in the citizens themselves was rejected, could the revolution in thinking started by Descartes and Bacon become a widespread social psychological phenomenon with application to every sphere of human endeavour.[14]

However, as de Tocqueville observes, no man really is an island unto himself and can really fix the standard of his own judgement in himself alone. As he says, "If man were forced to demonstrate for himself all the truths of which he makes daily use, his task would never end" (II.8). For this reason, de Tocqueville notes, "A principle of authority must then always occur, under all circumstances in some part of the moral and intellectual world" (II.9). While the American's belief in his own equality and independence of thought means that no American will automatically submit his judgement to the authority of another particular individual or class of people, in the absence of such authority, individuals tend to seek the truth in people like themselves who are easily found, almost by definition and due to its overwhelming power, in the majority. As de Tocqueville points out, "by whatever political laws men are governed in the ages of equality, it may be foreseen that faith in public opinion will become for them a species of religion, and the majority its ministering prophet" (II.11).

Modern Canadians, no less than their American cousins, proudly believe in the independence of their own thinking and that they fix the standards of their own judgment alone. While there may have been a time when the populations that united to form the Canadian regime looked back to traditions predating the American War of Independence and sought to preserve them north of the 49th parallel, that is certainly no longer the case. Anglicanism, love of King and Empire, the parochial education of Catholic Quebec, and the esteem in which the priests of that province were held, have all given way in the Canadian public domain. The recognition of this back in 1965 led George Grant, perhaps Canada's most renowned philosopher, to write his famous *Lament for a Nation*, a lament for the demise of Canadian sovereignty and a certain shared, old-world vision of the public good that Grant saw as a noble attempt to fend off the excesses of American individualism and materialism.

Addressing how and when that demise came to be and whether it is to be welcomed or lamented, would take me far beyond the story I have already told and would leave me on far less certain ground.[15] But I think it is fair to say that the deep irony de Tocqueville discovers in the American culture of his own day is no less true of the Canadian culture of our own. Deeply convinced of our own independent judgement, we Canadians are as prone to allow ourselves to be governed by public opinion as any other good, modern democrats. This is perhaps most especially true of our publicly held belief in the importance of independent judgement and our publicly held belief in our essential dissimilarity from our cousins south of the border.

And, of course, we also share the belief in indefinite human perfectibility and material well-being identified by de Tocqueville as essential to the American psyche. The first, of course, is another name for our belief in progress that sees us as always improving on the past, ever moving towards a more promising future (II.33-34). Impatient of philosophical and moral contemplation, however, our sense of progress is bound up most especially with technological innovation and the conquest of nature. As de Tocqueville puts it:

> The greater part of men who constitute [democratic] nations are extremely eager in the pursuit of actual and physical gratification. As they are always dissatisfied with the position they occupy and are always free to leave it, they think of nothing but the means of changing their fortune or of increasing it. To minds thus predisposed, every new method that leads by a shorter road to wealth, every machine that spares labour, every instrument that diminishes the cost of production, every discovery that facilitates pleasures or augments them, seems to be the grandest effort of the human intellect (II.45).

The differences between Canadians and Americans, and there remain some, are interesting and worth pondering, it seems to me, but the lessons I take from de Tocqueville have to do with our essential similarities. What is interesting about those similarities is, first of all, given our different histories, that those essential similarities are there at all. Remember, the populations that united to form the Canadian regime did so on the initial understanding that they were working together to preserve something old, an old world that the new American regime sought to displace.

A conclusion one might draw from de Tocqueville, however, is that the very presence of democratic institutions and customs, established by the British in the Canadian colonies, would serve to undermine the old worlds and authorities the Loyalists and French Catholics sought to protect. Indeed, he is seriously doubtful in the final chapter of *Democracy in America* that the old world of Europe itself, from which the idea of equality originally sprang and precisely because that is where it originated, can cling to its ancient ways. Canada, therefore, offers an interesting case study in the irresistibility of the new world, despite valiant and self-conscious efforts on the part of those who knew that world first-hand to keep it in abeyance. It is especially significant, for instance, that even the things that Canadians currently believe distinguish themselves from Americans are not advanced on the grounds of some old world sensibility but rather on the grounds of a superior commitment to equality and progress. It is equally significant that the Canadian parliament adopted something called The Charter of Rights and Freedoms as the cornerstone of its Constitution Act of 1982. America did not bring the map of modern democracy with its disavowal of all ancient authority to Canada. What is interesting is that Canada in spite of herself, in thinking she was going somewhere else, got there all by herself.

Is this a good thing? Well, de Tocqueville was not sure that the rise of the new and unprecedented world he saw coming was a completely good thing, although he was not so sure it was completely bad either. What he did know was, once it came, there would be no going back (II.333-334). The world he maps out for us is, indeed, recognizable as a world which is not so much American as it is modern, with America having been the first to get there. To take a position on this world, to make a moral evaluation of it, is particularly difficult because we are thoroughly modern men and women, living in a world that has virtually nowhere remained untouched by the modern. For me, attempting to judge whether the modern world is a good thing or not requires me to try to stand outside of it. As I alluded to earlier, this is a bit like trying to get outside of my own skin.

This is where it seems to me, the virtues of a core text education for us who are moderns is especially valuable. As de Tocqueville himself says, "No literature places those fine qualities in which the writers of democracies are naturally deficient in bolder relief than that of the ancients; no literature ought to be more studied in democratic times" (II.63). By the ancients, of course, he is referring to the Greeks and the Romans, though, as his invocation of them makes clear, any literature that would illuminate the deficiencies of democratic times would be most timely in those times.

Is it that such literature holds timeless truths that the modern world and modern democracy tend to veil? I am not at all sure. It might or some of it might, or it might not. But de Tocqueville maps out many of the limits of the modern world, limits, given its character, that are impossible to see from within. The greatest of these is the limit this new world places upon the recognition of the need for self-knowledge. I find de Tocqueville's analysis of the special self-deception of us moderns quite chilling. Unlike our ancient forebears, his claim is that we believe the seat of moral and intellectual judgement rests solely within our very selves. And, for this very reason, we are unlikely to see the extent to which, in fact, it rests upon our appropriation of the moral and intellectual judgements of the majority of others. Believing that we already think for ourselves, thank you very much, we in fact allow others to do the important task of thinking for us. This might not be such a bad thing, save that we are also committed to ignoring the past in the name of an infinitely perfectible future, perfectible not through wonder and the contemplation of what is good and true, but through the conquest of nature via the most amazing technological arsenal the world has ever seen, an arsenal through which we attempt to master the world and everything in it, including ourselves.[16] If only to raise some cogent voices that might point out how perhaps we have not thought things out as well as we might, that might illustrate the possibility of a human excellence outside of the mastery of things, or that might make us wonder whether all this mastery in the hands of the unreflective is compatible with freedom, it seems to me that a core text education in the modern world remains crucial.

But I am also under no illusions that such an education is likely to ever be widespread or powerful enough to change the modern trajectory in any significant way, given the very nature of the beast. De Tocqueville goes much further and suggests that such an education might even be dangerous to the collective good of modern societies. He worries that, as an education that did nothing more than immerse students in the ancients "would give them everyday a sense of wants, which their education would never teach them to supply, they would perturb the state, in the name of the Greeks and Romans, instead of enriching it by their productive industry" (I.63). De Tocqueville, therefore, does not simply rest where one might expect him to, namely, with a prediction that an education designed to reveal the deficiencies of modern democracies could never become predominant in modern democracies. He actually strongly recommends that the education of the greater number of citizens in a democracy should be "scientific, commercial, and industrial rather than literary" (II.63).

On the one hand, the democrat in me recoils at the notion that the opportunity to map out the deficiencies in modern democratic societies should not be made available to all, if not insisted upon for all. On the other hand, the same democrat in me agrees that an immersion in a form of education that would serve largely to undermine the modern democratic world that we share is a troublesome notion as well.[17] Are old maps fair guides to new worlds? I do not know. As Yogi said, "You gotta be careful if you don't know where you're going because you might not get there." Maybe. But then again, as teachers and students in core text programs, maybe we just might.

Notes

1 In fact, I often wonder whether the impulse to reduce Canadian history to what all parties can agree to is what makes the learning of it so boring in school. I

am fairly certain that the fact that so many Canadians find their history boring has some bearing on Canada's fairly high degree of historical amnesia.

2 On his map, Champlain names a set of rapids near Montreal "Lachine." Both
he and Cartier failed to navigate them. Both believed they were part of the
route to the Far East.

3 Champlain was, of course, also interested in settlements in the new world
which would provide the old world with various commodities. Such outposts were outposts of the old world, however, and were meant to serve the
old world without starting anything new of and on their own.

4 The French colony of Acadia (covering Canada's maritime provinces) had
come into British hands in 1713. In 1755, the Great Expulsion of 15,000
Acadians began, most of whom ended up in Louisiana where they became
known as Cajuns. The Acadians had wanted to remain neutral in Britain's
war with France in North America and refused to swear an oath of loyalty
to the British crown. They were allowed to return in 1764 though most did
not. Acadia held a small population of Scots in the mid-1600s, and, after it
was regained by Britain from France in 1713, Scots from New England
were encouraged to emigrate there by the colonial governor. In the late
1770s, the Highland Clearances brought many more. The role of the Scots
in the formation of the Canadian nation was highly significant. My account,
for brevity sake only, is silent about them. The thinking of many of the
eighteenth-century Scots who arrived in North America is well chronicled
in Arthur Herman's *How the Scots Invented the Modern World*. In his biography of Canada's premier "founding father," *John A: The Man Who Made
Us*, Richard J. Gwyn offers an interesting account of the disproportionately
significant contributions made by Scots to the emergence of Canada as a
political entity. Among the peculiar cultural baggage they imported from
Scotland to British North America was their ability, as a British minority, to
forge a special relationship with its French population.

5 See John Mitchell's 1775 map.

6 See Thomas Kitchin's 1785 map.

7 An excellent book treating of the War of 1812 from the British North American perspective is Mark Zuehlke's *For Honour's Sake: The War of 1812
and the Brokering of an Uneasy Peace*.

8 See Alexander Keith Johnston, 1849.

9 See *Mitchell's School Atlas, 1866*.

10 See Blakie and Son, 1886.

11 In *John A: The Man Who Made Us* (400-403), Richard Gwyn provides fasci-
nating evidence that this phrase, inserted into the British North America Act
of 1867, was likely a typographical mistake made by the British legal
draftsman Francis Reilly. The 1865 draft of the Act included the phrase
"peace, welfare, and good government" which Reilly appears to have incorrectly transposed. As Gwyn notes, however, no one is on record as ever
having paid any attention to the error as the phrase likely meant very little
to anyone at the time. He calls it "a legal boilerplate that was routinely in-

serted into all kinds of British colonial constitutions." Gwyn maintains that it was only in the 1960s that the phrase became a slogan used in the ever-recurring Canadian cultural campaign to distinguish Canada from the United States. Gywn is likely right. He is, after all, an historian, and I am not. I will only note that, if he is right, the fact that "peace, order, and good government" never originally functioned for Canadians as did the phrase "life, liberty, and the pursuit of happiness" for Americans and if, indeed, it was not only mere legal boilerplate but also a typo no one cared enough to notice, then my implied description of the animating spirit of the newly created Canada is, I think, still valid. I hope the reader will forgive me for noting how this demonstrates that great democratic countries need not be founded upon great slogans.

12 The First Nations people of British North America played, of course, a huge role in the unfolding of its political history (that role, among other things, became a central bone of contention between the British and the United States in the War of 1812). Various historic rights of the aboriginal peoples of Canada, as well as the language rights of French and English speakers, are recognized in the Charter of Rights and Freedoms that forms part of Canada's Constitution Act of 1982. Debates about treaty rights and land claims continue to this day in Canada, especially in my own Province of British Columbia where large numbers of First Nations peoples never entered into comprehensive treaties with the Crown and yet, nonetheless, found themselves on reserves with their lands in the hands of others. Given the impossibility of treating the complex role of First Nations people in the political emergence of Canada in the short time allotted to me, I have left it out of my narrative. The omission, however, is glaring.

13 During a debate in 1854 about the regularization of religious holidays, Sir John A. MacDonald, the premier Father of Canadian Confederation in 1867, was reported to have made the following observation: "It was of the very greatest importance for the mutual comfort of the inhabitants of Canada to agree as much as possible, and the only way they could agree was by respecting each other's principles, and as much as possible even each other's prejudices. Unless they were governed by a spirit of compromise and kindly feeling towards each other, they could never get on harmoniously with each other" (*John A: The Man Who Made Us* 171). The British North American population at the time of Confederation was hardly more secular than their cousins to the south (though they are overwhelmingly more secular today). Indeed, the apparently sharp legal division between Church and State embraced south of the border appalled the majority of French and English alike. However, by reposing responsibilities for such things as education in general, and religious education in particular, to the provinces, MacDonald sought to keep religious debates from destabilizing or paralyzing the national government. He was largely successful. Debates between French and English, Catholics and Protestants, were transmuted into debates regarding

the relative jurisdictions of the federal and respective provincial govern-ments.

14 De Tocqueville describes Descartes's work as "philosophy properly so called" perhaps to distinguish the looser or ironic sense in which he refers to the "philosophical method" of the Americans.

15 De Tocqueville himself spent a couple of weeks in Lower Canada. His jour-nal notes are available on the web at <<http://english.republiquelibre.org/notes-of-alexis-de-tocqueville-in-lower-canada.html>>. One sees in his ob-servations some of the seeds of the current state of Canadian affairs.

16 The importance of medicine, bioengineering, and cognitive neuroscience is worth thinking about in this context, as is the importance of the contempo-rary social sciences to the ancient arts of management and politics.

17 Here I am tempted to segue into a series of reflections on the character of democracy as presented by Socrates in Book VIII of Plato's *Republic*. There, democracy is described by Socrates as being "the fairest" of the re-gimes in no small part due to its lack of compulsion and the fact that it con-tains "all the species of regimes." Socrates describes it as a general store wherein a man can choose the regime that pleases him (557c-558c). I will resist my temptation to pursue any detailed reflections on this passage, save only to suggest that there may be a resolution to my enigma here. That reso-lution, however, would require the democrat in me to see my attachment to democracy as legitimate not because a democracy is worthy in and of itself but only insofar as it functions as a means to engage in something else. This, though, is perhaps not so much a resolution to my enigma as it is an-other enigma.

Works Cited

Blakie and Son. 1886. <<http://library.lib.mcmaster.ca/maps/images/raremaps/107357.jpg>> Accessed April 2008.

de Champlain, Samuel. *1632 Map of New France.* <<http://www.usm.maine.edu/~maps/exhibit2/17.jpg>> Accessed April 2008.

Grant, George. *Lament for a Nation: The Defeat of Canadian Nationalism.* Toronto: McLelland and Stewart, 1965.

Gwyn, Richard J. *John A: The Man Who Made Us.* Toronto: Random House, 2007.

Herman, Arthur. *How the Scots Invented the Modern World.* New York: Three Rivers, 2001.

Johnston, Alexander Keith 1849. <<http://library.lib.mcmaster.ca/maps/images/raremaps/107395.jpg>> Accessed April 2008.>>

Kitchin, Thomas. *1785 Map.* <<http://library.lib.mcmaster.ca/maps/images/raremaps/107301.jpg>> Accessed April 2008.

Mitchell, John. *1775 Map.* <<http://www.usm.maine.edu/~maps/mitchell/full1.jpeg >> Accessed April 2008.

Mitchell's School Atlas, 1866. <<http://www.lib.msu.edu/coll/main/maps/mapscan/na1967m.jpg>> Accessed April 2008.

de Tocqueville, Alexis. *Democracy in America*. 2 volumes. Toronto: Vintage, 1990.

Zuehlke, Mark. *For Honour's Sake: The War of 1812 and the Brokering of an Uneasy Peace*. Toronto: Knopf, 2006.

Freedom, Democracy, and Empire: Are We Imperial Athens?

James Wood
Boston University

Thucydides famously declares at the beginning of his *History of the Peloponnesian War* that his work is "not a piece of writing designed to meet the taste of an immediate public, but was done to last forever" (I.22). His reasoning is that history is not just a record of the past but a guide to the future because what has happened once is likely to happen again, "human nature being what it is" (I.22). Since Thucydides was an Athenian and consequently wrote his history with a particular focus on the role of Athens in the war, his history proves most useful not just in understanding the nature of war, its sources and effects, and related issues of international relations and conflicts, but more particularly in understanding the role of a democratic, commercial, and imperial power in such situations of international crisis and conflict. It can hardly escape the notice of a contemporary reader of Thucydides that the one nation that most resembles imperial Athens in the world today is the United States of America and that his tale of the internal degeneration and external defeat of Athens is therefore a serious warning to us. If we are to make use of Thucydides as he wished, then, it behooves us to consider what lessons he has to offer us as a nation, whether the tragic downfall of his city is a risk we face, and if so whether there is anything we can do to avoid the same fate.

Let us note in the first place the character of Athens as described by various Athenians and non-Athenians in Thucydides' account. In the speech of the Corinthians to Sparta urging them to war, the Athenian character is described in the following way: "An Athenian is always an innovator, quick to form a resolution and quick at carrying it out.... Then again, Athenian daring will outrun its own resources; they will take risks against their better judgment, and still, in the midst of danger, remain confident." They are "always abroad," regard what they seek as theirs already, turn from both failure and success to the pursuit of new enterprises, work without rest, and in sum, "they are by nature incapable of either living a quiet life themselves or of allowing anyone else to do so" (I.70). The Athenians themselves, in response to this speech, do not dispute this characterization at all, but rather highlight the glorious and self-sacrificing actions of their city in defending Greek liberty against Persian aggression, point out that they did not seek imperial power but responded to desperate pleas for Athens' leadership, and emphasize that once in possession of imperial power they behaved as anyone would in keeping it, that they treated their subject states more generously and moderately than others would, and that it would be too dangerous, dishonorable, and contrary to the national interest to jettison such power once theirs (I.75-77).

Pericles in his funeral oration then offers an account of Athenian democracy, as what he calls the "constitution and way of life which has made us great" (II.36), "a model to others" (II.37), and "an education to Greece" (II.41). He praises, for example, the following features of the Athenian democracy: "power is in the hands not of a minority but of the whole people"; "everyone is equal before the law"; and "what counts is not membership of a particular class, but the actual ability which the man possesses" (II.37). He also points to the freedom, tolerance, and openness of Athenian society: "Just as our political life is free and open, so is our day-to-day life in our relations with each other"; "we are free and tolerant in our private lives; but in public affairs we keep to the law"; "we are in a position to enjoy all kinds of recreation for our spirits"; and "our city is open to the world" (II.38). Finally, he describes the public-spirited, generous, and independent character of the Athenian: "Each individual is interested not only in his own affairs but in the affairs of the state as well"; "when we do kindnesses to others, we do not do them out of any calculations of profit or loss: we do them without afterthought, relying on our free liberality"; "each single one of our citizens, in all the manifold aspects of life, is able to show himself the rightful lord and owner of his own person, and do this, moreover, with exceptional grace and exceptional versatility" (II.40). The upshot is that Athens' greatness derives from "the power which our city possesses and which has been won by those very qualities which I have mentioned" (II.41).

The similarities between Athens so described and the United States are striking. Like the Athenians, we pride ourselves on our dynamic, innovative character, our enterprising work ethic, our uncalculating generosity, our open and cosmopolitan spirit, our cultural contributions and opportunities, our freedom and democracy, our past liberation of the world from aggressive tyranny and present defense of international democracy, and our status as a model and education to the world – the "shining city on a hill" and the world's "indispensable nation." Like Athens too, our geopolitical influence and military strength is a direct consequence of our commercial dynamism and success. Like Athens, the United States gained her present geopolitical prominence in the course of a great war, in which she was invited by her allies to take a leading part and after which she was invited to continue her leadership as the defender of free states, a leadership which has now taken the form of direct military aggression against sovereign political powers to the end of installing friendly democratic regimes. Like Athens, we find ourselves unable to retract our international position and ambitions, both because we continue to believe in our special international responsibility and because doing so would be, as we perhaps rightly suppose, disadvantageous, dangerous, and dishonorable. And like Athens, we find ourselves increasingly the target of international resentment and hatred, and for reasons that Pericles himself understood very well: "No doubt," he tells the Athenian people, "[our greatness] will be disparaged by people who are politically apathetic; but those who, like us, prefer a life of action will try to imitate us, and, if they fail to secure what we have secured, they will envy us. All who have taken it upon themselves to rule over others have incurred hatred and unpopularity for a time; but," he adds, "if one has a great aim to pursue, this burden of envy must be accepted, and it is wise to accept it. Hatred does not last for long; but the brilliance of the present is the glory of the future stored up for ever in the memory of man" (II.64). Pericles is quite right that the glory of Athens will not be forgotten, but this is a glory that for us is grounded in Athens' cultural and intellectual achievements, not in her empire; and what we remember of her imperial glory is equally counterbalanced (thanks to Thucydides) by our memory of that empire's destruction and by our sense of the defects in and degeneration of the Athenian character and state that contributed to that destruction. But what was the nature of those defects and that degeneration? And can we see parallels to our own case?

In the first place, it seems evident that we suffer, if to a lesser degree, from the same tension between internal freedom and external coercion as imperial Athens did, though this tension is less obvious for us because we convince ourselves, to some extent justifiably, that our control over world affairs is in the service of the liberty, self-determination, and prosperity of the world's nations. Our empire is of the "soft" variety, as it has been called, because our projection of international power does not directly seek the permanent subjugation of other nations. Nevertheless, as we sometimes admit to ourselves, we do seek to make the world's nations democratic and capitalistic after our model, because nations who share our political and economic system will be less likely to oppose us internationally and more likely to open their markets and trade with us on advantageous terms; and when nations determine themselves economically or politically in ways disadvantageous to us, we are far less welcoming of their choices and often actively oppose them. The tension, in other words, is that we seem all too willing to play the democrat with ourselves and the autocrat with others, and it is plain enough that this tension risks subverting freedom and democracy at home, as indeed some would say is already happening. In the case of Athens, Thucydides describes the overthrow of the democracy once it is perceived as an obstacle to winning the war and preserving the empire (VIII.45 ff.), and this is a collapse prepared for well in advance by the undermining of Athenians' respect for the liberty of nations abroad and the increasingly unjust application of Athenian power (captured above all in the Melian dialogue: V.84-116). It is no doubt true that we cannot simply stop projecting our power internationally without serious risk to our national interests, but it is equally true that continuing to project our power as we are doing also carries serious risk, for maintaining our international presence and military power consumes enormous national resources at the same time as it increases the hatred and resentment of significant portions of the world against us. This is the dilemma of empire: that, in Pericles' words, even if "it [was] wrong to take it, it is certainly dangerous to let it go" and that "you cannot continue to enjoy the privileges of empire unless you also shoulder the burdens of empire" (II.63).

Not only does Thucydides show how the maintenance of an empire threatens freedom and democracy at home; on the other side, he also points to internal weaknesses in democracies that threaten their ability to preserve an empire. The first of these is inconstancy of political will. The fact that, as Pericles proudly notes, the people rule in a democracy means that it is more difficult for the polity to maintain consistent policy in the face of adversity. Thucydides observes that what the people enthusiastically favored initially, such as war with Sparta and the Sicilian expedition, they subsequently turned against, undermined, or failed to support adequately because they could not maintain a long-term perspective, were overwhelmed by their individual distresses, and irrationally turned against their own leaders. The reason for this fickleness is that, in spite of Pericles' exalted rhetoric of self-sacrifice and public-spiritedness, most people view affairs of state through the lens of their personal concerns, becoming temporarily public-spirited for the most part only through patriotic appeals; and as they resist taking responsibility for public affairs, they tend to blame their leaders for their problems. So, following the plague, the Athenian people tried to sue for peace and blamed Pericles for their suffering, even though their suffering was in part an expected consequence of the war they supported and in part due to the plague, which was no one's fault (II.59-65). Similarly, while the people were swept into a nationalistic fervor by the prospect of conquering Sicily, they failed to provide the expedition adequate support, according to Thucydides (II.65), and contributed directly to its defeat by their persecution of its principal and most gifted general, Alcibiades, mainly because of their envy and fear of Alcibiades' extraordinary talents and lavish lifestyle (VI.12, 28, 60-61). Such envy and fear arose in Athens as it has arisen and will likely continue to arise in democracies wherever and whenever they exist, because a sovereign *dēmos* does not want to think of itself as inferior to anyone. The people will therefore resist the rise of extraordinary leaders and promote the elevation of the mediocre by exerting an enormous pressure for their leaders to mirror them, flatter them, and cater to their whims. Such behavior, to say the least, does not tend to promote either consistent or competent foreign policy.

This consideration leads us to a related weakness in democracies: their vulnerability to demagoguery. Since, as just noted, it is very much in the interest of politicians to tell the people what they want to hear, even when the people are wrong, a skilled demagogue will gain power by flattering the mob while still manipulating it into supporting his own policies. Thucydides points to such demagoguery in the case of Cleon's speech in support of a harsh retribution against Mytilene's rebellion and Alcibiades' speech in favor of the Sicilian expedition. Pericles, in contrast, is described as a successful democratic leader ironically because of superiority to the people and his ability to oppose them:

> Pericles, because of his position, his intelligence, and his known integrity, could respect the liberty of the people and at the same time hold them in check. It was he who led them, rather than they who led him, and, since he never sought power from any wrong motive, he was under no necessity of flattering them: in fact he was so highly respected that he was able to speak angrily to them and to contradict them.... So, in what was nominally a democracy, power was really in the hands of the first citizen. But his successors, who were more on a level with each other and each of whom aimed at occupying the first place, adopted methods of demagoguery, which resulted in their losing control over the actual conduct of affairs. (II.65)

As this passage suggests, the worst impulses and weaknesses of democracy are best held in check by a leader who both respects democracy and rises above the *dēmos*; but because such a leader will be unlikely to attain power in the first place or to keep it once he has it, Periclean democracy will remain a very rare and fragile phenomenon. Moreover, a Periclean *imperial* democracy is not exempt from the tension between internal freedom and external coercion described above, and may be more vulnerable to it, since respect for democratic principles does not easily coincide with pronounced superiority in a political leader, as evidenced above all by Alcibiades. And as much as Thucydides elevates Pericles over his mediocre and demagogic successors, even he does not escape his share of blame for what happened to Athens. He was, after all, one of the strongest supporters of Athens' imperial expansion and the principal impetus behind her entry into the war, both of which ultimately proved to be disastrous policies when Athens was defeated and stripped of both her empire and her democracy.

Democracies, in short, are fertile breeding grounds for demagogues because the people both resist taking responsibility for public affairs themselves and encourage the rise of mediocre, insincere, and self-interested leaders, who in turn undermine and subvert democracy by their drive for personal power above all else. Certainly, the United States is not exempt from this danger and has had its fair share of demagogues, although their effect has been limited by the deep roots and relative maturity of the American democracy and by the divisions and limitations of power wisely built into our constitutional structure. But the risk is there. Specifically, one sees the flattery of demagogues directed in one of two directions: toward people's patriotic sentiments, on the one hand, and toward their personal needs and liberties, on the other. The centripetal forces of democracy make it very difficult to maintain national cohesion without national self-assertion. This suggests that one of two courses tends to follow from the institution of democratic liberties: either national cohesion is maintained through national assertion, resulting in imperial expansion of some sort, or national cohesion gradually fades away, as the people increasingly tend to their private needs and desires at the expense of the public, resulting in the fading of the nation itself. Among contemporary democracies, the latter seems the stronger trend in Europe, the former in America, though this may be disputed in particular respects. Either course carries significant risks to democracy and on different levels. The inherently undemocratic assertion of national power can undermine respect for democracy internally, even as it increasingly exposes the state to the vulnerabilities of empire as described above. The spurning of national assertion, in contrast, can undermine public-spiritedness and weaken the nation to the point that it becomes subject to both internal dissolution and external domination. Tyranny lurks as a threat in either case, whether in a belligerent imperial presidency (US) or in a conflict-averse transnational bureaucracy (EU).

The question remains, however, whether anything can be done; whether there are lessons that can be learned from imperial Athens. Perhaps the lesson is that we need a Pericles, or a less imperialistic Pericles; in other words, the lesson is that democracy needs a wise, respected, and incorruptible statesman to preserve liberty, promote national cohesion, and guide its vigorous expression in just, beneficial, and sustainable directions. Such statesmen, however, are obviously rare and cannot simply be ordered up as needed. Moreover, dependence on them leaves the people vulnerable to less virtuous leaders in their absence because such dependence implies that the people are incapable of governing themselves. And if the lesson is that we should avoid empire, even of our "soft" variety, this does not seem satisfactory either, both because the *projection* of national power seems so naturally to be a consequence of *possessing* power, and that power in turn seems to be a natural consequence of the vigor, dynamism, and fruitfulness of a healthy democracy, and because the projection of our power does seem to be guided to a significant degree by the desire to promote freedom and democracy. However much that goal might coincide with our national self-interest, this coincidence is no objection so long as we are in fact consistently promoting the liberty of other nations.

If, however, we are to promote democracy both at home and abroad consistently, without hypocrisy, and in ways that avoid undermining our democracy, overextending our resources, and exposing us to our enemies, wise and virtuous leaders are not enough. *We* need to be wise and virtuous, for only then can we reliably produce such leaders. What is necessary to produce wise and virtuous citizens? The answer Thucydides suggests lies in the lines quoted at the beginning and is implicit in his very writing of the *History*: it is education and specifically the education of history. Imperial Athens is indeed a model and education for the world, both negatively and positively. By attending to Athens' imperialistic excesses, inconsistent and shortsighted policies, and vulnerabilities to demagoguery, we can more effectively avoid similar problems. On the other hand, we are relatively less public-spirited than imperial Athens, and our cultural life is less elevated. If we can come to view our national greatness more in terms of our cultural and intellectual achievements and less in terms of our material prosperity and military power and if we can take our greatness more as a call to national service and less as a license for empty bragging and complacency, we will have learned from Athens (even if a somewhat idealized Athens) in a positive sense. In short, we the people must learn to avoid envy, selfishness, and apathy in our politics and to view our national task as the elevation of excellence in ourselves. Only by becoming worthy of governing ourselves freely will we become capable of effectively promoting liberty beyond ourselves and of sustaining democracy both at home and abroad. The lessons of history alone are not sufficient for the education of a free people, but they are necessary. For a people notoriously uninterested in the past and therefore liable to repeat it in the worst ways, they are especially important. In sum, we have much to learn from Thucydides, and we ignore his tragic tale of imperial Athens at our peril.

Works Cited

Thucydides. *History of the Peloponnesian War*. Trans. Rex Warner. New York: Penguin, 1954.

Boiling Down the People: Democratic Reform in Aristophanes' *The Knights*

Richard Myers
Patrick Malcolmson
St. Thomas University

One obvious answer to the question "who are we?" is that we are democrats. As citizens of a democratic regime, our characters are defined by the view of the good life inherent in that regime. Aristophanes' comedy *The Knights* can help us to think through some of the implications of our democratic identity, for in it we see ourselves as typical members of the body politic that forms the foundation of democracy, the *demos*. More specifically, the play depicts a demos that has been corrupted. It is a democracy that has degenerated to the point that the demagogue – a man who lacks both learning and character – is mistaken for the true statesman.

Students quickly and easily relate the play to their experience, limited though it may be, as citizens in a democracy. It is certainly not difficult for them to recognize the various techniques that are typical of demagogues. The play includes five distinct contests between Kleon and the Sausage-seller, one at the outset in front of the two slaves and the knights, a second offstage in the Council, and then three separate contests in front of Demos. These contests depict a variety of examples of demagoguery, including calumny and character assassination, threats, lies, flattery, promises of future benefits, and declarations of dedication to the public good. Recognizing how Kleon makes use of each of these techniques and how the Sausage-seller is able to outdo him is both fun and profitable for students. And it is certainly not difficult to relate these techniques to the speeches so typical of electioneering or to the steady stream of moral indignation from the media. Aristophanes' comedy brings with it the recognition of some aspects of the typical vices of the democratic life and in so doing helps us to understand better who we democrats are.

Of course, that understanding leads to an even more important question: in recognizing who we are and in recognizing that we have problems, do we not then have to ask who we could be? Is there a solution to the problem of democratic degeneration? The action of the play turns on Demosthenes' plan to bring down the demagogue Kleon by recruiting an even greater demagogue who can beat Kleon at his own game. It is not difficult for most students to see the obvious problem in such a strategy, even if Aristophanes disguises it with a most improbable happy ending. Indeed, to the extent that the mission of the Sausage-seller is complete only once he has "boiled down" Demos (395, l. 1321; cf. 397, l. 1336), the happy ending actually depends on an act of *magic*. The real challenge for the students, then, is to grapple with the significance of this strange contest between Kleon and the Sausage-seller. What does it suggest about the challenge of reform? Who is this Sausage-seller, and how exactly does he rejuvenate this corrupt Demos?

Demosthenes and Nikias expect the Sausage-seller to beat the demagogue at his own game, to out-Kleon Kleon, as it were. In some respects, that is precisely what happens, but only in some respects. The key to understanding the play is to notice the way in which the Sausage-seller shifts the ground rules of the game. The first of the five contests between the two adversaries is a contest in shouting insults and threats – tactics that are Kleon's stock-in-trade. In this contest, the Sausage-seller holds Kleon to a draw. The Sausage-seller's first victory over Kleon comes only in the second contest, which takes place before the Council, and the key to his victory is a remarkable shift in tactics. Kleon reaches the Council first and decides to play the conspiracy card: he denounces the Sausage-seller as a "traitor." In the context of the Peloponnesian War, Kleon's accusation is a perfect example of what we would today call McCarthyism – the attempt to discredit one's rivals (and to enhance one's own power) by appealing to citizens' fears in relation to national security. This time the Sausage-seller does not try to match Kleon. In fact, he realizes that if the contest is to be fought on the terrain of conspiracy and national security, Kleon will certainly beat him (presumably due to his established credibility with the Council). The Sausage-seller, therefore, shifts gears, distracting the Councilmen with the news that cheap sardines have just arrived in the market and with advice as to how they might snap up all the sardines for themselves before the rest of the city finds out. In other words, he saves the Councilmen from being misled by Kleon on a question of national security by refocusing their attention on their own stomachs.

This *jujitsu* move at the Council forms the basis of the Sausage-seller's victory in the contests that follow. The third contest, which is the first contest before Demos himself, is a contest as to who renders Demos the greatest service. Kleon, of course, points to the political services he has rendered Demos, such as boosting public revenues, cooking the public books, and, most importantly, extending Athens' empire. The Sausage-seller trumps all of these with a simple gift that only a real man of the people would think of: a cushion for Demos' aching butt. Note that Demos refers to this gesture as a truly *philo-demos* act. What the demos truly loves is comfort. Note, too, that not only does this masterstroke allow the Sausage-seller to win the third contest. Demos also makes the Sausage-seller's standard – who best provides for the physical comfort of Demos – the sole criterion for the fifth and decisive contest.

It is therefore only partially accurate to say that the Sausage-seller has beaten Kleon at his own game; it would be more accurate to say that the Sausage-seller has beaten Kleon by revolutionizing the game. The Sausage-seller has understood that Kleon's game is to advance his private interest as a public figure by bamboozling the demos with respect to public issues. The Sausage-seller's game is to protect Demos from this kind of manipulation by appealing to the private concerns of the body so as to distract Demos from public issues altogether. This is the point behind the Sausage-seller's preference to hold the contest at the home of Demos rather than at the Pnyx: Demos is quite reasonable when thinking about his own private affairs but becomes quite irrational in the political arena. Indeed, Aristophanes conveys this point beautifully in the contest at the Council. Once Kleon realizes that the Sausage-seller's sardine trick is working, he goes for the Hail Mary pass: he announces that he, the leader of the war party, has lined up a truce with Sparta. Yet the Councilmen, who normally fall for whatever Kleon says, are now amazingly immune to Kleon's tricks. Their love of sardines frees them from the hold of the demagogue.

Now one might wonder how Aristophanes could see the depoliticization of Demos as a positive development. Would we not normally understand the substitution of private concerns for public ones to be the very essence of democratic decline? On this point, it is essential to view the events of the play in the context of the oracle that foretells them. The oracle Kleon has been hiding describes the city as passing through five stages: an original healthy state followed by steady decline from the rule of the rope-seller through rule by the sheep-seller, the leather-seller, and, finally, the sausage-seller. In other words, Aristophanes casts the action of the play as a comic reconstruction of Hesiod's five ages. The Sausage-seller's reorientation of Demos toward the private is indeed a kind of corruption, but it is the corruption of an already corrupt state, the final stage of decline that prepares the way for a return to the original golden age of the Marathon Men.

The Sausage-seller's "boiling down" of Demos, the magical act that makes Demos "young and beautiful" again, is literally a refining of him, a boiling away of the political ambitions that have corrupted his soul. If students read *The Knights* in conjunction with *The Prince,* one might express the point as follows. Kleon is an example of what Machiavelli calls "the noble humor," the desire to dominate. The play depicts him as advancing his own desire to dominate Athens by inculcating in Demos a desire to dominate not just Greece, but even Africa. The "boiling down" of Demos serves to return him to what Machiavelli calls the "popular humor," the desire for peace, comfort, and safety, by refining away all traces of the noble humor. The Demos we see at the end of the play returns to his farm and to a life characterized by comfort and pleasure. He is not necessarily opposed to war – his identification with the Marathon Men indicates that he will do his duty in wars of self-defense. But he no longer has any interest in the grasping politics of Athenian imperialism.

The question, of course, is what all of this means for the reform of real-world democracies. What concrete solutions emerge from Aristophanes' play? As authors of a first-year textbook in political science, we are unlikely to insert in the fourth edition a chapter on how to boil the people. For what, then, is the "boiling down" a metaphor? And who, exactly, is the Sausage-seller?

Our suggestion is that if the "boiling down" is a metaphor for stripping away Demos' attraction to the noble humor, the Sausage-seller is ultimately Aristophanes himself. For the best way of liberating people from a harmful prejudice – perhaps the only way – is to playfully ridicule it, to get them to laugh at their error. In a way, then, the real magic of *The Knights* (or perhaps the real trick in *The Knights*) is that Aristophanes has actually been boiling his audience as they watch his play.

Works Cited

Aristophanes. *The Knights*. In *Aristophanes, I, Acharnians. Knights*. Ed. and trans. Jeffrey Henderson. Cambridge: Loeb, 1998.

Tocquevillian Reflections on Liberal Education and Civic Engagement

Joseph M. Knippenberg
Oglethorpe University

Like many other colleges and universities, my institution is currently think-ing about how best to promote student civic engagement. As a political theorist who has given a good deal of thought to civic education, I should approve of this rediscovery of one of the original missions of liberal education on my own cam-pus and elsewhere. But as a contrarian who has given a good deal of thought to the relationship between theory and practice, I have some hesitations about this enterprise.

I initially formulated some of those hesitations in a talk I gave to colleagues a few months ago and restated them for a wider audience a little while later. My aim now is to see whether they bear scrutiny from a wider audience interested in pedagogy and scholarship.

I invoked the shade of Tocqueville because he is, after all, the great apostle of American civic engagement. Worried about the various threats to liberty posed by the equality of conditions that history was bringing his way, Toc-queville found in America a number of defenses against the tyrannical majorities and paternalistic governments he feared would succeed the old aristocratic re-gimes as they gave way to democracy.

But before I turn to a consideration of Tocqueville's recommendations, I would like briefly to sketch his analysis of what ails us democrats. Even casual readers of Tocqueville know that in his scheme the universal cause of almost everything (I exaggerate for the sake of clarity and emphasis) in America is equality of conditions. What he means by this is the absence of a rigid and fixed social structure in which everyone knows his or her place, not to mention the place of his or her parents, children, grandchildren, and so on. Equality of conditions is marked above all by a kind of social mobility, in which people rise and fall from one generation to the next and, indeed, over their lifetimes.

This has a couple of immediate consequences. First, since the hierarchical web of social relations characteristic of aristocracy is broken, people are much more on their own. Human relations are more voluntary and less obligatory, hence ultimately at least a little less reliable. As a result, people tend to be thrown back upon themselves. Self-reliance might seem to be a good thing, if the self on whom we are supposed to rely understands itself as competent and powerful. But, Tocqueville argues, the competent and powerful self is, in a sense, much more characteristic of an aristocracy. People with status and retainers to do their bidding feel empowered; they think, often rightly, that they can get things done. By contrast, democratic selves are relatively lonely. They lack many natural allies in a class identification, and they do not fit neatly into a social hierarchy where they can expect to receive assistance animated by a sense of *noblesse oblige* from above or call upon help from clients, dependents, and retainers from below.

Stated another way, for Tocqueville, a democratic age is marked above all by individualism, which he describes as "a reflective and peaceable sentiment that disposes each citizen to isolate himself from the mass of those like him and to withdraw on one side with his family and his friends, so that after having thus created a little society for his own use, he willingly abandons society at large to itself" (482; II.ii.2). This individualism, born of a sense of unconnectedness to one's fellows and of a sense of impotence in the face of the mass of one's fellows, has a number of consequences. First, it *disengages* us from anything other than the immediate arena over which we (think we) have control. We focus on friends and family. Second, we feel too weak to accomplish anything on our own, and, absent any countermeasures, we tend to lack what Robert Putnam has called the "social capital" to manage anything in conjunction with others.

Under the circumstances, if anything big is going to be done, it is likely to be accomplished by a paternalistic government. This is what Tocqueville calls "democratic despotism." Its principal consequence is a further slackening of any human effort to take responsibility for ourselves. We are nominally free but disinclined actually to exercise our freedom. As a result, the human prospect could be *radically* diminished as we sink further and further into individualistic domestic bliss and leave more and more to be accomplished by a government only too willing to do for us what we believe we are unable to do for ourselves.

A related problem is what Tocqueville calls "tyranny of the majority," which stems in part from the individual's sense of impotence in the face of what appears to be an undifferentiated majoritarian mass. In a society without stable classes and different sources of status, mass opinion is nearly impossible to resist. Here is one way that Tocqueville puts it:

> When a man or a party suffers from an injustice in the United States, whom do you want him to address? Public opinion? That is what forms the majority; the legislative body? It represents the majority and obeys it blindly; the executive power? It is named by the majority and serves as its passive instrument; the public forces? The public forces are nothing other than the majority in arms; the jury? The jury is the majority vested with the right to pronounce decrees.... (241; I.ii.7)

Lest anyone regard Tocqueville's diagnosis of the threat of tyranny of the majority as *merely* political, let me hasten to call attention to another observation he makes: "I do not know any country where, in general, less independence of mind and genuine freedom of discussion reign than in America" (244; I.ii.7). Already in the 1830s, there was political correctness:

> In America the majority draws a formidable circle around thought. Inside those limits, the writer is free; but unhappiness awaits him if he dares to leave them. It is not that he has to fear an auto-da-fé, but he is the butt of mortifications of all kinds and of persecutions every day. A political career is closed to him: he has offended the only power that has the capacity to open it up. Everything is refused him, even glory. Before publishing his opinions, he believed he had partisans; it seems to him that he no longer has any now that he has uncovered himself to all.... (244; I.ii.7)

Tocqueville thinks that the great antidote to individualism and its concomitant threat of democratic despotism is the development of a rich associational life and vibrant institutions of local self-government. This is, for Tocqueville, the great American contribution to our understanding of democratic self-government:

> Americans of all ages, all conditions, all minds constantly unite. Not only do they have commercial and industrial associations in which all take part, but they also have a thousand other kinds: religious, moral, grave, futile, very general and very particular, immense and very small; Americans use associations to give fêtes, to found seminaries, to build inns, to raise churches, to distribute books, to send missionaries to the antipodes; in this manner they create hospitals, prisons, schools. Finally, if it is a question of bringing to light a truth or developing a sentiment with the support of a great example, they associate. *Everywhere that, at the head of a new undertaking, you see the government in France or a great lord in England, count on it that you will perceive an association in the United States.* (489; II.ii.5)

Stated another way, associations are a democratic alternative to the individual empowerment of aristocrats, on the one side, and the paternalistic solicitude of government, on the other. Ordinary people join forces to do things together that

no one of them could have done on his or her own. To the degree that we cultivate the habit of associating, we take care of ourselves and tend to avoid the las-
situde associated with democratic despotism.

As I noted above, Tocqueville also has a very high regard for townships:

> The institutions of a township are to freedom what primary schools
> are to science; they put it within reach of the people; they make them
> taste its peaceful employ and habituate them to making use of it.
> Without the institutions of a township, a nation can give itself free
> government, but it does not have the spirit of freedom. (58–59; I.i.5)

When you give people power and responsibility to deal with problems with
which they are intimately acquainted and which they have to cooperate in order
to solve, you create a taste for self-government and help cultivate its habits.

It is tempting to argue, following Tocqueville, that colleges and universities
ought to do everything they can to shore up these institutions and the habits and
practices associated with them. In so doing, we educators would seem to be carrying out his prescriptions for how to preserve the liberty and genuine individuality that are threatened by equality of conditions. All we would have to do, it
would seem, is engage our students in the lives of our surrounding communities,
so that they could learn from local practitioners the habits of democratic self-
government and associational responsibility and self-help.

For this sort of civic education, colleges and universities would seem to be
little more than facilitators, middlemen, or midwives, introducing students to the
communities and associations from which they would learn the healthy practice
of democracy in America. But Tocqueville also has a theory of democracy in
America, so to speak, and that is where things begin to get interesting.

He notes quite frequently that there is little genuine diversity of thought in
America in large part because we, as individuals, lack the resources to think for
ourselves. Of course, that is only the most general way of putting it. In particular, because we all have to work for a living, we lack the time and the inclination
to engage in the kind of deep theoretical inquiry that conduces to the production
of new, different, and interesting ideas.[1] Instead, Tocqueville says, we buy our
opinions off the shelf, from the majority:

> In the United States, the majority takes charge of furnishing individu-
> als with a host of ready-made opinions, and thus it relieves them of
> the obligation to form their own. There are a great number of theories
> on matters of philosophy, morality, or politics that everyone thus
> adopts without examination, on the faith of the public.... (409; II.i.2)

In addition, we lack the secure self-confidence to disagree with the majority
of our fellows, on whose approbation we depend. Here is how Tocqueville chill-
ingly characterizes this aspect of what he calls "tyranny of the majority":

[I]n our day civilization has perfected even despotism itself, which seemed...to have nothing more to learn. Princes had so to speak made violence material; democratic republics in our day have rendered it just as intellectual as the human will it wants to constrain. Under the absolute government of one alone, despotism struck the body crudely, so as to reach the soul; and the soul, escaping from those blows, rose gloriously above it; but in democratic republics, tyranny does not proceed in this way; it leaves the body and goes straight for the soul. The master no longer says to it: You shall think as I do or you shall die; he says, You are free not to think as I do; your life, your goods, everything remains to you; but from this day on, you are a stranger among us. You shall keep your privileges in the city, but they will become useless to you; for if you crave the vote of your fellow citizens, they will not grant it to you, and if you demand only their esteem, they will still pretend to refuse it to you. You shall remain among men, but you shall lose your rights of humanity. When you approach those like you, they shall flee you as being impure.... Go in peace, I leave you your life, but I leave it to you worse than death. (244; I.ii.7)

Thus, Tocqueville says, "there is no freedom of mind in America" (245; I.ii.7). On the contrary, what we have come to call "political correctness" is, as it were, the occupational hazard of democratic citizenship.

To summarize: In America Tocqueville found immense pressures, some benign and some insidious, toward an intellectual conformity that would diminish the human spirit and lead us to squander the liberty that is our birthright. But he also identified the counterweights, and that is where colleges and universities come in.

First, to the degree that we are all prey to the demand for practicality and to the degree that we are all always busy acquiring credentials or deploying them in order to make a living, we need the kind of leisure that a genuinely higher education can afford us. Students need to be told that the constant credential-oriented agitation that has marked their lives as what New York *Times* columnist David Brooks once called "organization kids" should be suspended in favor of inquiry, thought, and discussion (see 434; II.i.10). The busyness will resume soon enough, but they have an opportunity to build up a kind of intellectual capital to sustain their individuality and freedom as they proceed through life. College students today can have a remarkable opportunity to be provoked into thinking for themselves, into examining and debating a variety of ways of regarding the world.

But we do not accomplish this primarily by sending them out into the community, busying them with the pressing affairs of others. To the degree that collegiate civic engagement is a substitute for leisurely thought and discussion, to the degree that it takes the place of the leisurely contemplation of great ideas, it hinders, rather than helps, the causes of freedom, individuality, and self-government.

But that is not Tocqueville's only piece of advice to educators. Here is another:

> In our day one must detain the human mind in theory; it runs of itself to practice, and instead of constantly leading it back toward the detailed examination of secondary effects, it is good to distract it from them sometimes in order to raise it to the contemplation of first causes. (438; II.i.10)

Our students' natural tendency is to seek the pragmatic and the useful, to prepare themselves for the life of work that awaits them. Regarded in this aspect, higher education is a kind of advanced trade school, dedicated to the preparation of young professionals.

While it would be folly simply to ignore this tendency, we educators should engage in a bit of pushback, insisting on the importance of theory for its own sake, as an end in itself. Stated another way, colleges and universities can play an important role in a democratic society by being countercultural. I do not mean to urge a return to the manner of the Sixties, which all too often simply exaggerated a certain kind of immediate pragmatism ("if it feels good, do it" is a plausible predecessor to the thought that "the one who dies with the most toys, wins"). Rather, I think that colleges and universities can pull a little away from the immediately practical, insisting upon the importance of the permanent things that provide an anchor for human freedom and individuality against the pressure of the everyday.

Tocqueville even has some suggestions about the content of a countercultural curriculum. People in democratic ages, he says, should read Greek and Latin authors, for they call to our attention the importance of individuals, their potency, and their consequent responsibility (see 450-452; II.i.15 and compare 472; II.i.20). By contrast, for example, modern historians tend to present individuals as victims of mass movements and impersonal social forces (469-472; II.i.20). We need reasons for taking responsibility for ourselves, our communities, and our nations, not excuses for why we cannot.

We seem to have arrived at a kind of paradox: Tocqueville is apparently the apostle of both civic engagement and collegiate disengagement, of immersion in community as a way of learning the dispositions and habits of responsible democratic self-government and of withdrawal from the pressures of busyness for the sake of cultivating a confident and responsible individuality.

Properly understood (to use a good Tocquevillian expression), there is a tension and not a paradox. Higher education should be understood as a *preparation* for a life of responsible individual citizenship. What it can offer us, perhaps uniquely of all American institutions, is exposure to the resources for cultivating genuine intellectual independence and individuality. To do so, it must, as I have said, fight against our tendency to disdain these resources as impractical and irrelevant to our need to get on with our daily lives.

Busyness of all sorts is inimical to the leisurely cultivation of individuality. That includes the busyness of working at a part-time job, the busyness of recreational pastimes (from ultimate Frisbee to ultimate partying to ultimate social networking to ultimate video-gaming), and the busyness of civic engagement as it is typically promoted on our college campuses, where community service offices provide a menu of opportunities that could engage or distract students every day of the week.

I will concede the point that there are better and worse forms of busyness, that the busyness of working in a homeless shelter or tutoring children at an elementary school is unquestionably superior to the busyness of beating level 47 of some video game. But unless we in higher education insist – for the brief time we have our students – upon the claims of genuine leisure over against *all* forms of busyness, we abdicate our unique position and in essence give away the game. We might as well bill ourselves as trade schools, dedicated to preparing cogs for our industrial (or post-industrial) and mass democratic machines. For we cannot any longer call ourselves *liberal* arts educators, called intransigently to insist upon the importance of leisurely contemplation for the cultivation of a genuinely free individuality.

If they are to be something other than trade schools, if they are genuinely to cultivate the *liberal* arts, colleges and universities have to be *different from* the society in which they are embedded. We should not deprecate, but rather to some degree celebrate, what we at my institution call "the bubble." What is more, the differences should not be further developments or exaggerations of the vices of democracy or equality of conditions, but rather the opposite – pulling as hard as possible in the other direction, insisting on leisure (*schole*), as opposed to busyness, theory as opposed to practice, and so on. We can rest assured that our best efforts to counteract the characteristic tendencies of our age (in a direction that Tocqueville frankly acknowledges is aristocratic – favoring liberty over equality) will serve only barely to moderate them. We might at best, if we are good and if we are lucky, help save democracy from its worst excesses.

I would further argue that there is a kind of civic engagement that actually helps colleges do their jobs (conceived as I have just stated). It is *not* in the first place sending people out into the community, which runs the risk of communicating the message that what goes on *intra muros* is of less importance than what goes on off campus, that our theory is in all respects inferior to real-world practice. Rather, it is making the best effort we can to engage our students with the immediate problems they confront in the world they inhabit. The campus is our township. Our student organizations are the associations that empower otherwise isolated individuals. The habits and understandings cultivated or confirmed here will be carried out, soon enough, into "the real world." And in the meantime, they will not be undercutting our countercultural message.

By all means, let us have some civic engagement, as a supplement to and occasion for thought. It is, for a variety of reasons, unavoidable. But let us also insist, against the pressures of the marketplace, upon the importance of reading, thinking, and conversation, all increasingly threatened in a world that demands that we always be *doing* something.

Notes

1 The relevant passages are found in I.i.3:

> I do not think there is a country in the world where, in proportion to popula-
> tion, so few ignorant and fewer learned men are found than in America.
> Primary instruction there is within the reach of each; higher instruction is
> within the reach of almost no one...Americans...can only give the first few
> years of life to the general cultivation of intelligence; at fifteen they enter
> into a career; thus their education most often ends in the period when ours
> begins. If it is pursued beyond this, it is then directed only toward a special
> and lucrative matter; one studies a science as one takes up a trade and one
> takes from it only the applications whose present utility is recognized....
> [W]hen one could have the taste for study, one does not have the time to
> engage in it; and when one has acquired the time to engage in it, one no
> longer has the taste for it. There does not exist in America, therefore, any
> class in which the penchant for intellectual treasures is transmitted with
> comfort and inherited leisure, and which holds the works of the intellect in
> honor...In America a certain common level in human knowledge has been
> established. All minds have approached it; some by being raised to it, others
> by being lowered to it. (51)

Works Cited

Brooks, David. "The Organization Kid." *Atlantic Monthly* April, 2001.
<<http://www.theatlantic.com/doc/200104/brooks.>>

de Tocqueville, Alexis. *Democracy in America.* Ed. and trans. Harvey C. Mans-
field, Jr. and Delba Winthrop. Chicago: U of Chicago P, 2000.

Putnam, Robert. *Bowling Alone: The Collapse and Revival of American Community.* New York: Simon and Schuster, 2001.

The Core and the Core of Persons

Good Cop, Bad Cop: Interrogating Human Nature with Xunzi and Mencius

Lawrence K. Schmidt
Hendrix College

> *"You know you are evil," Tom said. "There is not a good bone in your body. It's just me, me, me, all the time. You think you are pretty smart – conniving, cunning, and audacious. But, look where you are now – caught. Guilt is written all over your face."*
>
> *As Tom stamped out, John came in smiling and said, "Have a cigarette? Deep down I know you are good. You're not a misanthrope; you really do want to get along. You just got caught up with some lowlifes. They led you astray. Tell me all about it. You'll feel better."*
>
> *Just then Tom burst back in, grinning. "It's all set! We're going to nail him."*
>
> *Pulling Tom aside John whispered, but loud enough for all to hear, "That's fine Tom. I'm almost done. Just give me a minute – OK!"*
>
> *After Tom left, John turned saying, "It's your last chance. I know in your heart of hearts you are good. Just tell me how you were lead astray and I'll help you."*

We all know the debate between Hobbes and Locke concerning the natural state of human beings, although we may not have met them in the interrogation room. In order to infuse an Eastern perspective into discussions of who we are, I will introduce a similar debate concerning the natural state of humans that occurred 2,300 years ago in China between Xunzi and Mencius, two Confucian philosophers.

Confucius (551-478 BCE) lived in the middle of the Zhou Dynasty (1027-256 BCE), which began well and ended poorly. The final period of the Zhou Dynasty was appropriately called the Warring States Period (403-221 BCE) in the middle of which Mencius (372-289 BCE) lived, and Xunzi (312-238 BCE) lived at its end. Since they are both Confucian philosophers, I will begin by briefly noting those elements of Confucian thought that they shared.

Confucius argues that social order and peace can only be attained when the ruler rules by virtuous example. The central concept in Confucian thought is *ren*, humanity or authoritative conduct. A person who achieves *ren* is called a *junzi*, exemplary person. Confucius said, "As for filial and fraternal responsibility, it is, I suspect, the root of authoritative conduct (*ren*)" (*Analects* 1.2). For Confucius, moral education begins in the family. Confucius looks to the past to discover the proper way to live and rule society. *Li*, ritual propriety, is the code of conduct for virtuous behavior. Internally, one aims at realizing *yi*, righteousness. Education is central, beginning in the family and continuing throughout life. We would call it a liberal arts education. Xunzi and Mencius accept this Confucian foundation for their thinking. They agree on the importance of developing virtues, on the central importance of authoritative conduct or humanity (*ren*), on being appropriate or righteousness (*yi*), on following ritual propriety (*li*), on kingly government, and on the possibility that all humans could be good or attain the way (*Dao*) through study and the imitation of the sages. However, Confucius is not definitive concerning the natural state of human beings: "The master said, 'Human beings are similar in their natural tendencies (*xing*), but vary greatly by virtue of their habits'" (*Analects* 17.2). This left open the question of whether humans are naturally good or evil.

Mencius argues that humans are naturally good. Mencius argues, "If you let people follow their feelings (original nature), they will be able to do good. This is what is meant by saying that human nature is good. If man does evil, it is not the fault of his natural endowment" (6A6).[1] According to Mencius, our natural endowment includes four basic feelings that lead to four basic Confucian virtues. The feeling of commiseration leads to the virtue of humanity (*ren*), the feeling of shame and dislike to the virtue of righteousness (*yi*), the feeling of respect and reverence to the virtue of propriety (*li*), and the feeling of right and wrong (or affirmation and denial) to the virtue of wisdom (*zhi*) (6A6). These feelings are found in all people. Mencius presents three sayings to support his position. The ancient saying, "Seek and you will find it, neglect and you will lose it," means that one can develop one's natural endowment to differing degrees. He quotes from the *Book of Odes*[2] – "Heaven produces the teeming multitude. As there are things there are their specific principles. When the people keep their normal nature they will love excellent virtues." – and Confucius' statement that this writer knew the Way (*Dao*). Mencius' most famous example of the basic feelings concerns commiseration: "Now, when men suddenly see a child about to fall into a well, they all have a feeling of alarm and distress, not to gain friendship with the child's parents, nor to seek the praise of their neighbors and friends" (2A6). His point is that we naturally commiserate with the child and do so from our natural feeling of commiseration and not for some other ulterior motive. Mencius' contention is that humans have a specific principle and that it includes the four feelings.

In the next paragraph, Mencius acknowledges that sometimes young people behave well and other times they do not. However, "this is not due to any difference in the natural capacity endowed by Heaven. The abandonment is due to the fact that the mind is allowed to fall into evil" (6A7). This is supported by the concrete example of growing wheat. If the wheat is planted at the same time in the same field, its specific principle (i.e., by nature) would result in a good harvest. The differences we could find in different stalks of wheat would be the result of "differences in the soil," "unequal nourishment obtained from the rain," or "differences in human effort" (6A7). The same is true for humans.[3]

Having argued for his thesis that humans are good by nature in that they all have these innate, moral feelings, Mencius explains how it could appear that humans are not good by nature. He relates the story of the Niu (Ox) Mountain.[4] Originally the mountain was forested and beautiful. Because it was close to the capital, all the trees were cut down. With natural nourishment sprouts began to appear, but then sheep and cattle grazed the mountain. Today the mountain is bald, and people think that being bald is its true nature. The same is true for humans. A person loses "his originally good mind" as the trees are cut down, and "when there is repeated disturbance, the restorative influence of the night will not be sufficient to preserve (the proper goodness of the mind)" (6A8). In that case, man becomes like a beast, and people wrongly think that man "never had the original endowment (for goodness)" (6A8). Our original feelings require proper nourishment and care. He concludes by quoting Confucius, "Hold it fast and you preserve it. Let it go and you lose it" (6A8).[5]

Xunzi initiates his discussion of the nature of human beings by stating his thesis: "The nature of man is evil; his goodness is the result of his activity" (128).[6] He identifies the inborn nature to be "to seek for gain," to be "envious and hate others," and to possess "the desires of the ear and eye and [to] like sound and beauty.... Therefore to follow man's nature and his feelings will inevitably result in strife and rapacity, combine with rebellion and disorder, and end in violence" (128). To counter man's inborn nature, "the civilizing influence of teachers and laws and the guidance of propriety [li] and righteousness [yi]"[7] (128) are required and, if instituted, will result in deference, compliance, order, and peace.

Xunzi presents several observations and arguments. Concretely, he notes that crooked wood, implicitly what naturally occurs, must be worked on to become straight. Activity on the part of the artisan is required to make what is good. Similarly, since humans are by nature evil, they need "teachers and laws to become correct and achieve propriety and righteousness" (128). Without these there will be "rebellion, disorder, and chaos" (128). The sage-kings recognized this state of human affairs and so "created the rules of propriety [li] and righteousness [yi] and instituted laws and systems in order to correct man's feelings" so that humans could "become disciplined and conform with the Way

(*Dao*)" (128). The superior man has put forth this effort to conform to the proper way, while inferior persons have given "rein to their feelings," i.e., their evil nature (128).

To support his conclusion, Xunzi begins with an important distinction. Quoting Mencius,[8] "'Man learns because his nature is good'" (129), Xunzi disagrees, claiming that Mencius has not properly distinguished what is by nature and what can be caused by human activity. What is by nature, he argues, "cannot be learned and cannot be worked for" (129). For example, the clarity of vision is set by nature, and we cannot improve our vision by trying to learn how to see better. Similarly, "by nature man desires repletion when hungry, desires warmth when cold, and desires rest when tired" (129). These are, as Xunzi says later, "natural reactions to stimuli and do not require any work to be produced" (130). In contrast, to act in a way opposed to one's natural desires requires learning and effort. "[W]hen a man is hungry and sees some elders before him, [and] he does not eat ahead of them but yields to them," this action is "contrary to original nature and violate[s] natural feeling" (129). Rather, one must learn and work to behave properly according to propriety and righteousness.

Xunzi defines goodness to mean "true principles and peaceful order" and evil to mean "imbalance, violence, and disorder" (131). He says Mencius is wrong to think man's nature is good, for then man would follow true principles and be peaceful. If that were the case, then we would not need sages (to teach us the way) nor would we need propriety and righteousness (as moral prescriptions) since we would naturally act for the good.

There is still the question of how the good came to be if we are naturally evil, even if only in our desires. Xunzi has someone ask, "'If man's nature is evil, whence come propriety [*li*] and righteousness [*yi*]?'" (130). His answer is that they came from the activity of the sages. The example of the potter who pounds the clay to form the pot demonstrates that the pot is the result of activity and does not come to be by nature. The same is the case with propriety and righteousness. Xunzi says, "The sages gathered together their ideas and thoughts and became familiar with activity, facts, and principles, and thus produced propriety and righteousness and instituted laws and systems" (130). In the typical Confucian manner, Xunzi credits the earlier sage-kings with developing the good moral and political system. His point is that it was by studying how human beings behave and through their own activity that the sages discovered the rules of propriety and righteousness and incorporated these into the structure of the political system to counter humans' natural tendency towards evil.

As we have seen, Xunzi, like Hobbes, argues that humans are by nature evil and require a strong government to provide order and peace. Students of Xunzi helped end the Warring States period and unite China for the first time in the Qin Dynasty (221-206 BCE), which was known for its excessive law-and-order mentality. Xunzi's influence continued throughout the Han Dynasty (206 BCE – 220 CE) before fading until modern times.

Mencius, like Locke, argues that humans are good by nature. Unlike Locke, Mencius still supports the Confucian ideal of virtuous ruling, which is hierarchical without being authoritarian. Similar to Locke, Mencius is also known for supporting the people's right to remove a bad government.[9] After the Han Dynasty, Mencius' thought influenced Chinese thinking until the present; his text was included with Confucius' in the national examination system. Of course, the cause for humans' being good by nature is different in each.

Locke and Hobbes emphasize the use of individual reason to discover the laws of nature, whereas Mencius and Xunzi, while also using reason and arguments, argue for the need for the rules of correct behavior and governance, although the sage-kings already established these rules. There is also a major difference concerning their respective understanding of who we are. The Europeans understand the self to be primarily an isolated individual with autonomy, whereas the Chinese understand the self to be fundamentally constituted by relationships to others. Perhaps this is why Mencius and Xunzi do not need the social contract to establish a commonwealth, since one is necessarily already embedded within social relations. For this reason, as well, Mencius may avoid Locke's problem of making the state of nature so good that government would not be required.

Notes

1 Chan notes, "*The Book of Mencius, Meng Tzu* in Chinese, is divided into seven books, each subdivided into two parts [A and B]" (51 n15). The quotations here come from book 6 part 1, so 6A and then the paragraph number.

2 Chan notes this is ode no. 260 (54 n30).

3 He cites several specific examples. Without knowing the foot size of the buyers, a shoemaker does not make shoes the size of baskets, since we all have similar feet. Also, concerning our taste for food, our taste for music, and our appreciation of beauty, there is a standard and common agreement. We do not find humans whose taste for food differs as greatly as dogs' and horses' tastes differ from humans' tastes. Mencius asks rhetorically, "Can it be that in our minds alone we are not alike?" (6A7). No. What is common in our minds is "the sense of principle and righteousness (*yi-li*, moral principles)" (6A7).

4 Chan notes that this mountain was outside the capital of the state of Ch'i (56 n38).

5 To answer the question why some people do not follow their innate feelings but act incorrectly, Mencius says that when we use our senses without thinking, they "are thereby obscured by material things, the material things act on the material senses and lead them astray" (6A15). This appears to mean that when humans are guided in their actions by only the senses and without thinking about the moral dimension of what they are doing, they are led astray not by something internal but by the external influence of the material things on their senses. For example, the meat itself affects our sense of taste by tasting good and makes us desire more. If the mind does not control

our desire so stimulated, we are in danger of overindulging. As Mencius says, "The function of the mind is to think" (6A15). By thinking, we can do what is right by controlling our desires.

6 Xunzi (in Wade-Giles transliteration Hsün Tzu) discusses the nature of human beings in chapter or essay 23 of his work *The Hsün Tzu*.

7 I have inserted the Pinyin transliterations of major terms to show the connections with the *Analects*.

8 Wing-Tsit Chan notes that this is a paraphrase and not a direct quote of Mencius (129 n42). He also notes that there is no evidence that Xunzi and Mencius ever met (116).

9 See Chan, 62.

Works Cited

Chan, Wing-Tsit, ed. *A Source Book in Chinese Philosophy*. Princeton: Princeton UP, 1963.

Confucius. *The Analects of Confucius: A Philosophical Translation*. Trans. Roger T. Ames and Henry Rosemont, Jr. New York: Ballantine, 1998.

Mencius. *The Book of Mencius*. In Wing-Tsit Chan. *A Source Book in Chinese Philosophy*. Princeton: Princeton UP, 1963.

Xunzi. *The Hsün Tzu*. In Wing-Tsit Chan. *A Source Book in Chinese Philosophy*. Princeton: Princeton UP, 1963.

Aristotle (versus Kant) on Autonomy and Moral Maturity

Molly Brigid Flynn
Assumption College

On the one hand, we are persons, thus free morally, and we are capable of becoming morally mature. On the other hand, we are social animals. Often these sides of human life seem at odds. I will compare Kant's modern view with Aristotle's classical view of freedom and moral maturity to illustrate that how we philosophically describe our freedom makes a difference for how we understand our goal of moral maturity.

Kant emphasizes autonomy as the essence of morality, and this autonomy or freedom contains both a negative *from* aspect and a positive *to* aspect. The individual's moral life is free *from* two things especially: desires and other people. He emphasizes freedom from the passions because the passions, as entwined with the body, are one way in which we are determined by the laws of physics. This aspect of freedom is especially emphasized in the *Groundwork* and in the second *Critique*. According to his epistemological metaphysics, we have no direct access, as knowing beings, to the noumenal, to the real in itself. It is in the moral life alone, through our willing of the moral law, which we break through into the noumenal. The will, in willing the rule of reason, is free from the phenomenal realm and its laws, but when we allow our passions to determine what we do, we give ourselves over to the phenomenal and to physics and are thus not free. In "What is Enlightenment?" freedom from others is Kant's focus. To be morally mature is to be autonomous from other persons. This, also, is grounded in Kant's conception of the moral law. Each person, having reason, has equal and easy access to the moral law, the categorical imperative. The equality of access here is important. The moral law is built into reason, and the willing of the moral law is in fact nothing other than the willing of reason. Because all persons have reason, we all have the moral law given to us directly, rather than through others. The ease of access is important here, too. Kant claims to merely formalize and defend philosophically, what we all know intuitively: the golden rule, consistency of action, treating persons as persons. Making some individuals more authoritative morally offends against both the ease and the equality of access to the moral law. Being determined by desire subjects the will to the laws of physics; by looking to others as moral authorities, we abdicate our sovereign throne as persons with reason and as containing the moral law within us. In both cases, freedom *to* exercise our essential dignity as persons requires freedom *from* desires and others lest we displace our own inner moral authority, estranging ourselves from the moral law and from our own authenticity as persons with reason. Of course, in being truly free, we are also bound. Instead of advocating lawlessness as freedom, Kant maintains that freedom is binding oneself to duty. Thus, moral maturity is giving oneself the law that defines one's essence as a person and gives one dignity.

Kant's ethics focuses on autonomy or moral maturity as rationality and freedom from heteronomy. Aristotle's ethics does not focus on these concepts, but rather on the inborn human *telos*, happiness, the virtues and their exercise, prudence, friendship, and contemplation – anything that goes into a human life turned out well, to use Robert Spaemann's rendering of *eudaimonia* (19). I would like to force Aristotle to speak in our modern idiom. What does he have to say about us in terms of autonomy and moral maturity?

If we focus on the end of *De Anima* III.11-12 (434a and 434b), we see that freedom first arises for Aristotle in the non-rational voluntary movement of animals. Having sensation, animals also experience pleasures and pains. The lowest level animals have touch and an indefinite imagination, but lack the distant senses of sight, hearing, and smell and lack the capacity for forward movement. Even these "imperfect animals," like jellyfish, perform the voluntary local motion of taking in desired things and rejecting undesired things. So-called "perfect" animals, having some distant senses, also perform forward movements, exercising a mobility to pull toward or push away from objects that cause pleasure or pain. This is a freedom *to* move, but it is not a raw freedom – it is bound to a particular sensed thing as it shows up as good in pleasure and desire. At the next level, most animals also have a definite imagination, a quasi-sensory discernment of objects not immediately given to the five senses. This is an additional level of freedom: freedom *from* the immediate, sensed present and freedom *to* pursue or flee the sensible thing not here but just around the corner. By rejecting as absurd the denial of voluntary movement to children and brutes, Aristotle insists that all this movement in response to sensed and imagined things is willed movement. It is on this ground that true, human freedom is built. The highest level of animal life is the adult human, but it remains part of this continuum of animals. As *De Anima* III.10 explains (433b), we have not just a sensory imagination but also a "calculative" imagination by which we can consider and weigh several goods together, and with a deeper memory and longer sense of the future, we discern many more goods to compare and weigh. With reason we can recognize the best and decide upon certain goods among many. This opens up the possibilities of continence and incontinence, and of deliberation and of choice. In *De Anima* III.9-12, reason appears mostly as multiplying the number of things that we can discern and desire. From *Nicomachean Ethics*, we also know that reason opens up new type of goods: reason itself as both practical and theoretical is good, and it is so not merely as a new tool to get more of the same lower-level goods.

At each level of animal life, voluntary movement involves two key factors, a faculty of discrimination or knowledge (e.g., touch, sight, imagination, and thought) and a faculty of desire (e.g., hunger, fear, and wish). Voluntary movement requires a particular object to be apprehended and to be desired, so voluntary movement is always bound to how things appear to us. Notice how Aristotle distinguishes between touch and taste, on the one hand, and sight, smell, and hearing, on the other; then between sensation and imagination; then between a sensory and a calculative imagination; and then between imagination and thought. These are all faculties of discrimination, but at each level the animal increases its range, apprehending objects further away in space or time. Aristotle hierarchically orders the levels of animal life according to the degree of freedom from the immediately discerned and desired sensory objects. At each level, the expanded range of discrimination out of the sensed present opens up a new range of freedom, and that means a new set of desirable objects shows up. But movement is still always bound to an object apprehended and desired. For Kant, we must in being morally mature not allow our will to be determined by particular desired goods. For Kant, we must, rather, declare independence from the appearances and always will the good will itself. In contrast, for Aristotle, our sensory apprehension of and desire for goods do not undermine freedom or voluntariness but form its ground.

For Aristotle, reason both enhances and catapults us beyond this apprehension and desire for material goods. Thought, wish, and choice are part of the hierarchy – the continuum, in animal life of the discernment of objects, the desire for goods, and self-movement – but reason also transforms all of this upon which it is built. In the adult human, thought often opposes desire for material goods sensed or imagined, giving rise to continence and incontinence. Most of the practical virtues deal with mundane material or interpersonal goods, many of the same type that animals can discern and desire, such as food, safety, victory, power, and sex. But we have the ability to deal with these animal goods in a human way, by infusing our desires and actions with reason. In doing so, we can get not only more of these goods or get them more securely, but we also get to accomplish noble or beautiful actions with them. One need only recall one's last activity involving such animal goods as sex, food, or power to realize the extent to which reason humanizes these goods, transforming them and making our actions with them more beautiful or more ugly than any animal movement could be. Like his account of voluntary movement, Aristotle's ethics allows us to understand both the continuity of human life with brute life and the radical changes that reason brings to the animal aspects of our lives. Because Aristotle does not share Kant's conception of the forces of matter as completely and perfectly deterministic, freedom for him does not require autonomy defined against the desires the way it does for Kant. Freedom for Aristotle arises within nature, not against it, and in action we are always aiming for a particular good as it appears to us through the imagination. The morally mature man is not free from the apparent good, but he is the one who uses reason to ensure that the good appears to him truly.

What about autonomy from others? Authority is the function of those capable of directing others to the true or the good. The virtuous person successfully trains his desires to harmonize with the good. This training must start in childhood. The need for others' authority, especially in childhood, follows from the non-rational foundations of voluntary movement. Virtue does not consist in the mere habituation of one's desires, but it does require it. And this starts in childhood by means of authorities praising or blaming our non-chosen but voluntary movements, so that we begin to understand responsibility and so that our pleasures and pains are connected with their proper objects.

That chosen virtuous actions by adult humans emerge out of the pre-chosen voluntary movement of children shows that others' authority has a positive, even crucial, role in ethics, at least in childhood. What about adulthood? For Aristotle (as for Kant), the virtuous person is autonomous from others' direction and is a law unto himself (*Politics* 1284a14). But as Aristotle claims in the *Rhetoric*, the moral law is not expressible in any finite formula. Our best access to this moral law is the matured faculties of the virtuous person. The virtuous person is the measure, and like the measuring stick from Lesbos, he bends with the oddly shaped situations to measure them correctly when the letter of the law fails because of its generality and inflexibility. Although raised by others and by the law, the virtuous person has not merely adopted others' views or assimilated well to his culture. With their help, he has acquired for himself a sensitively tuned faculty to discriminate the good and bad in his own and in others' actions. He can even recognize the inadequacies of the law that have cultivated this sensitivity in him. Though Kant sees as necessary, for a historically limited time, a tough but enlightened authority, like Frederick II of Prussia, who can set the ground for a people to progressively enlighten themselves, Aristotle does not think the multitude of people can reach moral maturity. For Aristotle, virtuous people really are permanently invaluable as moral authorities for the multitude, which is stuck in the middle in continence or incontinence.

Aristotle denies both the equality and the ease of access to moral correctness, the two features of Kant's categorical imperative that allow Kant to denigrate, as a form of immoral heteronomy, the exercise and honoring of moral authority. Many people do not become fully virtuous, and for them the law and others' authority remains important throughout life. In the *Nicomachean Ethics*, Aristotle quotes Hesiod: "Altogether best is he who has insight into all things, / But good in his turn is he who trusts one who speaks well. / But whoever neither himself discerns, nor, harkening to another, / Lays to heart what he says, that one for his part is a useless man" (1095b). Although autonomous insight is best, we who lack insight into all things are foolish if ungrateful for authorities with better understanding than ourselves. Aristotle also denies the ease of knowledge of right and wrong. In a rejection of anything like the categorical imperative, Aristotle denies that any formula or single principle is an infallible guide to moral action. All actions deal with particulars, and general principles are good but imperfect guides. The morally serious and virtuous person may not need moral authorities, but the difficulty of knowing the best course of action may make other virtuous people epistemically useful even to the morally mature man. Aristotle tells us that it is easier to perceive, and thus enjoy contemplatively, the good actions of others. Moreover, in good friendship decent people make each other better "by putting their friendship to work and by straightening one another out, for they have their rough edges knocked off by the things they like in one another" (1172a). It might also be easier to perceive the *imperfection* of actions done by others. Other people's opinions and actions would then take on a positive role in Aristotle's ethics, even for the virtuous person. The happy life of the person who puts virtue to work throughout life is "self-sufficient" (1097b), but this self-sufficiency requires the virtue and happiness of friends, as well.

Finally, Aristotle does come closer to Kant when he denies that reason is merely another natural thing. For Kant, the radical independence of reason from nature makes freedom and a good will the ultimate goods for us: it is with reason's freedom that I attain the real me, affirming the authentic dignity of my personhood, and here I break away from the appearances and get through to the really real. We need to understand reason and freedom as radically different from nature in order to be persons, and to be free from the determinism of nature, according to Kant.

Likewise, for Aristotle, I am most truly my intellect, and true self-love means acting reasonably, serving and exercising this highest part of me most of all. And likewise for Aristotle, reason is not just another part of nature. It is ultimately god-like and immaterial. It is simultaneously part of us and beyond us, and with it we can really, though imperfectly, be united with the most real beings in and behind the cosmos. Nevertheless, Aristotle draws a quite un-Kantian conclusion from the non-naturalness of reason and the identity of the core of the person with the intellect. After all, Aristotle does not have a problem explaining free movement *within* the physical world, as Kant does. Rather, it is in the *theoretical* operation of the intellect that the moral life is culminated and surpassed, in our knowing and not in our doing. Moral maturity and autonomy of the person, for Aristotle, is found most of all not in willing but in knowing, in this superhuman ability in which we only share but in which we should strive to share as much as possible.

For both Kant and Aristotle the person is most of all his reason, and moral maturity requires a certain autonomy from desires and from others' opinions. But for Aristotle our freedom arises out of nature rather than as a completely separate domain. Because of this and because knowledge of the moral law is not given easily or equally, to act morally we need a prudence that is based in the full maturation of our animality (i.e., our desires) and a willingness to submit to proper authority when it speaks. A deterministic view of nature mixed with a dedication to the freedom and dignity of persons leads Kant to distance the person from his animal side, and Kant's view of the ease and equality of access to the moral law leads him to denigrate authority and others' roles in our moral activity. But does not moral maturity require maturation of the whole person, including the animal side? And is it not morally mature to recognize when others speak with authority in an arca new to us and to recognize that others are an integral part of our own moral life? Kant would doubtless also answer these questions affirmatively, but Aristotle's psychology and ethics allow us to recognize these facts more easily than Kant's do and so better illuminate human freedom and autonomy for us. Aristotle allows us better to understand our complex nature as part of the continuum of animal life, while also showing how reason transforms and allows us to surpass the merely animal. Moral maturity is not just the autonomous rule of reason, but it is really the maturation of the whole person: animal, social, and rational.

Works Cited

Aristotle. *Nicomachean Ethics*. Trans. Joe Sachs. Newburyport: Focus, 2002.
---. *On the Soul*. Trans. J.A. Smith. In *The Complete Works of Aristotle* I. Ed. J. Barnes. Princeton: Princeton UP, 1984.
Spaemann, Robert. *Happiness and Benevolence*. Trans. Jeremiah Alberg. Notre Dame: U Notre Dame P, 2000.

Two *Meditations* on the Nature of Self

Roosevelt Montás
Columbia University

"Who am I?" is about as basic a question as one can ask. But, in the spirit of Descartes's attempt in the *Meditations* to dismantle all assumptions about his own knowledge and reduce his attention to the most elementary level of inquiry possible, we might propose the more fundamental question "What am I?" The relative pronoun "who" already carries in it a set of assumptions – ultimately metaphysical assumptions – about the nature of the kind of thing that can answer the question. Specifically, the pronoun "who" carries ontological presuppositions – embedded in the logic of human languages and perhaps in the cognitive structures of our brains – about personal identity and agency. Not just anything can answer the question "who?" Only a discrete, personal – or personalized – agent can answer to that pronoun. The notions of unitary identity and agency are so indispensable to the way we interact with the world that their metaphysical foundations are virtually invisible. In the technical sense of "taking for granted what one sets out to prove," to ask "who am I?" is already to beg the question at the most elementary level. So, to think about this subtlest of questions in Descartes and Marcus Aurelius, I want to shave it down to elementary form, "What is the self?" *That* is the question that I want to, as it were, thread through the two texts called *Meditations*.

Descartes is closer to us than Marcus Aurelius both in time and in the metaphysical worldview he assumes. His ontological assumptions are very much like our own, despite the fact that, as we all know – and Nietzsche made explicit – God did not survive the epistemological revolution Descartes himself helped launch in the seventeenth century. So let us look first at Descartes and at the answer we get to the question "What am I?" in his brilliant *Meditations on First Philosophy* of 1640/41.

Descartes begins his *Meditations* with a mental exercise in which he tries to doubt everything – and he means *everything*. To help this exercise, he imagines an all-powerful evil genius that can deceive him about everything – even about mathematical truths: he grants that he can even be deceived in "counting the sides of a square" (61). But Descartes quickly tells us that the one thing he cannot bring himself to doubt, even with this evil genius working on him, is his own existence. And he cannot doubt his own existence because the very act of doubting – that mental operation – immediately establishes existence. So he declares that "this pronouncement 'I am, I exist' is necessarily true every time I utter it or conceive of it in my mind" (64). This is a very compelling argument. Sometimes I taunt my students to refute it. I ask them to close their eyes and imagine themselves not existing. They soon discover that the effort is futile. What Descartes sees here, and where he directs our attention, is the doubling upon itself that is consciousness. As James Joyce said in *Ulysses*, "thought is the thought of thought" (21). To be conscious is, first of all, to be. Being and consciousness are analytically embedded concepts. Consciousness is, in itself, already an ontological condition.

Note that what we get in *Meditations* is not the argument "I think, therefore I am," which is the more famous formulation of Descartes's *cogito* and which one finds in the *Discourse on Method*. What we get in the *Meditations* is "I think, I exist," which is not an argument. We get simply *"cogito, existo,"* without the *ergo*. And Descartes is serious and deliberate about this omission. To depend on an *ergo* – a "therefore" – would be like counting the sides of a triangle; in any argument, the evil genius can intervene in the movement from premise to conclusion and deceive Descartes. His skepticism must be absolute. There is no reasoning in "I think, I exist," no movement from premise to necessary conclusion. These two concepts, "consciousness" and "being" have a relation of *emanation* – not of logical necessity, which is rendered suspect in the all-encompassing skepticism of the first Meditation. Later in the *Mediations,* Descartes is going to pose an analogous relationship between the existence of "I" and the existence of a supreme being: the famous ontological argument for the existence of God. But that would be the subject of a different paper.

Before saying something about how Marcus Aurelius's conception of the self contrasts with and challenges Descartes's views, let me point out two striking features of Descartes's *cogito*: (1) to get at any truth, that is, at a truth that is un-doubtable, one has to turn inward. The outside world could be entirely a deception. Our perceptions of the outside world are not necessarily reliable, and only by looking within can one hit epistemological bedrock – unshakable truth. This means that (2) truth, ultimate Truth, has to be phenomenal, i.e., truth is not going to be interpretive, but simply perceptual. One is not allowed to interpret what one sees and claim that *it* exists or that *it* is true. Only the raw phenomenon, without interpretation, undoubtedly exists and is true, at least *as* phenomenon. In other words, at this early stage of the *Meditations*, which is as far I want to go, I cannot know *what* I am, but I cannot doubt *that* I am.

That argument seems quite unassailable. But I want to take a shot at it through Marcus Aurelius's conception of the self. The stoicism for which Marcus Aurelius is a spokesman is a philosophical tradition that flourished in the West for centuries but was then digested by Christianity. Christianity, while absorbing many elements of stoicism, also discarded many others. One of the things it discarded was a metaphysical view of the cosmos as essentially integrated; a metaphysics that collapsed subject and object – the observer and the observed – into one entity immanently divine. The conception of self that this orientation to the universe implies is much closer to Eastern spiritual traditions such as Buddhism than it is to the dualistic and more typically Western metaphysics we find convincingly articulated in Descartes. And this dualism in Descartes is subtler and more deeply ingrained than one realizes on a first reading. When one thinks of Cartesian dualism, one usually thinks of the famous mind-body split, of Descartes's discovery in *Meditations* that there are two types of things in world, *res cogitans* and *res extensas*, thinking things and extended things. But there is a more basic Cartesian dualism that is already embedded in "I think, I exist."

Faced with Descartes's *cogito* demonstration of the existence of a unitary self – "I am, I exist" – I can imagine Marcus Aurelius challenging what Descartes might mean by the pronoun "I." Marcus Aurelius might grant Descartes that there is "thought" and that there is "existence," but he might object to Descartes's automatic postulation of an independent and self-contained agent – an "I" – behind "thinking." Marcus Aurelius might be more comfortable with the simple statement "there is thought" rather than with "I think" and with "existence" rather than "I exist."

Perhaps the most prominent tenet in Marcus Aurelius's *Meditations* is that everything is changing, which includes in it his other master-theme: mortality. There is no constant; there is nothing that is unchanging. The only constant is change. Like Montaigne, Marcus Aurelius understood that when one looks at a boulder sitting somewhere, what one sees is very slow movement. Everything is constantly changing from one thing to another. But everything is also interlinked – changes are not random; everything is interconnected and changing together in a complex and beginningless chain of causation. Everything is interlinked, claims Marcus Aurelius, *rationally*. The self, for him, is a phenomenon that arises from a mix of pre-existing elements and that, like everything else, changes and decays, becoming some other new phenomenon. Marcus Aurelius often thinks of existence as a kind of ontological wax. This is how he puts it: "Universal nature uses the substance of the universe like wax, making now the model of a horse, then melting it down and using the material for a tree; next for a man; next for something else" (61). Man here, and the metaphysical notion of self, has no independent or permanent existence – no existence that persists from moment to moment, no identity, properly speaking. Cartesian self-contained identity is, for Marcus Aurelius, a metaphysical fiction.

For Marcus Aurelius, the self is inseparable from the rest of the cosmos. Two of his key understandings – the ceaseless changing of all things and the rational interconnectedness of all things – in effect undermine Descartes's notion of a unitary and consistent agent standing behind mental experiences. This is something Nietzsche also grasped, as he says in the *Genealogy of Morals:* "there is no 'being' behind 'doing'…'the doer' is merely a fiction added to the deed – the deed is everything" (45).

Another metaphor Marcus Aurelius returns to again and again is that of a river: "Existence," he writes, "is like a river in ceaseless flow, its actions a constant succession of change, its causes innumerable in their variety" (42). Instead of a Cartesian "self" observing phenomenal reality, Marcus Aurelius understands consciousness as itself immersed in and inseparable from the river of ever-changing existence. Existence, he says, is a "river…in which there can be no foothold" (48). Elsewhere he notes to himself (just as everything else in the *Meditations* is to himself): "You yourself are subject to constant alteration" (87) and "consider any existing object and reflect that it is even now in the process of dissolution and change" (99). The self, for Marcus Aurelius, is in perpetual dissolution.

Marcus Aurelius and Descartes give us two very different understandings of the notion of self. Together, they shine a bright light on each other and suggest a way of thinking that has over time become unfamiliar in Western metaphysics: the way of immanence, which is also the way of perpetual change.

Works Cited

Descartes, René. *Discourse on Method and Meditations on First Philosophy.* Trans. Donald A. Cress. 4th ed. Indianapolis: Hackett, 1998.

Joyce, James. *Ulysses.* The Gabler Edition. New York: Vintage, 1986.

Marcus Aurelius. *Meditations.* Trans. Martin Hammond. New York: Penguin, 2006.

Nietzsche, Friedrich. *On the Genealogy of Morals and Ecce Homo.* Trans. Walter Kaufman. New York: Vintage, 1967.

Montaigne and the Limits of Human Reason

Montague Brown
Saint Anselm College

The question "Who are we?" is fundamental to education. And so we pursue answers through science, philosophy, sociology, theology, and literary narratives. But the question is even more fundamental, perhaps, when it pertains to the possibility of education. For if we are mere animals or, more basically, mere matter in motion, then all pretence to make sense of this question in a distinctively human sense is an illusion. Michel de Montaigne provides us with a forum for discussing this matter. In his long essay *Apology for Raymond Sebond*, he defends the arguments for the existence of God both by way of the traditional Catholic view of faith seeking understanding and by a more radical move of undercutting the objections of those who reject such arguments. In an odd move, he invokes a radical skepticism to defend reasoned arguments for the existence of God, thus both commending reason and insisting that it is wholly inadequate. Since a proper assessment of reason is important to a liberal arts education that tries to answer the question "Who are we?" let us try to figure out what Montaigne means and whether he is right.

In the opening paragraph, Montaigne makes four main points: (1) knowledge is good; (2) those who despise knowledge are stupid; (3) knowledge does not have the power to make us good; and (4) science (that is, knowledge) is not virtue, nor ignorance vice. The first two points commend knowledge; the last two question its adequacy. These two approaches indicate the general plan of the work.

The ostensible occasion for the work is filial piety on the part of Montaigne. A few days before his death, Montaigne's father had asked Montaigne to translate a book entitled *The Natural Theology of Raymond Sebond*. The book is basically a representation of the natural theology of Thomas Aquinas. Being the dutiful son, Montaigne honors his father's wish that the work be translated, and after his father's death, he takes up the defense of the book.

Montaigne says that two main objections have been leveled against Sebond's work. The first is that it is simply wrong to base belief on human argument. To do so is an act of pride and impiety. Montaigne's response to this objection is an appeal to the tradition of faith seeking understanding proposed by St. Augustine and clearly followed by St. Anselm and St. Thomas Aquinas, among others. This traditional position holds that the mysteries of Christianity are indeed embraced by faith alone; however, once we believe them, we want to understand them, and the effort to do so is good. Montaigne writes, "We must accompany our faith with all the reason in us, but always with this reservation: we should not suppose that faith depends on us, or that our efforts and arguments can achieve so supernatural and divine a knowledge" (4). Montaigne goes on to mention Plato as one of those who have shown us that atheism is unnatural (8) and then presents the rudiments of an argument from design for the existence of God, saying, "It is not credible that the whole machine should not bear some marks imprinted by the hand of the great architect, and that there is not some image in the things of this world somehow relating to the workman who built and formed them" (9). Montaigne quotes the passage from Romans 1:20 where Paul says that the invisible things of God can be known from the things that are made. Since Scripture itself supports the ability of humans to know God from creation, such arguments for the existence of God cannot be impious and therefore wrong.

The second objection against Sebond's arguments is that they are weak and fail to lead to the conclusions he has in mind (10). Montaigne's answer to this objection occupies him for the rest of the essay, some one hundred and fifty pages as compared to the ten pages of his introduction and response to the first objection. In addressing this second objection, Montaigne makes a very clever, but questionable, move: he states that the objections against Sebond's arguments fail because reason fails. Montaigne admits the danger of such an argument and later counsels against its general use. He warns, "This last fencing trick is never to be employed except as an extreme remedy. It is a desperate thrust, in which you must abandon your arms in order to make your opponent lose his" (119). It is, indeed, a desperate (literally hopeless) move, for if the opponents' arguments are no good because reason is an illusion, neither are Sebond's (nor indeed anyone's including, of course, Montaigne's). Not only does Montaigne recognize that this move is contradictory in terms of theoretical reason; he also sees that it is an act of immense pride and as such immoral. He writes, "It is great temerity for you to destroy yourself in order to destroy another" (119). Why then does Montaigne make this move? Is there any justification for it?

When Montaigne introduces this response to the second objection, he does so in the name of morality and faith. It is an act of hubris to think that one can know divine things. In other words, Montaigne goes back on his reply to the first objection – the measured distinction between what reason can and cannot do in relation to the truths of faith. He says, "The means I take to beat back this frenzy, and which seems to me most appropriate, is to crush and trample underfoot human vanity and pride; to make them feel the inanity, the vanity and the nothingness of man; to snatch from their hands the miserable weapons of their reason; to make them bow their heads and bite the dust beneath the authority and reverence of divine majesty" (11).

The kinds of arguments Montaigne makes in defense of his thesis are a rehash of the skeptical arguments presented by Epicurus, Lucretius, and the Pyrrhonists. He denies the idea that the human being has a special importance as the end of the universe in the Aristotelian and Thomistic sense (13); he equates human beings with the animals (15-47); and he presents the twin puzzles of the apparent incompatibility of freedom and providence and the problem of evil in a good creation as counterarguments to those who would prove that God exists (22, 83). Philosophically, his main gripe is with the Stoics (as it was with the Epicureans). The Stoics claim that it is reason that sets us apart from the animals and that, if we will only turn to reason, we can be saved. Such an attitude seems both wrong and presumptuous, filled with pride and vanity. It is wrong because it does not seem to be true that knowledge (the fruit of reason) is virtue and ignorance is vice. On the contrary, for an action to be morally evil in the strict sense, it seems that the agent must know what he or she is doing, know that the act is wrong, yet still choose to do it. It is presumptuous and impious because one is claiming to be able to save oneself. Montaigne quotes Seneca: "Oh, what a vile and abject thing is man, if he does not raise himself above humanity" (164). In a way, there is nothing wrong with this ambition, for we should aspire to virtue and perfection. Montaigne would agree with this. But we cannot raise ourselves above humanity; only God can do it. He says, "It is for our Christian faith, and not for Stoic virtue, to aspire to that divine and miraculous metamorphosis" (164).

We must be humble before God if we are to be raised up. As Montaigne puts it, "Only humility and submission can produce a good man" (49). There is something right about this, not just for religion but also for philosophy and for education in general. Clearly, humility and submission are appropriate before the God of creation – they follow from an admission of one's being a creature. But they are also appropriate for all education: one must be humble and submissive before the truth. As Socrates so famously said, if one thinks one knows, one cannot learn (*Apology*, 29ab).

However, Montaigne's favored philosophy seems to go against this insight. He claims that the end of all philosophy is tranquility, saying, "On this there is general agreement among the philosophers of all sects: that the sovereign good consists in tranquility of soul and body" (50). If this is so, then our happiness lies within our reach. All we have to do is to find out how to be tranquil in mind and body, and we will be happy – we can save ourselves. Such an act of hubris in the face of the obviousness of our being creatures, is indeed immoral. Montaigne has the Stoics in mind mostly for this condemnation. They thought that however bad things got one could always retreat into one's reason and find peace. But this claim that tranquility is the ultimate end is also true for the Epicureans and the skeptics. Indeed Montaigne's arguments (such as they are) are meant to convince the reader that it is impossible to know what is true. The upshot is that one should abandon the quest for truth and thus attain tranquility – the *ataraxia* of the skeptics (64). Indeed, Montaigne seems to see even Christianity in this light. He says, "Man's plague is the belief that he has knowledge. That is why ignorance is so highly recommended by our religion as appropriate for belief and obedience" (50).[2] But Montaigne is wrong on two scores here. It is not true that all philosophers seek tranquility of mind and body as the sovereign good. It is not true of Plato and Aristotle. For them, the true, the good, and the beautiful are the objective ends in which our happiness lies. Nor is it true that ignorance is recommended by Christianity: "You will know the truth, and the truth will make you free" (John 9:32).

Montaigne is correct when he says that the Stoics' confidence in their ability to save themselves is a signal instance of pride and vanity to be firmly rejected. Such a position is anti-religious and anti-philosophical and so can reasonably be criticized. It is clearly bad for liberal arts education, and will make it impossible for us to know who we are. Just as it is clearly inadequate to predetermine the truth about God based entirely on what we know about ourselves, so also it is inadequate to predetermine the truth of any kind before we pursue it. But this is a moral flaw, not a flaw in reason.

Clearly, to abandon reason is not reasonable, philosophically or religiously. Such an abandonment makes it impossible to know who we are. In the first place, such a move is contradictory and thus absurd. There can be no good reasons to abandon reason. Montaigne tells many entertaining stories about silly positions people have held, but none of them is an argument against reason, for no such argument can be mounted without using reason. But in the second place, making such an argument is also immoral. Because it is absurd to reject reason, such a rejection must be a mere act of willful, unreasonable pride. Such a rejection we call sin. It is but a false humility and a mere pretense of obedience. Thus, Montaigne's legitimate reason for cautioning about the adequacy of relying entirely on our understanding is undercut. As Montaigne himself says, "It is a great temerity for you to destroy yourself in order to destroy another" (119).

Notes

1 This doctrine is a main theme in Erasmus' *In Praise of Folly*.

Works Cited

Bible (NRSV). New York: HarperCollins, 2007.

Montaigne. *Apology for Raymond Sebond.* Trans. Roger Ariew and Marjorie Grene. Indianapolis, IN: Hackett, 2003.

Plato. *Apology.* Trans. G.M.A. Grube. In *Plato: Five Dialogues.* Indianapolis, IN: Hackett, 1981.

Othello in Context: Who Are We? Who Do We Think We Are? Who Are They? How Do We Know?

Ann Dunn
University of North Carolina at Asheville

Like Shakespeare's vibrant and diverse London, *Othello* is a play full of sex, violence, race, politics, power, money, jealousy, murder, and philosophy, but, for me, it is not about any of those things. They are all foils or metaphors for the real subject. For me, the play is about two things: the formation and transformation of human identity and the highest thing one can do with that identity once formed, love – love oneself and love another. *Othello* is sad because the marvelous identity the hero formed for himself by the beginning of the play is transformed into its base opposite by the end and because both kinds of love are present in the beginning of the play and are destroyed by the end. Identity is destroyed by its opposite – a shape-shifting shadow-dweller. Love is destroyed by its opposite – hatred. *Othello* is a tragedy in the Aristotelian sense because, in the end, both identity and love are reclaimed, or at least understood to have been lost, too late. Indeed, I take *too late* to be the defining words of tragedy. The phrase involves both a permanent loss and a terrible awareness of the value of that which is lost.

From Iago's "I am not what I am" in Act One to Othello's "Speak of me as I am" in the final soliloquy, Shakespeare probes the nature of human identity: the constructs we make as individuals, as individuals in love with a single other individual, and as individuals in a historic-socio-political context of many individuals. Our students arrive at college with identities fashioned by the worlds they come from, are trying to find true stories to tell about themselves, are in search of love, and want to do some service for the world. *Othello* speaks directly to these personal issues. Further, because the play is a tragedy, it asks, "What went wrong?" and, by extension, "What can go wrong in our own worlds of interacting selves?"

The play has two contexts, external and internal. The external context of *Othello* included the Italian Renaissance and its spread north, the idealistic Protestant Reformation and Catholic Counter Reformation, the witch craze, the expanding Ottoman Empire (Rhodes, LePanto, Vienna), the undeclared war with Spain (1585-1604), the burgeoning Conceptual Revolution in science and philosophy, the exploration and exploitation of new worlds and markets, the unique literary English Renaissance, the unique, un-idealistic, and pragmatic English Reformation, and both perceptions about and the presence of black Africans in European culture.

I am interested here in the Conceptual Revolution. Shakespeare wrote on the cusp of a great revolution in ideas – in ways people thought about themselves and the world. Increasingly, old world views (faith-based, text-based, hierarchical, teleological, and communal) were coming into conflict with nascent modern world views (based on empirical observation, reason, and the authority of the individual). Shakespeare seems to me to be less interested in the rightness or wrongness of these views than he is in the creative tension inherent in them – the dramatic possibilities. How often does he express the old, possibly now superstitious, views in the words of venerable, good, if slightly foolish elderly men, and the new reasonable views in the words of eminently intelligent, young, if slightly evil, characters? The new ways of thinking were simply a new stage for him, to throw characters onto and see how they respond. Shakespeare is the Iago in the wings of this play.

And what of the play's inner context? There is a geographical context: the two worlds of Venice and Cyprus, the great civilized realm of civic law, where reason and good council yield justice and the Edenic garden paradise where Othello and Desdemona, like Milton's Adam and Eve, make and lose their love bower. There is a political-social context: the two melded worlds of Othello and Desdemona – military and domestic, public and private, state and family, general and particular. But I want to focus on what I see as the psychological context of the play, a strange realm indeed: Iago's mind.

Shakespeare's character Iago achieves nothing less than a complete conceptual revolution within the hero, Othello. We all think about ourselves and the world in which we find ourselves in a certain way, and we change our behavior based on our way of thinking. Our perceptions about ourselves and our sense of good and bad affect our relationships to each other. I find it useful to look with students at the way Othello perceives himself and his love in Acts One and Two and at the way his perception changes and makes it possible for him to act. After the seduction scene, 3.3, Othello is no longer the level-headed general: "Othello's occupation is gone." How he sees Desdemona, and therefore what it is possible for him to do to her, changes. She is no longer sacred and chaste. She is a profane whore.

Wherever we are in this play, we are in Iago's world because, like Milton's Satan, he carries hell within him and can make a hell of heaven. Look how he makes ambiguous the urban heaven of Venice. Brabantio, in disbelief that anything terrible could happen in the city, exclaims simply, "This is Venice!" And we, with Othello, have seen with our own eyes the reasonableness of civilized governance. But Iago collapses our and Othello's faith in our own experience when he insinuates, "In Venice they do . . . ." And he transforms the heaven of the bridal bed to the hell of the murder couch.

So, what do we initially learn about this territory we and the characters will inhabit? Iago's first and almost last words are profane curses: "Sblood" and "Zounds." His first advice about himself, and incidentally a reflection of his opinion of himself, is: "Abhor me. / Despise me." The first and only emotion to escape him is "hate." We learn that his weapons are words – language. He "tells" people things. His first prediction is his final act and has to do with words: "You'll not hear me." "From this time forth I never will speak a word." But his first and primary syntactical construction, the conditional, casts into ambiguity everything he says: "If," "If." Thus, in the first eight lines of the play, in utter darkness but for a torch, we hear the world the characters will inhabit from the mouth of its creator. When Brabantio hears his voice out of the darkness, he recognizes Iago's true nature: "What profane wretch art thou?" By the end of the first act, we have seen that he is a completely egocentric shape-shifter, "seeming" for his own "peculiar end." He swears by "Janus," the two-faced god of beginnings. He goads others into action: "Call up her father." He uses, ruthlessly, the people around Othello to "poison his delight." He understands neither self-love (1.3.116) nor love (1.3.334). He considers himself self-created: "Our bodies are gardens...." He aligns himself with the prince of Hell and boasts that he has access to "all the tribes of hell." He perpetrates evil for "sport." He is an improviser who has no plan but never lets slip an occasion: "Tis here, but yet confused." Like the dramatist himself, he is a keen observer of human nature who absorbs words and events as though the whole human drama is nothing but potential weaponry in his arsenal. He is a big fan of "reason." He speaks in metaphors, questions, and innuendos, rather than straightforward description ("Barbary Horse"). And above all, he is as invisible in the whole play as he was in the darkness of the first scene – as invisible as hypocrisy always is, a subject Milton will also deal with in a similar way. In *Aereopagitica,* Milton will claim that in any open encounter with truth, falsehood will lose. So a smart falsehood must be circumspect. As Iago says of himself, "Knavery's plain face is never seen til used." His epithet, which he wears like Harry Potter's invisibility cloak, is "honest." Iago's mind and his imposition of it on the world he will ruin remind me of many of Flannery O'Connor's characters and her comment that her "subject in fiction is the action of grace in territory held largely by the devil" (O'Connor 118).

I want now to look at the character of Othello. Iago may claim to be self-created, but, again like Milton's Satan, his whole problem in the beginning of the play is that he is at the mercy of his commander in chief and cannot tell the difference between servitude and service. The most self-fashioned character in *Othello* is Othello. I am currently working on the ways I think the character is initially modeled on the positive images of the black male as noble, princely, spiritual, and free – images that coexisted side by side with negative images and that existed from antiquity to the Trans-Atlantic Slave Trade, when there was another conceptual shift. Here I will argue that three strands weave together to form an identity: nature (in modern terms, both genetics and what we are given as children by parents, school, etc.), merit (choice and deed), and magic (what we imagine and invent about ourselves).

What do we learn about Othello at the beginning? I skip the clearly vitriolic first scene, except to note its impact, by contrast, on our first glimpse of Othello and except to note that when Iago speaks in soliloquy, he calls Othello a man "of a free and open nature." Othello, we learn, is a black African, a man of mature years, and an important general in service to the Venetian state. He is "royal," self-raised by "merit" to a "proud fortune," "free," and in love with "the gentle Desdemona." If we look at deeds to infer character, let us compare Iago's mean, sneaky, invisible deeds of scene one with Othello's in scene two. Othello accepts the consequences of his choices ("I must be found"), honors the years and standing of his father-in-law, does not act rashly ("Put up your swords"), and remains calm and dignified in the face of disgusting prejudice and false slander (he is neither a "bond-slave," a "pagan," or a wielder of potions). Othello submits to the rule of law and is associated with justice from the beginning. He does understand the meaning of service to a higher authority than himself and acts at all times as though he is indeed his own gardener. He speaks in direct declarative sentences that make us believe him and that make his epithets ("brave," "valiant") ring true. He does understand both self-love and selfless love for Desdemona. The only two potential cracks in his character armor (cracks Iago sees right through as he, almost invisible, listens from the corner of the room) are his reference to the "vices of his blood" and the fact that he sees himself reflected in Desdemona's adoring and admiring eyes ("I did love her that she did pity them"). At least part of his love for her has to do with the way her love for him reinforces the value of the story he tells about himself. How many of us have loved "unwisely" because we were loved?

How did Othello fashion this admirable identity? A twenty-year-old student once told me that when he sees a movie with a character in it that he really likes, he becomes that character for a couple of days. He tries on selves to see how they fit. We will never know how Othello became Othello. All we have is his story about himself – a linguistic myth he explicitly connects with the "witchcraft" of words. Anyone who has ever created a poem, a story, a drama, a piece of music, a ballet, or a painting knows, has experienced, magic. Without the oft-invoked muses, there is nothing. The sense of being a magician is palpable in the act of creation, self or otherwise.

I think one thing can safely be said about how Othello became a virtuous individual, since I speak here in an educational context. Experience was a good teacher for him. I am reminded of Montaigne's essay "On Education," when he speaks of Alexander's acquisition of virtues: "Aristotle did not amuse his great pupil so much with the trick of constructing syllogisms...as by instructing him in the good precepts concerning valor, prowess, magnanimity, and temperance, and the security of fearing nothing, and with this ammunition he sent him, still a child, to subjugate the empire of the whole world" (Montaigne 121). Alas, Othello is about to run into a bad teacher whose method is, precisely, tricks of constructing false syllogisms, in which the authority in the false first part of the initial premise is the new god, Nature. Act Three, scene three is one big list of such syllogisms.

We have looked at the fashioning of a good self. How do we fashion a good union of two selves? Again, I argue that, in this play, the three strands woven together to form a good love are nature (individual character and sexual attraction), merit (choices made relative to each other), and magic (the mysterious "faith" or "trust" the characters speak of). Iago must pervert each of these in order to uncreate love.

Othello and Desdemona, in spite of the "gross" picture painted by Iago and Rodrigo, are "soul to soul," "mind" to "mind," "most fortunate in each other," only have eyes for each other, and are in perfect harmony with each other and with the spheres (2.1.200). They are partners in the enterprise of their relationship. She is "half the wooer." Her descriptor is "divine," she swears by "'r Lady," she is the bearer of mercy ("no-one, I myself"), and Cassio sings an Ave Maria to her and praises her in Petrarchan mode (2.1.63-87). Thus their love is connected with the celestial and sacred. But it is also rooted in the human. She is both unfallen, sensual Eve and chaste intercessor, Mary. She is the Goddess of Love, Venus, and their bower is on Venus's sacred island, Cyprus. Their natural sexual union in the garden of Cypress will make all right with the world, says Cassio (2.1.82-84). They try to steal "but an hour of love" before shipping out to war. Othello says, "my life upon her faith," and language – in a play partly about the potential and limits of language – fails him when he tries to describe his joy (2.1.196). Above all, their union puts the universe in a new order, for each of them, and they can never go back to their previous individual orderings. Their disunion would not cause the dissolution of worlds, but, as Othello says "when I love thee not, / Chaos is come again." If there is a crack in their love armor, it is, as Othello realizes too late, that he loves her too much (a theme Milton will expand upon with Adam and Eve). Their love is personal to them and is the new most important thing in their mutual hierarchy. How many of us, and our students, have experienced such a reshuffling in a love relationship, one that leaves us stranded with no frame of reference when that new order is shattered? That personal urgency, selflessness, tenderness, and absoluteness is what makes Othello and Desdemona's love, and its sad dissolution, a good one to look at with students.

What goes wrong? Well, Iago clearly goes wrong. But more importantly, how does he succeed? We teachers are in the business of helping young people reveal and create individual adult selves. We hold mirrors up to them through literature, art, science, history, and philosophy. Part of our project is to try to teach our students to read well, by which we mean critically, to reason for themselves, and to formulate responses based on those acts of reading and reasoning. The relationship between reading, reasoning, and choice (or action) is at the heart of what goes wrong in *Othello*.

If this is a play that on some level shines a light on the power of language to create and uncreate, it must then deal with the act of reading, as well. There is a lot of misreading in this play, from the beginning. Brabantio misreads his daughter. Othello and Desdemona selectively read each other. The significance of an over "seen" conversation, a handkerchief, and a suit on behalf of a friend are misread. And everyone misreads Iago. In fact, the only person who reads everything almost correctly throughout the whole play is Iago, who writes the script. I say almost. We will see why in a moment.

In the beginning, Iago sets reason and passion at opposite ends of a balance beam. He leaves something out of that equation: faith, or in the secular world, trust. The balance beam must rest on some fulcrum. What name can we give that point? Faith, magic, mystery, trust are not concepts Iago is comfortable with, except as possibly useful weapons. They are squishy. "A Fig," he would say. He works "by wit and not by witchcraft." But these concepts turn up again and again in this play.

We do see reason and passion operating in the traditional polar way (1.3 and 2.3). But Othello and Desdemona's passion for each other is presented, early, as a good thing, approved by the reasonable state, a passion that will heal a war-torn world. And Shakespeare, inheriting Montaigne's distrust of reason, seems to be at least ambiguous about the value of reason, demonstrating repeatedly the ways human nature can pervert any value, new or old. Reason is, in fact, Iago's secret weapon. His if-then construction does two things. *If* asks a question where none was. *Then* poses an answer to the non-existent question as though it is the only possible alternative. Iago teaches people how to interpret a text before he sets that text in front of them. He then lets them think they are reasoning their way through it. This is a play in which "all that is spoke is marred," first by mis-reading, then by mis-reasoning.

In fact, Shakespeare suggests there is a great deal of the mysterious in self-fashioning and in fashioning a love. It is when Othello and Desdemona falter in their mysterious love bond, which hinges on trust of each other, that both reason and passion go haywire (she lies about the handkerchief, and he, well, look at 3.3). And it is this very mysterious element that will, in the play's last moment, pull right reason and loving passion back up out of Iago's muck – the magic that happens in a kiss and in an act of mercy. Iago has been holding a mirror up to all and showing them his own filthy interior landscape so that they think it is theirs. Othello finally holds his own mirror up to himself, looks squarely, reads truly, and acts honorably. It seems to me that Iago's project collapses, in the end, because of his great initial misreading of the mysterious human potential for both self-love and selfless love.

How do we know what we know? What can we do to sniff out and foil the evil of invisible egocentric hatred? I do not know. Perhaps we cannot. Perhaps Milton is right and not even angels can spot hypocrisy. The word hypocrisy derives from the Greek for "play-acting, "feigning," or "dissembling." Perhaps Othello could have asked questions back. A child's first question would be a good place to start: "Why?" In fact, he finally does ask "why?" But it is *too late*. Like Iago, I will close with a question. How, in fashioning good and secure identities and loves, in territory held largely by the devil, can we achieve vigilance without cynicism, can we balance the beam of reason and passion on the fulcrum of trust, can we strive for justice, but be merciful when we fail, as we will? How can we feel fully, read the world critically, think carefully, and trust ourselves?

I think one answer Shakespeare offers is that we can choose our mirrors carefully. One aspect of our identity must respond to the values of the world in which we must succeed and be happy and to the way the world sees us. What is the name of the mirror in which we gaze at any given moment? When the "I" that is not what it seems has slunk from the field in silence, will our students be able to say, with Othello, "I am"?

Works Cited

Montaigne. "Of the Education of a Child." *The Complete Works of Montaigne.* Ed. and trans. Donald M. Frame. Stanford: Stanford UP, 1943.

O'Connor, Flannery. *Mystery and Manners.* Eds. Sally and Robert Fitzgerald. New York: Farrar, Straus & Giroux, 1962.

Shakespeare, William. *Othello. The Complete Works of Shakespeare.* 4th ed. Ed. David Bevington. New York: HarperCollins, 1992.

Doch – Alles, was dazu mich trieb / Gott! war so gut! ach war so lieb: Pleasure and Obligation in *Faust*

Christopher Beyers
Assumption College

About two-thirds of the way through the first part of Johann Wolfgang von Goethe's *Faust*, Gretchen goes to the community well to draw water. She meets Lieschen, who tells her about a mutual friend, Barbara, who was impregnated then abandoned by her lover. Lieschen mocks Gretchen for feeling pity for such a person and admires the young man who is not so foolish as to stick around after he has gotten what he wants. After Lieschen leaves, Gretchen remembers that she used to think that way. Now she finds herself in the same situation as Barbara. She concludes the scene by sighing, "Yet – everything which drove me to this pass / God! was so good! Oh! Was so dear."

I have always thought this the most philosophical moment in the play, though I find I am in a minority in this regard. Most focus on the heart-rending scene at the end of the first part, where Gretchen awaits punishment for murdering her child and begs Faust to stay with her in the dungeon. Barker Fairley cautions against the "temptation" to "judge the Gretchen tragedy morally" (522) but very few (including, by the way, Fairley) have been able to resist the temptation. The dominant view – and the moral stakes involved – is suggested by August Wilhelm von Schlegel's summary: "A girl who lives alone in modest seclusion and childish contentment attracts [Faust] and falls victim to his passion. He destroys her domestic peace; this good, weak creature perishes from love and remorse" (434). When the more recent feminist critic, Barbara Becker-Cantarino, concludes that the tragedy is a "celebration of patriarchy in an atavistic interpretation of woman's sexuality" (520), she is deploring Schlegel's assumptions while endorsing the view that the reader is supposed to take sides in a socio-moral allegory.

The problem with these sorts of readings is that they are basically saying that Lieschen is right and agreeing with Gretchen's brother, Valentine (the male version of Lieschen) who in his dying utterances calls his sister a slut, lectures her on the consequences of what she has already done, and then complacently breathes his last, assured he has died an honorable, soldier's death. While I do not claim to be sure of much regarding Goethe's masterwork, I do feel strongly two things: first, I do not want to agree with two of the story's most nasty characters; second, I do not think we are supposed to ignore or suppress the great bliss that Gretchen so poignantly expresses.

In saying these things, I fear I am falling in the trap that I think too many readers of *Faust* never escape – the notion that Goethe had written some sort of proto-existential work that is all about choice, with the corollary that the reader must render judgments as to the debates presented in the work. As my first principle, I am convinced *Faust* is constructed according to the principle articulated by Louise Nevelson, the creator of monumental abstract sculptures. When asked about what, precisely, her work was trying to express, she replied that she was not trying to make a definite statement; "the question mark" she said, "is very valid for me" (Taylor 71).

I take a rather Nevelsonian view of the Gretchen story: it is not a drama with a moral but rather an exploration of a human problem. In saying this, I am putting the tale in the same category I would put *Paradise Lost* and *The Iliad*: that is, for all their elaborate machinery, these stories are, at their heart, affecting tales of human beings acting in recognizable ways. The genius of *Paradise Lost* is not Satan's rhetoric, but the fact that Milton portrays the mythical Adam and Eve as rather normal humans making choices that seemed to them reasonable at the time. Homer climaxes his tale of wars on earth and in the heavens not with heroics on the battlefield but in the unlikely reconciliation of grieving men.

Thus, to understand the Gretchen story, we must take our direction not from Schlegel, Nietzsche, or Sartre, but from that great American actress and philosopher, Elizabeth Taylor. Once in an interim between failed marriages, so the story goes, somebody asked her why she kept on getting married. "I don't know what it is," she is reported to have replied, "but whenever I sleep with someone, I just *have* to marry him."

The feeling that Taylor was expressing is one that I expect is fairly universal; it is a restatement of what Gretchen is sighing by the well. Although this is not true for people like the ex-governor of New York, for most of us, sexual acts can be so intense, so intimate, so pleasurable, so overwhelming and fulfilling, that we assume it just *has* to mean something. It just *has* to lead to something else. Walt Whitman would have us know that sex is a mixing of body and soul with the supreme result of procreation. What could possibly be more meaningful?

The problem, of course, is that most of what is communicated in sexual acts is nonverbal. And in this regard, the relationship between Faust and Gretchen is doomed. For centuries, critics have asserted that the relationship is a very unequal one, pitting an innocent person against a worldly one. While I agree with the pattern, I say that most have the roles backwards. Let us think about Faust for a second: he has, for all his life, been a diligent scholar in an institution of higher learning, yet in all this time he has, apparently, had no wife, no children (in or out of wedlock), no adulterous relationships, no mistresses, no lovers of any sex, no real friends, no family since childhood – no significant relations with anybody. He does not even have a substance abuse problem. Talk about a triumph of the German imagination!

While it is true that Gretchen is ignorant in subjects in which Faust is expert, it is also true that she has the equivalent of a common-law doctorate in human relationships. While she does not have a boyfriend, it is clear that she has been instructed about the dangers of men for all her life. Thus, she knows immediately, as Faust apparently does not, that the relationship he proposes is improper. She tells Faust that Mephistopheles is no good. She knows what *can* happen, is *likely* to happen, and what *does* happen, and she admits as much by the well.

So, you are thinking, *now you are telling us that it is all Gretchen's fault.* But that would be taking sides. What I am really trying to say is that the story shows us the predictable results when two people do something that both feel is filled with tacit meaning: Gretchen views sex, as Faust does, as an act which inextricably mixes passion and love, body and soul. But her socialization has led her to expect that Faust would also understand what she thinks sex has obliged him to. Ultimately, it is an entrance, in her view, to a life of self-sacrifice and compromise to the inevitable. Since she has seen that Faust is, or tries to be, nice, she assumes that he knows what, in her view, *everyone* knows is the nice response.

Unfortunately, Faust is the least likely person on this earth – perhaps the least likely character in all of artistic creation – to know this. He can honestly claim that he never suggested that he would ever accept the strictures Gretchen views as certain. Faust, who has had *no* meaningful human relationships, assumes that lovers interact like students and professors in the lecture hall, or participants at a conference, through words, the open exchange of ideas, with clear statements of premises, evidence, and reasoning. He is completely unprepared to enter a world ruled by the tyranny of human feeling. Faust's obtuseness in this regard mirrors that of Milton's Eve, who risks pain because she has never felt it. Faust has the learning to know how babies are made but not the experience to understand the consequences of conception.

At this point, I am expected to say that the misunderstanding causes the Gretchen tragedy, but I am not inclined to say this, mainly because I do not feel her tale is really that tragic. First, she is saved by God in the end, so that would give the story a happy ending. Granted, terrible things happen to her, but is her intense suffering more pitiable, more horrid, than the long, enervating life she would have led had she never met Faust? She had been destined to a life of poverty and unending care, lorded over by a mother who is repressive and apparently a loan shark. Further, who, exactly, will she marry? A noble soldier like her brother who regards her sexuality as a badge of his honor? Or perhaps she should choose among the rioters of Siebel, Altmeyer, Frosch, and Brander.

My point is that if we are going to assign dignity to Faust's claim that "Feeling is all," we should take just as seriously Gretchen's lament near the well. Surely, Goethe is not trying to show us the virtues of exhausting resignation. Instead, the problem *Faust* explores is foreshadowed by Faust's earlier attempts to translate John 1.1. Dissatisfied with "In the beginning was the Word," he tries out "In the beginning was the Mind" (since there had to be a mind to think the word), then "Power" (since there had to be an impulse to think), before settling on "Act." Ultimately, I think we are to see, there is the action. We can assert whatever moral or philosophical system we want, but what meaning we ascribe to it is always an act of translation.

Works Cited

Becker-Cantarino, Barbara. "Goethe and Gender." *Cambridge Companion to Goethe*. Ed. Lesley Sharpe. Cambridge: Cambridge UP, 2002. 179-92.

Fairley, Barker. "The Gretchen Tragedy and the Young Goethe." Hamlin, ed. *Faust. A Tragedy*. Trans. Walter Arndt. Norton Critical Edition. NY: Norton. 1976. 519-23.

Goethe, Johann Wolfgang von. *Faust. First Part*. Trans. Peter Salm. NY: Bantam. 2007.

Hamlin, Cyrus, ed. *Faust. A Tragedy*. Trans. Walter Arndt. Norton Critical Edition. NY: Norton. 1976.

Schlegel, August Wilhelm von. Review of the *Fragment* 1790. Hamlin, ed. *Faust. A Tragedy*. Trans. Walter Arndt. Norton Critical Edition. NY: Norton. 1976. 434-35.

Taylor, Robert. "The Style, Spirit and Vision of Louise Nevelson." *Boston Globe*. April 19, 1988.

The Person in Society

Who Are We, *Whose* Are We?
Women as God's Agents of Change in the Hebrew Bible

Tina Wray
Salve Regina University

"Who am I?" is a timeless, existential question of self-identification. Modern women might explore this question in terms of the concrete realities of the Great Juggle: family, career, and the struggle to carve out a sliver of time devoted to self. In the world of biblical antiquity, however, women would likely answer the question "Who am I?" in terms of belonging to a particular man: the daughters of Lot; Job's wife; the sister of Absalom; the mother of Samson. A deeper reading of the Hebrew Bible's women stories, however, presents us with a larger question beyond "Who am I?" The real question for biblical women is "*Whose* am I?" and the answer is a resounding: "You belong to God."

Some scholars speculate that the Bible's stories about women are actually allegorical, reflecting the status of Israel, as a nation, for Israel, like her women, was often powerless against her enemies, both foreign and domestic. Weak and marginalized nations and people often resort to devious means to survive. It is not surprising, then, that many of the women stories in the Bible feature a trickster type character who uses unorthodox means – including lying, cheating, and others forms of deception – to bring about God's plan. As such, tricksters are both admired and respected in the Bible for their skillful use of manipulation. The three women profiled in this paper – Rebekah, Tamar, and Rahab – are representative of the types of women stories found in the Hebrew Bible, and they are tricksters. Like most of the women stories in the Bible, these women act as agents of change.

The wife of Isaac, Rebekah (Gen 24:10-67; 26:6-16; 27:5-38; 28:5-6;

29:12-13; 35:8; 49:31), is known for her cleverness and single-minded devotion to her son, Jacob, who represents the continuation of God's promise to Abraham. This promise (Gen 12: 2-3) assures the acquisition of the land, an enduring relationship with God who will extol blessings upon future generations, and a proliferation of descendents.

After twenty years of barrenness (in the Bible, viewed as a curse or punishment from God), Rebekah conceives twin sons, whose in-utero jostling portends their future conflict. Rebekah asks the Lord about the brawling in her belly, and the Lord responds with an oracle:

> Two nations are in your womb, and two peoples born of you shall be divided; the one shall be stronger than the other; the elder shall serve the younger. (Gen 25:23)[1]

This oracle designates *Jacob* – who is the *second* twin born – as the one who will continue God's promise. Rebekah makes the fulfillment of this oracle her life's mission. Jacob's brother, Esau, is presented as a hairy, dull, wild man who likes to hunt, while Jacob is a mama's boy who is interested in more domestic chores, like cooking. His culinary skills prove profitable when he jokingly offers his brother some lentil soup in exchange for Esau's birthright and the hungry Esau readily gives away his birthright for the soup (Gen 25:29-34).

Apparently, Esau can still gain his inheritance if he receives his father's final blessing. Isaac, old, blind, and on his deathbed, asks his favorite son, Esau, to hunt and prepare a meal for his father so that Isaac can bestow his special blessing upon Esau. Rebekah, like many women in the biblical world, gathers information by eavesdropping, and when she learns of Isaac's plan to give Esau the blessing, she enlists the help of Jacob, and together they pull off one of the Bible's most amazing hoodwinks. While Esau is off hunting, Rebekah takes a kid from the herd and prepares a meal for Isaac. Next, she disguises Jacob in his brother's gamey smelling clothes, covering his smooth skin with the hide of the kid to give him the wooly feel of Esau, should Isaac touch him. Although Isaac is initially suspicious, Rebekah's plan works, and Isaac gives Jacob Esau's blessing.

When Esau finds out, he vows to kill his brother. Again, Rebekah works to fulfill the oracle, arranging to send Jacob to Haran and out of harm's way (Gen 27:42-45). While modern readers may object to Rebekah's favoritism and deceit, the biblical author would disagree. Rebekah does what she must to protect the bearer of the Promise and thus fulfill God's plan for Israel.

Like Rebekah, Tamar manipulates events to help bring about God's plan – in this case, she will bear a son in the line of King David. Tamar's first husband, Er, does something – the Bible does not tell us what – that greatly offends God, and God kills him (Gen 38:7). Under the law of levirate (Deut 25:5-10), which decrees that a surviving brother must marry his dead brother's widow, Judah (Tamar's father-in-law) gives Tamar to Er's younger brother, Onan. If Tamar has a son with Onan, according to the Levirate law, her firstborn son is recognized as *Er's* and assumes primacy over Onan when it comes to inheritance. Obviously, it is not in Onan's best financial interest to have a child with Tamar, so he practices *cotius interruptus*, an action that prompts the Lord to kill him too (Gen 38: 9-10). It is not Onan's sexual behavior that provokes the Lord; rather, it is his refusal to honor the law of levirate.

Tamar is once again without a husband, but she is still entitled to have children from Judah's family. The law of levirate demands that Judah give her his only remaining son, Shelah, who is too young to marry. Judah sends Tamar away to her father's house – single and barren, both viewed as great humiliations in the world of biblical antiquity – to wait until Shelah is old enough to wed (Gen 38:11). At least this is the story he tells Tamar. The reader, however, knows the real story. Judah thinks Tamar is a toxic bride and fears losing another son (Gen 38:11). It is clear that he has no intention of allowing Shelah anywhere near Bridezilla, not now, not ever.

Time passes, Shelah grows up, and Tamar eventually realizes her father-in-law's betrayal. Her situation seems desperate, but things change quickly when she hears that Judah will be passing through town (Gen 38:13). Tamar seizes the opportunity and swings into action to take what is rightfully hers – a child from the family of Judah. Removing her widow's garb and covering her face with a veil, Tamar waits on the side of the road, the place of streetwalkers, beggars, and unescorted women with dubious reputations (Gen 38:14). Her disguise reminds us of Rebekah's hoodwinking of Isaac with the Esau costume she pieced together for Jacob.

When Judah spies her on the side of the road, he approaches the faux hooker, and the two talk business:

> Judah: "Come let me come in to you."
> Tamar: "What will you give me, that you may come in to me?"
> Judah: "I will send you a kid from the flock."
> Tamar: "Only if you give me a pledge, until you send it."
> Judah: "What pledge shall I give you?"
> Tamar: "Your signet and your cord, and the staff that is in your hand." (Gen. 38:16-18)[2]

To leave his signet and cord with her in pledge is the modern equivalent of giving her his driver's license, and Judah will come to regret this lapse in judgment. Three months later, Judah, who holds a position of authority in the local government, receives word that "Tamar has played the whore...she is pregnant as a result of whoredom" (Gen 38:24). The penalty for adultery is death (Deut 22:23-24; Lev 21:9), and Judah demands that Tamar be burned. As she is brought out for execution, she comes face-to-face with the father-in-law who betrayed her. But Tamar holds the ultimate trump card. Producing the items Judah left in pledge during their brief sexual encounter, she says: "It was the owner of these who made me pregnant...Take note, please, whose these are, the signet and the cord and the staff" (Gen 38:25). And with that, the condemned Tamar is vindicated. Like Rebekah, she gives birth to twin sons, Zerah and Perez, the latter an ancestor of the great King David (Ruth 4:18-22).

Our final trickster, Rahab (Josh 2; 6:16-25) is the courageous courtesan who helps continue the original promise God made to Abraham, in this case, the assurance of the land (Gen 12:1-4). Rahab's story begins as the epic adventure of Israel's exodus from Egypt and forty-year sojourn in the wilderness draws to a close. Joshua leads the Israelites to the edge of the Promised Land, but there seems to be slight problem: apparently, there are people already living in the land that God deeded to Abraham (Gen 12:6-7).

Joshua sends out two spies to assess the situation. Upon entering the city (Jericho), Joshua's spies head immediately to the local whorehouse (Josh 2:1). The story does not tell us why the men decide to make a pit stop at the bordello. Perhaps those forty years of wandering in the wilderness has something to do with it, or maybe they sought to gather secret information about the city that the working girls sometimes coaxed from clients in the throes of passion.

The Madam, Rahab, becomes their protector, confidant, and friend. The king of Jericho learns of the spies' presence in his town and orders Rahab to turn them over (Josh 2:3). Rahab lies and says that the men have already left, when in reality, she has hidden them safely on her roof, under stalks of drying flax.

When the coast is clear, this not-so-good Canaanite girl reveals her motives for protecting the enemy, saying, "The Lord, your God is indeed God in heaven above and on earth below" (Josh 2:11). Rahab's confession of faith makes her the first convert in the Promised Land. Of course, prostitutes do not give away their services for free; Rahab asks the spies to spare her and her family when the Israelites attack Jericho (Josh 2:12-13). The spies agree, and when the city is attacked and the inhabitants slaughtered, Rahab and her family are indeed spared. Modern readers cannot help but note that Rahab betrays her own people and that her treason brings about much death and destruction. But, from the perspective of the biblical author, Rahab is a great heroine, for her actions allow Israel to take possession of the Promised Land.

Rahab, the unlikely heroine who heralds Israel's occupation of the land, reminds us of Rebekah (Genesis 24-27) and Tamar (Genesis 38), sister tricksters, whose resourcefulness and cleverness play a part in God's ultimate plan for Israel. The greater message, of course, is aimed at the reader, who is also called to serve the ineffable, unknowable God.

Notes

1 All quotations are from *The New Oxford Annotated Bible*. For other Bibles consulted, see Works Cited.

2 See Tikva Frymer-Kensky, 269.

Works Cited

Berlin, Adele and Marc Zvi Brettler. *The Jewish Study Bible*. New York: Oxford UP, 2004.

Kensky, Tikva Frymer. *Reading the Women of the Bible: A New Interpretation of Their Stories*. New York: Shocken, 2002.

The New Oxford Annotated Bible with the Apocrypha. Eds Bruce M. Metzger and Roland E. Murphy. New York: Oxford UP, 1994.

Senior, Donald and John J. Collins, eds. *The Catholic Study Bible: New American Bible*. 2nd ed. New York: Oxford UP, 2006.

Who We Are Through Family and Friends

Fr. John R. Fortin, O.S.B.
Saint Anselm College

Ezra Pound wrote the following in a letter to his fiancée Dorothy Shakespear: "The real meditation is...the meditation on one's identity. Ah, voilà une chose!! You try it. You try finding out why you're you and not somebody else. And who in the blazes are you anyhow? Ah, voilà une chose!" (April 21, 1913). He wrote to a friend who would soon become family, viz., his wife. In pursing the question of who are we, it seems natural to examine the roles of various social communities in shaping our identity. Of these communities, two, family and friends, will be considered here from the perspective of two individuals from two great traditions: Abraham and family from the Hebrew tradition as found in the Book of Genesis and Achilles and friends from the Greek tradition as found in Homer's *Iliad*. An examination of these texts in regard to family and friends reveals a pronounced exclusivity: it appears that Abraham discovered who he was in family and Achilles discovered who he was in friendship. The question to be asked is: can one find one's true identity in answer to Pound's question, "Who in the blazes are you anyhow?" exclusively in familial relations or in friendly relations, or must one have both?

We begin with Abraham. Abraham almost completely identified himself with his family. As Abram, he responded to the call of God in Genesis 12 to leave the land of his ancestors and settle in a new land, Canaan. But he was to take family with him: "his wife Sarai, his brother's son Lot...and the persons they had acquired in Haran" (Gen 12.5). Even as he journeyed through the Negeb, Egypt, Bethel, Ai, and elsewhere, Abram was with and was only concerned for his family as it grew and expanded. Most of the story of Abraham is a presentation of the development of his family in the context of the promises and the covenant God made with him. All of the central figures in the Abraham story have familial connections, whether they are united with or removed from the family: Sarah, Hagar, Ishmael, Isaac, and Rebecca.

Abraham's dealing with non-family members is situated in the context of family. Three examples will suffice. First, the only reason given for Abram's willingness to fight the battle of the kings was that his nephew Lot and his family had been captured in the raid on Sodom (Gen 14.12). When the battle was won, Abram took no gift from the king of Sodom because he did not want to enter into any kind of compact or relationship with a non-family member (Gen 14.22-24). Second, the only reason he entered into a pact with Abimelech over a well was to preserve its use for the Abrahamic family (Gen 21.25-32). Though Abimelech recognized the greatness of Abraham as one favored by God, he also was aware that he could get close to Abraham as a friend. Finally, Abraham's deal with the Hittites for a burial place for Sarah was for the purposes of having an exclusive site separate from the burial plots of the Hittites, which were first offered to him for Sarah's burial. Abraham's family was not to intermingle with outsiders, and separation was preserved even in death: "Ephron's field in Machpelah, facing Mamre, together with its cave and all the trees anywhere within its limits, was conveyed to Abraham" (Gen 23.17-18).

For Abraham, family was central; friendship was non-existent. His influence on succeeding generations in this regard appears to be dominant. Only one direct descendant of Abraham in the Genesis narrative is spoken of as having a friend. That is Judah, a son of Jacob, who, shortly after the selling of Joseph to the Midianites, moved away from his family, perhaps ashamed of the treachery against Joseph and Jacob, and settled in with and married foreigners: "Judah parted from his brothers and pitched his tent near a certain Adullamite named Hirah. There he met the daughter of a Canaanite named Shua, married her, and had relations with her" (Gen 38.1-2). His friendship with Hirah is mentioned three times in Genesis 38 (1, 12, 20), but not in any succeeding chapter. By the time of the famine and the need to go to Egypt for grain (Gen 42), Judah was back with the family and led the delegation to purchase grain; he was clearly in charge on the second trip (Gen 43) and thus fully reintegrated with the family, as Abraham would have wanted it.

Thus it appears that for Abraham and for the tradition he established, friendship really had no place, and family alone, all others being barred or prohibited from inclusion, was what is central to one's identity as a child of the covenant. As Leon Kass has written, "Friendship and marriage-and-family are mutually exclusive alternatives.... Friendship (especially male-male bonding) belongs to the ways of others" (531).

"The ways of others" includes the Greek tradition, and the practice and celebration of friendship in Homer's *Iliad*, in particular in the life of Achilles, is a clear example of one of these other ways. Throughout the text, there are many instances of addresses to fellow warriors and assemblies beginning with "My friends." This is no throwaway phrase but an expression of the bonds of fellowship and dependency necessary in time of war. Achilles, although he stands alone and above all others as a warrior and as a hero, as one whose prowess and skill excel all others on the battlefield, is a man with many friends. Most of those who know him acknowledge and are awed by his martial arts, and they are honored to be counted among his friends: he fights alongside them; he feasts with them; he parleys with them; he listens to their counsel. This is seen, for example, in the visit of the delegation of Odysseus, Nestor, Phoenix, and Ajax (Book IX) when the delegation tries to persuade Achilles to return to the battlefield.

But the one friend most associated with Achilles is Patroclus. While still a boy, Patroclus killed his friend Clysonymus during an argument. His father Menoetius fled with Patroclus into exile to avoid revenge and took shelter at the palace of their kinsman King Peleus of Phthia. There Patroclus apparently first met Peleus' son Achilles. They became childhood companions and fellow students of Chiron. Patroclus, perhaps a bit older than Achilles, would be Achilles' lifelong and beloved friend. The close friendship of Achilles and Patroclus is evident throughout the text. It was Patroclus who brought Briseis to Agamemnon (Book I); it was Patroclus who was present when the delegation came to plead with Achilles to rejoin the battle (Book IX); it was Patroclus whom Achilles sent to learn from Nestor how the battle by the ships was going (Book XI); and it was Patroclus who donned Achilles' armor in an effort to drive the Trojans away from the Achaean fleet (Book XVI). But it was especially in Achilles' mourning the death of Patroclus that the profound loss of this particular friend and the painful awareness of mortality as never before felt are expressed by Homer. Though Patroclus was beloved by many, as witnessed in the defense of his body by Menelaus, Ajax, and others (Book XVII), it was the leonine but desperate cry of Achilles' grief that reached to the heights of Olympus and the depths of the sea (Book XVIII). The fierceness and mercilessness when Achilles reentered the battle with his new armor (Book XX), the attempt to fight even the god Scamander (Book XXI), the ferocity of his revenge upon Hector (Book XXII), the elaborateness and savagery of the funeral rites and the magnanimity at the funeral games (Book XXIII), and even the pity shown to Priam and the return of Hector's body (Book XXIV), all revealed Achilles' love for Patroclus and his identification of himself as Patroclus' bereaved friend. Though Automedon, his charioteer, and Alcinus, a son of Ares and an attendant on Achilles, became closer to him than any other comrades after the death of Patroclus (Book XXIV), no one could replace Patroclus.

For all the value he placed on friendship, Achilles appeared to have small regard for family. His relationship with his mother was, to use a modern phrase, dysfunctional at best. A sea nymph who cannot live on the earth, Thetis was there for him in the *Iliad* to comfort and console, to advise, and to defend before the gods. But he cannot do anything for her: he cannot live with her, he cannot support her, and he cannot look after her. It is a one-way relationship. Indeed, in

one account of the legend of his birth, Peleus interrupts Thetis in the act of burn-
ing the mortality out of the baby Achilles, and Thetis abandons them both in her
rage.

As for his father, Peleus, Achilles, often identified as "the son of Peleus" in
the *Iliad*, had a deep respect for him, but their relationship appears not to have
been a matter of great consequence. Peleus was not present at Troy, though
Achilles wore his armor, used his spear, and drove his god-given steeds for his
chariot. Peleus is more a memory of a great warrior honored by Achilles as well
as by others[1] and less a real presence in Achilles' life. In Book XIX, Achilles
says that Peleus is either dead by now or "what little life remains to him is op-
pressed alike with the infirmities of age and ever present fear lest he should hear
the sad tidings of my death" (ll. 398-401). In Book XXIV, when Priam comes to
beg the body of Hector, Achilles responds in part by speaking almost mourn-
fully of his father:

> the gods endowed him with all good things from his birth upwards,
> for he reigned over the Myrmidons excelling all men in prosperity
> and wealth, and mortal though he was they gave him a goddess for
> his bride. But even on him too did heaven send misfortune, for there
> is no race of royal children born to him in his house, save one son
> who is doomed to die all untimely; nor may I take care of him now
> that he is growing old, for I must stay here at Troy to be the bane of
> you and your children. (ll. 623-634)

Achilles had no wife, only war-prize lovers like Briseis, and his only child
was Neoptolemus, who was present at Troy but was not protected from the
fighting as was Patroclus. Neoptolemus was the child of Achilles and Dieda-
meia, the daughter of Lycomedes, king of Scyros, with whom Achilles, disguised as a woman, was staying at the connivance of Thetis to keep him out of
the Trojan War. It was Neoptolemus who killed Priam in the attack on Troy, but
he is not even mentioned by name in the *Iliad*. Achilles' home among the Myr-
midons appears to be no more than a staging area for his heroic warrior exploits.
Clearly, Achilles found in his friends, in particular his friend Patroclus, and not
in his family that social circle by which he came chiefly to establish his identity.

The contrast between Abraham and Achilles when answering the question
"Who am I?" is indicative of significantly divergent trends in the two great traditions from which Western Civilization and the Great Books of that civilization
come. For Abraham, family was tantamount. The covenant the Lord established
with him was seen only in the context of family, and the centrality of the family
plays out throughout the Hebrew tradition.[2] For Achilles, friendship was tantamount, and his superiority as a warrior, while severely limiting his familial relations, allowed him to select friends who would show him the honor due him as a
warrior and who would fight beside him. The centrality of friendship plays out
throughout the Greek tradition.[3]

As inheritors of both of these traditions, we in the West have given weight to each. We might well argue that both family and friends are necessary and important for an individual to develop a proper sense of identity. Abraham and Achilles would disagree and wonder how it is possible to form a proper identity with both family and friends. Each would claim that to answer Pound's question a person must choose one or the other, family or friends, but not both. As inheritors of both of these traditions, we are left to determine the weight that each must bear as we search for the answer to Pound's question: "Who in the blazes are we anyhow?"

Notes

1 Nestor (Book VII) and Phoenix (Book IX) speak highly of their friend Peleus.

2 The notable exception in the Hebrew tradition is the relation between David and Jonathan, the account of which begins in I Samuel 18.1-4 and extends to Jonathan's death in I Samuel 31.2.

3 Socrates at his death prefers to be surrounded by his friends, having said goodbye to his wife and children. Aristotle devotes two books to friendship in his *Nicomachean Ethics* (VIII and IX) but gives minimal space to a discussion of family (e.g., Book VII.6 and Book IX.2). Treachery and discord in families is the substance of many Greek tragedies (e.g., the House of Atreus and the House of Laius).

Works Cited

Homer. *Iliad*. Trans. Robert Fagles. New York: Penguin, 1990.

Kass, Leon R. *The Beginning of Wisdom: Reading Genesis.* New York: Free Press, 2005.

The New American Bible. New York: Thomas Nelson, 1971.

Pound, Ezra. *Ezra Pound and Dorothy Shakespear: Their Letters 1909-1914.* Eds. Omar Pound and A. Walton Litz. New York: New Directions, 1984.

Rethinking Rites-Music Relations in Confucian Tradition

Rachel Chung
Columbia University

Given our conference theme of "Who Are We?" I wanted to take this occasion to challenge the often held notion of Confucianism as simply conservative, but from the relatively little discussed perspective of music (樂) and rites (禮). So many have touted the so-called inherent conservatism of Confucianism that it has almost become accepted as fact. In the nineteenth and twentieth centuries, this notion of Confucianism was held by critics of Confucianism anxious for radical social change, both within and without. More recently, they have been joined by those interested in suppressing social unrest in the name of Confucian "harmony." It is true that Confucianism has always held harmony to be the ultimate goal; what is at issue is how harmony is to be understood. And as I will argue, to define Confucian harmony in terms of orderliness, regulation, and stability is to see only half the picture – and the lesser half, at that.

Since time immemorial, Confucian tradition considered music and rites to be two of the most powerful instruments of governance. They were featured prominently in the governance of legendary Yao and Shun, and according to the *Record of Music*,

Music is the harmony of Heaven and earth, rites are their order. Through harmony all things are transformed; through order all are distinguished.... When music and rites are fully realized, Heaven and earth function in perfect order.... If Music reaches the ultimate, there are no grievances. (I.168)[1]

Consequently, every dynasty from its inception established separate – and often massive – bureaus at court for music and rites and invested heavily in maintaining exclusive authority to prescribe "correct" music and rites for the state. It was also understood that music and rites worked in concert, with complementary but different functions. Confucius said, "In putting at ease those above and governing the people, nothing is better than ritual. In altering customs and changing habits, nothing is better than music" (*Yegi* II.235; my translation). It is worth noting that even though rites were thought essential to the smooth functioning of human relations, it is music with its ability to alter customs and change habits that was thought to promote harmony. Harmony, in other words, had little to do with the status quo.

Of course, more was meant by music and rites than a performance by the Beatles or the niceties of etiquette. In Confucian tradition rites encompassed almost every area of human activity ranging from offering seasonal sacrifices to consuming barley rather than rice in the summer, from mourning the death of one's parents for three years to not sitting unless one's mat was straight. Rites had their basis in giving appropriate outward expression to one's sense of reverence (敬) for all under Heaven, including one's self. Since rites are about propriety, however, expression of reverence had to be adapted to particularities of each relationship. What is appropriate in one context is not necessarily appropriate in another, and to meet mutuality of ritual expectations one needed to have a clear – and shared – sense of differentiation and proper degree of partiality ("rites differentiate;" *Yegi* II.215).

The category of music known as *yue* (樂), on the other hand, referred to the art of sound giving expression to the highest level of moral existence, which might be described as joy in the unity of all things: "Music unites" (*Yegi* II.215). The unity spoken of here is not the kind of collective emotionalism one experiences at a concert or a rally, however.[2] It is rather the unity of quiescence (靜, stillness) and impartiality that are the shared root of human nature: "Music comes out from within, ritual comes into being from without. Music is thus still (靜); ritual is thus ordered" (*Yegi* II.216). According to the Confucian worldview, every human being is born with this original stillness of mind. The stillness is subsequently broken or moved to different feelings by external stimuli. But the potential to return to that impartiality and stillness remains, and it is the basis of harmony:[3]

Before the feelings…are aroused is called [the state of] centrality (中). After [they] are aroused, if they preserve centrality it is called [the state of] harmony. (*The Mean* 1.746)

Unity of – and in – our original given nature: this was the harmony aspired to in *yue*, and the ultimate function of governance was to create an environment that supports a return to impartiality in all human beings. Confucian impartiality, however, bears little resemblance to laissez-faire indifference. On the contrary, it means actively adhering oneself to no predispositions except public good.

Whereas ritual aspires to rightness (義) in given relations or context, music on the level of *yue* functions to remind us of rightness *in* human nature itself.

But could and did such lofty aspirations ever have any real impact beyond rhetoric? In 1943, after nearly a century of passionate experimentation with implementing *yue* in practice, one dynasty codified its findings in a musico-political document called the *Akhak kwebŏm* (樂學軌範) or the *Model for Study of Music*. The text came at an interesting juncture in the history of the dynasty. Although the Chosŏn dynasty (1392-1910) of Korea had enjoyed a century of cultural renaissance founded on revitalization of Neo-Confucian learning and values, by this time it was also beginning to see sprouts of problems to come. Its ambitious scale of social mobility based on merit was beginning to give way under the pressure of competition for access to coveted government positions, while at court itself a group of elite ministers threatened the delicate balance of power in their favor (*A New History of Korea* 204).

In reaction to these problems, one might expect to see growing conservative tendencies, whether from those interested in maintaining their hold on power or others interested in moral reforms. As an official state-commissioned text responding to the situation, however, the *Model for Study of Music* put forward an extraordinary political argument set in musical terms:

[T]he two added variant tones (變音) erode the true tones, and the four added high tones (i.e., beyond the octave) divest the fundamental tones so that there is confusion and disorder among ruler, people, affairs, and things.[4] However, for sounds to have variants and high tones is like food and drink having blandness and saltiness. It is *not acceptable* to have only Daigeng (i.e., soup without any seasoning) and Xuanjiu ("black wine," i.e., water). (126-27, my emphasis)[5]

Even without going into complexities of Confucian modal theory, which I explain in detail elsewhere, the intent of the passage affirming difference, tolerance, and respect for the basic dignity of the human individual is clear. Elsewhere the text puts forward the view that the ruler's role is not to exact moral conduct from the people but to empower them to "come [back] together in unity" (117). Variant tones and tones above the prescribed octave will cause confusion and disorder, but to insist therefore on using only the fundamentals negates the very idea of civilization and civility. In reaching for the highest harmony expressive of the stillness of human original impartiality, "there are no grievances" – not even against variants that supposedly depart from it. How well Confucian Chosŏn Korea kept to this principle during its subsequent centuries is beyond the scope of this brief paper. But the *Model for Study of Music* stands as a remarkable document of liberal ideology, especially coming from the fifteenth century.

The true range of *yue*'s influence over Confucian governance and thought is only beginning to be studied. But given the official nature of the recognition and institutionalization it enjoyed over the centuries as the great essence of Confucian harmony, further study of *yue* may be able to provide a meaningful counterpart to the more individual-oriented aspects of liberal tradition emphasized in studies of Confucianism to date. As Wm. Theodore de Bary and others have so eloquently argued, Confucianism has endured in part because it nurtured such qualities as principles of cultivated personhood, voluntarism, and exercise of autonomous conscience in interpreting tradition.[6] How music in government – as principle, as political institution, as philosophy and aesthetic – helped define and support those individual and collective experiences of harmony in freedom should allow for our fuller understanding of what it takes to be a civil society.

Notes

1 For the original Chinese text, I referred to *Sinwanyŏk* edition of *Yegi* 禮記 as well as *Sibu beiyao* edition of Kong Yingda's (574-648) *Liji zhengyi*. *Record of Music* is the earliest extant text on music from the Confucian tradition, believed to have been compiled in the second and first centuries B.C. or earlier. For an excellent background on the *Record of Music* in English, see Scott Cook, "*Yue Ji* 樂記 – *Record of Music*: Introduction, Translation, Notes, and Commentary."

2 That kind of collective emotionalism belonged to another category of music known as *yin* (音).

3 "The radiance of the original substance [nature] is never lost, and one who pursues learning need only keep to what emerges from it and clarify it, so as to restore it to its original condition" (Xi, 725).

4 Variant tones refer to the two *extra* tones in the pentatonic modes only half steps apart from the neighboring tones. They were considered deviant and unstable, and rarely used in ritual music. High tones refer to those notes beyond the fixed octave plus two tones considered the proper range of ritual music.

5 The translation is based on the earliest extant version of the *Model for Study of Music* from before the 1592 invasion of Korea, which was discovered in the Hosa Bunko Library in Japan in 1968 and made available in facsimile editions from Yŏnsei University Press (1969) and Publishers of Asian Culture (1975). The earliest extant version of the text housed within Korea is from 1610, now kept in the Rare Books Collection of the Seoul National University Library.

6 See, for example, de Bary's *Learning for One's Self: Essays on the Individual in Neo-Confucian Thought* and Weiming's *Way, Learning, and Politics: Essays on the Confucian Intellectual*.

Works Cited

Cook, Scott. "*Yue Ji* 樂記 – *Record of Music*: Introduction, Translation, Notes, and Commentary." *Asian Music* 36.2 (1995): 2-96.

de Bary, Willam Theodore. *Learning for One's Self: Essays on the Individual in Neo-Confucian Thought.* New York: Columbia UP, 1991.

de Bary, Wm. Theodore and Irene Bloom. *Sources of Chinese Tradition* I. 2nd ed. New York: Columbia UP, 1999.

Lee, Ki-baik. *A New History of Korea.* Trans. Edward W. Wagner. Cambridge: Harvard UP, 1984.

The Mean. In *Sources of Chinese Tradition* I. 2nd ed. Eds. Wm. Theodore de Bary and Irene Bloom. New York: Columbia UP, 1999.

Model for Study of Music. In "Sŏng Hyŏn's *Model for Study of Music* and the Historical Development of the Neo-Confucian Concept of Music (*Yue*) in Fifteen-Century Chosŏn Korea, with Translations of the "Introduction" and Excerpts from the *Investigation of Music* in the *Late Chosŏn Reference Compilation of Documents on Korea.*" Rachel Chung. Ph.D. Dissertation: Columbia University, 2002.

Record of Music (樂記). In *Sources of Chinese Tradition* I. 1st ed. Eds. Wm. Theodore de Bary, Wing-Tsit Chang, and Burton Watson. Trans. Burton Watson. New York: Columbia UP, 1960.

Weiming, Tu. *Way, Learning, and Politics: Essays on the Confucian Intellectual.* New York: SUNY, 1993.

Xi, Zhu. "Commentary to the Opening Line of the *Great Learning.*" In *Sources of Chinese Tradition* I. 2nd ed. New York: Columbia UP, 2000: 725.

Yegi 禮記. *Sinwanyŏk* edition. Seoul: *Myŏngmundang*, 1993.

Yingda, Kong. *Liji zhengyi.* Edition *Sibu beiyao.* Shanghai: Zhongghua shuju, 1934-6.

Politics, Principles, and Death in *Antigone*

Kieran M. Bonner
University of Waterloo

Tragedy is not melodrama; rather, as it has been remarked, tragedy is more like a battle of mighty opposites. *Antigone* is an excellent example of this battle. The struggle between Antigone and Creon is not "a confrontation of the forces of darkness and the forces of light, but a clash of two great imperatives that underlie all political action, the needs of the individual and the needs of the State" (Taylor xlvii) or between "public and private morality" (Taylor xiv). The Greek audience would have understood the significance of both imperatives. As Creon says, "indiscipline, anarchy, disobedience, what greater scourge than that for humankind" (160). Yet, they would also have understood that, as Antigone says, "laws that [the State] enact[s] cannot overturn ancient moralities or common human decency" (151). Both the bond that ties us to the past and the preservation of peace and order are sacred to the Greeks. As a result, we see the drama as a battle between a civic politics and a moral duty, a battle placing politics and morality in opposite camps. The tragedy of the play points to the universal problem when the demands of individual conscience and the need for political order and stability are placed in irreconcilable conflict. As such, while it may not, according to Aristotle, be the greatest of Sophocles' tragedies, "no one has put the nature of the conflict more succinctly, or demonstrated the price that must be paid on both sides with more unrelenting honesty" (Taylor xlvii). In the words of the theme of this conference, *Antigone* provides a "timeless answer" to "who we are" when faced with a conflict of this nature.

However, I want to argue that this particular tragedy can serve another important pedagogical function as a core text. It provides an opportunity to see politics and morality as not just in conflict but also as belonging together. On this reading of *Antigone*, conscience and political interests are not opposed. Instead, Antigone's action in the play can help us recognize how certain actions can be – even need to be – both ethical and political simultaneously. As a result, pedagogically speaking, *Antigone* can be used in a core text course to serve two purposes. It can, like other similar great texts, serve as an instance of what tragedy means. The same play, however, can also be an excellent example of what action that integrates the moral and the political looks like.

The tension between Creon and Antigone in this tragedy can fruitfully (for pedagogical purposes) be read as raising the question of the difference between the tragic hero and the moral and political hero. The tragic hero embodies suffering and learning through suffering. The moral and political hero embodies action and the principles brought alive through action. In the case of Antigone, her commitment to defying the law established by Creon and so her willing and knowing risk of death for the sake of what she believed in are not unrelated to the media image of the suicide bomber. Both kinds of actions, according to Emile Durkheim's classic study, would qualify as suicide and would lead many of us to agree with Antigone's sister Ismene's accusation that such acts reveal insanity. It has been decreed by Creon, Antigone's uncle and the ruler of Thebes, that her brother Polyneices should not be buried as a punishment for betraying the city. Her other brother, Eteocles, who fought for the city and died in battle with Polyneices, is to be buried with full state honors. When Antigone tells Ismene that she intends to defy the law and bury her brother Polyneices, Ismene says, "You must be mad" (135). Ismene goes on to say that "this obsession will destroy you. You're certain to fail." This prospect of certain failure makes the action proposed by Antigone seem insane. Through a dialogue with the action of the play and with the help of Hannah Arendt, this paper addresses the issue of the relation between action, principle, and the courage to risk death.

What can a liberal arts approach tell us about the difference between a dangerous obsession and a principled action? From a conventional social science perspective, we could say that Antigone's extreme actions are shaped, to say the least, by the very dysfunctional family that she came from. Such an interpretation is sustainable; yet, in taking this interpretive path, are we as teachers failing to take up an opportunity to understand Antigone's action in a way that could disturb and challenge our contemporary era rather than confirm cultural prejudices? An alternative way of looking at the play is to see Antigone as not just acting out dysfunctional instincts but rather as acting on principle. To develop this reading requires thinking through the relation between principle and action.

Arendt addresses the idea of principle in her essay "What is Freedom" in *Between Past and Future*. "Action," she says, "insofar as it is free is neither under the guidance of the intellect nor under the dictate of the will – although it needs both for the execution of any particular goal – but springs from…principle…. Principles do not operate from within the self as motives do – but inspire, as it were, from without" (151). Principles, Arendt says, "are much too general to prescribe particular goals, although every particular aim can be judged in the light of its principle once the act has been started" (151). Throughout the drama and as a response to those who challenge her defiance of the law, Antigone defends herself with appeals to, variously, "ancient moralities," "common human decency," "the approval of the dead," "natural justice," and "the rights of the dead." Dead traitors, she accepts, may be treasonous, but they are not animals.

From Arendt's perspective, it is Antigone and not Creon who is the political actor, as it is she whose actions bring alive a principled relation to the dead. Antigone's action takes away some of the force of the distinction between life and death by bringing death and life together. Both are seen to be oriented to the same end: keeping alive a certain general principle. This orientation is what most distinguishes the approach of Creon and Antigone to their respective relation between their beliefs and actions. It is Creon's belief that the fear of death will prevent all but the insane from disobeying the law. But the insane and the principled seem to have in common a willingness to act that risks their own security. Creon acts on the belief that the worst thing that can happen to people is that they will die; death therefore becomes his ultimate threat. This is how he threatens the soldier who first reports the burial. "Money will not save your life," he says (146). Creon describes the actions of those who defy him as motivated by greed (the soldier) or arrogance (Antigone). The threat of death is therefore aimed at resisting the kind of self-interest (greed) or the self-absorption (arrogance) that threatens public order. The death threat does not humble Antigone, and she continues to assert her duty to defy the law, which is seen by Creon as "lunacy" (155-56). From the perspective of life, says Arendt, "we should be the first to condemn courage as the foolish and even vicious contempt for life and its interests, that is for the allegedly highest of all goods" (156).

From the perspective of life, the most powerful distinction is between life and death; as a result, our greatest commonality is that we share life with all who currently live (this is one meaning of the term *humanity*). Humans share the fundamental togetherness of humanity by virtue of being alive on Mother Earth. In turn, the greatest separation is our difference from those who are not alive, those who have passed on. Thus, Creon can be seen to be acting not from political principles but rather from the perspective of life that makes the courage needed to act on principle seem foolish and contemptuous. The idea of the rights of the dead putting the obligation of human decency on the living, an obligation that calls on one to risk one's life, seems foolish to the extreme. So, he contemptuously says to his son Haemon, "let her find herself a husband that suits her among the dead" (159).

However, the action that brings the principle of the "rights of the dead" to life shows that we can have a community with those who are dead and be essentially out of community with some who are alive. That is, vis-à-vis the principled demand for human decency that ancient moralities put on us, the difference between life and death is secondary. From the perspective of the relation between action and principle, Antigone can be heard to say, *if a principle is truly worth living for, it is also worth dying for.* Her actions demonstrate that the major difference in life is not between death and life but between being principled and unprincipled. As she says, "some deaths are more honorable than others" (137). Blum and McHugh have also taken up this notion of principle in their work. "A principled actor," they say, "orients to the (essential) significance of his action in that he understands its being undertaken as a sign of value" (118). As they say, "a principled practice can fail without being a failure of principle," and "practice can succeed without being a morally committed practice" (118). For Antigone, to fail to act on principle or to let it be violated would be to make a lie out of her life; "if I die in the attempt," she says, "I shall die in the knowledge that I have acted justly" (136).

Having the courage to act on a principle shows that, in the political world, the distinction between life and death is secondary. In describing the development of the Greek *polis*, Arendt says, "whoever entered the political realm had first to be ready to risk his life, and too great a love for life obstructed freedom, was a sure sign of slavishness. Courage therefore became the political virtue par excellence" (*Human Condition* 36). If principle inspires action, action can be recognized in the distance it shows from the love of living per se. Courage is "indispensable for political action...because in politics not life but the world is at stake" (*Past and Future* 156).

The distinction between life and death is a powerful distinction: our whole medical science system is oriented by it. The victory of modern medical science is the victory of overcoming particular diseases and, most of all, extending life. All measurements of quality of life place life itself as the highest of goods. To Creon it is central; the fear of death will bring people into line and turn potential traitors into law-abiding citizens. Yet, Antigone says, "death is the worst thing that can happen. And some deaths are more honorable than others" (137). Antigone, in defying the law of the state, argues for the principle of the rights of the dead. Her action of burying her brother is not a brute deed, like a bomb in a crowded square. It is a deed supported with words and defended on the basis of its principle rather than its outcomes. Thus, here too we have a way of distinguishing between the deeds of a terror campaign and the deeds inspired by principled action. While both may be grounded in an opposition to the necessary laws that support the stability of the state, a terror campaign, insofar as its aim or goal is to demoralize the enemy, is focused on consequences. Action, however, as developed by Arendt, is done for its own sake ("its being undertaken as a sign of value" in the words of Blum and McHugh), such as for the universal principle of defending the rights of the dead, rights that require one to treat corpses with human decency. Thus, Antigone's action brings into being or into the world the principle of common human decency, the principle that the distinction between the animal and the human applies even to traitors. The Thebans, in turn, judge her particular action in light of the principle by which it was inspired, saying, "In burying her brother...she did something most people consider decent and honorable.... She should be given a medal for it, those same people say, and her name inscribed on the roll of honor" (160). Here again we see another feature of action that Arendt articulated – the boundlessness of an act, its potential to change the horizon in both irreversible and unpredictable ways. As Arendt points out, "the smallest act in the most limited circumstances bears the seed of...boundlessness, because one deed, and sometimes one word, suffices to change every constellation" (*Human Condition* 190). Where before Ismene saw the attempt to act as insane and bound to fail, she "is now proud to stand with [Antigone] in the dock" (155). The fundamental or deep truth revealed by Antigone's actions shows that the power of action can be more powerful than the actions of those in power and as such can provide a way of grounding the power of the actions of twentieth-century heroes like Martin Luther King and Gandhi.

Antigone, as a core text, can thus serve two important pedagogical purposes. First, it can serve as an example of the genre of tragedy and the insight that tragedy gives us into the human condition. This approach to tragedy is essentially polytheistic invention and shows the gods standing "monumentally aloof, as the human actors hurl themselves against their immutable laws and unalterable predictions and smash themselves to pieces. They neither help nor hinder. Simply, they know how the story will end, and they stand back and contemplate the tragic protagonists as they find their way by however indirect a route to that prophesied ending" (Taylor xxxvii). However, *Antigone* in particular is also a good example of the way that the moral and political can be seen as essentially belonging together and not in opposition to each other. The latter approach to *Antigone* makes a place for a lifeworld that undermines the urgent forces of life. This lifeworld gives us some distance on the claim Meurseault makes in *The Outsider* that "nothing mattered" because we are all "condemned" to die (115-16).

Works Cited

Arendt, Hannah. *Between Past and Future: Eight Exercises in Political Thought.* New Jersey: Humanities Press, 1968.

---. *The Human Condition.* Chicago: Chicago UP, 1958.

Blum, Alan and Peter McHugh. *Self Reflection in the Arts and Sciences.* New Jersey: Humanities Press, 1984.

Camus, Albert. *The Outsider.* Middlesex, England: Penguin, 1942.

Durkheim, Emile. *Suicide.* 1897. Glencoe, IL: Free Press, 1951.

Sophocles. "Antigone." *Sophocles: The Theban Plays.* Trans. and intro. Don Taylor. London: Methuen, 1986.

Self-Cultivation and the Chinese Epic: Confucian, Taoist, and Buddhist Themes in *Journey to the West*

Jane Rodeheffer
Saint Mary's University of Minnesota

In addressing the theme of the 2008 ACTC conference, Professor Theodore de Bary suggested that the question of personal and collective identity is central to the Confucian classics, insofar as they address the rich correspondence between the ordering of the self and the ordering of the world. As Professor de Bary pointed out, such a correspondence lies at the heart of the Ming epic *Journey to the West,* which is attributed to Wu Cheng'en. While the novel is often appreciated for its comedy and satire, such a facile reading fails to uncover the deeper riches that a reading of *Journey to the West* can offer to one who may be approaching a classical Chinese text for the first time. In what follows, I will explore the ways in which the thematic tension between self-cultivation and social harmony in *Journey to the West* invites the reader to explore not only the Confucian tradition, but also the Taoist and Buddhist traditions, all of which are vividly and often comically interwoven throughout the novel.

Journey to the West reworks and expands on numerous folk tales that developed around the historical journey of the Tang Buddhist Monk Hsuan Tsang (Sung Tan) who traveled to India in 629 C.E. to bring the original Buddhist scriptures back to China. His sixteen-year odyssey and subsequent devotion to translating the scriptures from Sanskrit into Chinese became the subject of numerous mystical and fantastic legends. In Wu Cheng'en's version of the legend, Buddha asks the Bodhisattva Kuan-Yin to find a pilgrim who is willing to make the long and dangerous journey to the west (India) to receive the scriptures from the Buddha, take them back to China, and "explain them to the people and change their hearts." (Waley 78). As she is portrayed in the novel, the character of Kuan-Yin is in keeping with a long Buddhist tradition in which she is venerated as a Bodhisattva: a spiritual being who postpones her own entry into enlightenment in order to help others progress in their spiritual development. In *Journey to the West*, Kuan-Yin commissions the Buddhist monk Hsuan Tsang to retrieve the scriptures, giving him the religious name Tripitaka, which refers to the three "baskets" or categories of Buddhist Scriptures. Tripitaka is accompanied on his journey to India by a band of immortal animals named Monkey, Pigsy, Dragon-Horse, and Sandy, all of whom have fallen into disfavor with heaven because of their evil deeds and undisciplined natures. Kuan-Yin convinces them to serve as Buddhist disciples to Tripitaka on his journey by promising that their good works will gain them the merit and redemption needed to attain enlightenment and freedom.

The characteristics of both Tripitaka and Monkey suggest that they are both quintessential pilgrims. An ill-tempered and cowardly mortal, Tripitaka is entirely incapable of recognizing the true reality behind sensible phenomena, despite his Buddhist credentials. His primary guardian and disciple, also in search of enlightenment, is the redoubtable Monkey, whose physical prowess is matched only by his ego. The narrator informs us that prior to joining Tripitaka, Monkey had gained tremendous magical powers and had even learned the secret of immortality under the tutelage of the Taoist sage, Sumbodhi. At the end of this process, Monkey declared himself "Great Sage Equal of Heaven." When his mischievous monkey-ways caused such havoc in heaven that Buddha himself was required to intervene, Monkey was removed from heaven and imprisoned beneath a mountain for 500 years. He is still serving out his sentence when Kuan-Yin approaches him. Knowing that Tripitaka will need assistance on his journey, Kuan-Yin offers Monkey freedom as well as the possibility of redemption if he will serve as the protector and guide of Tripitaka. As suggested above, the narrative structure of *Journey to the West* stands on its own; nevertheless, an appreciation of the philosophical and religious traditions underlying the concepts of self-cultivation and enlightenment can be very instructive for the reader unfamiliar with the Eastern classics.

Confucian scholars have traditionally argued that there is no Confucian teaching on self-cultivation outside of the *Ta Tsueh* (*Great Learning*). This brief work, which consists of no more than 250 characters, is understood as the gate through which all people must walk to become fully cultivated human selves:

> The ancients, who wished to illustrate illustrious virtue throughout
> the kingdom, first ordered well their own states. Wishing to order
> well their states, they first regulated their families. Wishing to regu-
> late their families, they first cultivated their persons. Wishing to cul-
> tivate their persons, they first rectified their hearts. Wishing to rectify
> their hearts, they first sought to be sincere in their thoughts. Wishing

to be sincere in their thoughts they first extended to the utmost their knowledge.... From the Son of Heaven to the mass of the people, all must consider the cultivation of the person the root of everything besides. It cannot be, when the root is neglected, that what should spring from it will be well ordered. (Legge 355)

This passage from the *Great Learning* sheds light on two important aspects of Confucianism as an underlying motif in *Journey to the West*. With regard to the ordering of the self, the reader soon realizes the extent to which the cowardly and peevish Tripitaka consistently fails not only to rectify his heart or become sincere in his thoughts, but also to extend his knowledge beyond the sensible phenomena that enslave him. The fact that he is nevertheless granted Buddhahood at the end of the journey is part of the comic brilliance of the novel. The world order outlined in the *Great Learning* also serves to underscore the fact that for the author of *Journey to the West* the self under cultivation is really a corporate self, a self writ large. As the Confucian text makes clear, the cultivation of one's own person takes place in an unfolding web of relationships. Tripitaka needs his pilgrim disciples if he is to complete the journey and overcome the monsters, demons, and other hurdles in his path, and his pilgrim disciples in turn need one another. When they finally reach the "further shore of salvation," Monkey tells his companions,

> "Every one of us...is equally indebted to the other. If the Master (Tripitaka) had not received our vows and accepted us as his disciples, we should not have had the chance to do good works and win salvation. If we had not protected the master and mounted guard over him, he would never have got rid of his mortal body." (Waley 282)

Monkey's insight bears witness to the Confucian values of filial piety and honor, as well as to the social context in which all true self-cultivation takes place.

To fully appreciate Monkey's spiritual growth both before and after the journey to the west, the reader must set the Confucian view of his self-cultivation against the background of popular religion in the Ming period, which, as Eva Wong points out, "blended Taoist and Buddhist spiritual values with fantasy" (88). The *Tao Te Ching* is traditionally attributed to the Taoist sage Lao Tzu who had, by the Ming period, attained the status of a deity. Lao Tzu was viewed as the source of the power behind the forces of change that sustain the universe. In Taoist cosmogony, the *Tao* or "Way" of the universe was understood as an unending creative transformation of the "ten thousand things": a process in which yang, or tranquility, is unified with yin, or movement, and these in turn are made harmonious with the five agents of water, fire, wood, metal, and earth. The author of the *Tao Te Ching* is at pains to preserve the essential mystery of this process:

> The universe is like a bellows
> It stays empty yet is never exhausted

It gives out yet always brings forth more. (Star 18)

In the Ming period, this eternal cosmological process of transformation became the foundation for a method of internal transformation – a kind of internal alchemy. Believing that all of the necessary ingredients for achieving immortality can be found within the human body, Taoists believed that "as nature renews itself by following the principles of the Tao, mortals too can renew themselves and attain immortality by living in accordance with these principles" (Wong 68). Readers of *Journey to the West* see this process at work in the very opening lines of the epic, in which we are told,

> There was a rock that since the creation of the world had been worked upon by the pure essence of Heaven and the fine savours of Earth, the vigour of sunshine and the grace of moonlight, till at last it became pregnant and one day split open, giving birth to a stone egg, about as big as a playing ball. Fructified by the wind it developed into a stone Monkey, complete with every organ and limb. (Waley 1)

A steely light emanating from Monkey's eyes makes the Emperor of Heaven take notice and acknowledge that the forces of change that sustain the universe (yin and yang) have been replicated within an earthly being. Monkey's first efforts at spiritual growth, undertaken prior to his pilgrimage with Tripitaka, bring him only temporary success. While his efforts at internal alchemy under the tutelage of the Taoist sage Sumbodhi do bring him immortality and a place in heaven, the mischievous elements of his inherent Monkey nature remain, and it is these that eventually lead to his banishment from the realm of the immortals. The fact that Buddha punishes the banished Monkey by imprisoning him under a mountain, only to send Kuan-Yin, the Bodhisattva of compassion, to free him later on, suggests that he is saving Monkey for an even greater task than the achievement of his personal immortality. As Whalen Lai points out, Monkey's early efforts in internal transformation via Taoism have allowed him to acquire only his "premoral, childlike, monkey nature," which, while innocent, is ineffective (55). Although the author of *Journey to the West* is clearly engaging in a certain amount of satire in suggesting that the internal alchemy of the Taoists is a complex and ridiculous failure, the background information provided by these early chapters allows for a seamless transition to the Buddhist trajectory of the pilgrimage, to which we now turn.

As previously mentioned, the animal Monkey was originally a stone monkey whose transformation into a living being comes about as a result of the mysterious forces of yin and yang at work in the universe. During his first spiritual instruction under the Taoist sage Sumbodhi, Monkey's lack of natural parentage is revealed, and when the time comes to bestow a religious name on Monkey, Sumbodhi recognizes him as "a child of nature...as nameless as nature itself" (Lai 48). Sumbodhi names him "Awareness of Vacuity." Monkey's birth out of a stone allows the author of a *Journey to the West* to play on both Taoist and Buddhist conceptions of true nature. Monkey symbolizes both what Lao Tzu would call the "uncarved block" and what the Buddhists would call "Buddha nature." The latter concept connotes awareness that all aspects of human existence are characterized by emptiness. It is in his second pilgrimage, as a disciple of Tripitaka, that Monkey undertakes the process of Buddhist self-cultivation, which involves the disciplining of his monkey-mind and an increasing awareness of the "vacuity" or emptiness of the phenomenal world. The term *monkey-mind* is used by Buddhists to refer to the chaotic procession of thoughts that clouds awareness of our true Buddha nature. From the vantage point of Buddhism, therefore, Monkey's initial Taoist transformation from a stone monkey to a living and breathing monkey with magical powers has only brought him part of the way toward the ultimate goal of enlightenment. As we will see, it is Monkey's Taoist knowledge that enables him to protect the naïve Tripitaka on their journey. In order to reach his true spiritual potential, however, Monkey's impulsive monkey-mind must be brought under control so that a Buddhist awareness of the emptiness of sensible phenomena can emerge and Monkey can fulfill his mission of protecting Tripitaka and bringing the Buddhist scriptures back from the west.

After Monkey is freed by Kuan-Yin and he and Tripitaka set out on their journey, the two pilgrims immediately encounter dangerous situations and treacherous demons that threaten their lives. Monkey is forced to use his Taoist knowledge of alchemy in order to transform himself into protective beings as the situation requires. Otherwise, Tripitaka will never make it to the west. But Tripitaka's compassion for all beings and his constant reprimanding of Monkey make it difficult for Monkey to engage in the type of death dealing necessary to protect Tripitaka, and Monkey quickly becomes frustrated by his master's failure to see phenomenal appearances for the dangers they are. His impulsive monkey-mind gets the best of him, and he attempts to abandon the journey altogether. At this point in the novel, Kuan-Yin again intervenes in order to ensure the success of the journey. She provides Tripitaka with a magical cap for Monkey. The cap is fitted with a metal band, and every time Monkey indulges in evil thoughts, Tripitaka chants a spell that tightens the band, causing Monkey immediate head pain. In this way, his monkey-mind is eventually disciplined, and his Buddha nature freed.

Monkey's enlightened awareness that "form is emptiness and emptiness is form," manifests itself most notably at the end of the journey, as the pilgrims are faced with the final crossing to reach the further shore of salvation. Just as Monkey is trying to convince his unwilling companions to follow him across a rickety bridge, they spy a boat. Monkey is the only pilgrim to recognize the ferryman as the "Conductor of souls," whose bottomless boat separates the physical body from the enlightened self, and he quickly pushes a reluctant Tripitaka into the bottomless boat. While Tripitaka complains that Monkey has gotten him wet, the other pilgrims notice that the monk has lost his body, which is floating in the water beneath the boat:

Tripitaka stared in consternation. Monkey laughed. "Don't be fright-
ened, Master," he said. "That's you." And Pigsy said "it's you, it's
you." Sandy clapped his hands. "It's you, it's you," he cried. The ferryman too joined in the chorus. "There you go!" He cried. "My best
congratulations...." Tripitika stepped lightly ashore. He had discarded his earthly body; he was cleansed from the corruption of the
senses, from the fleshly inheritance of those bygone years. His was
now the transcendent wisdom that leads to the further shore, the mastery that knows no bounds. (Waley 282)

A reader familiar with the early Buddhist scripture known as the *Heart Sutra* will recognize the above passage as a metaphor for the attainment of perfect
wisdom, which is the "heart" or goal of all Buddhist endeavor. The content of
perfect wisdom is an awareness of the emptiness of all being, as illustrated in the
passage in which Tripitaka loses his mortal form. According to the *Heart Sutra*,
"form is emptiness, and the very emptiness is form; emptiness does not differ
from form, form does not differ from emptiness; whatever is form that is emptiness, whatever is emptiness that is form. The same is true of feelings, perceptions, impulses, and consciousness" (Conze 162-3). Even the exclamatory cries
of the pilgrims in the bottomless boat mimic the tone of the *Heart Sutra*, the
conclusion of which suggests that the teaching on perfect wisdom is like a spell:
"It runs like this: Gone, Gone, Gone beyond, Gone altogether beyond, O what
an awakening, All hail!" (Conze 164).

When, at the end of the novel, Tripitaka and his disciples reach the "further
shore" of enlightenment, the Buddha rewards each of them for his role in successfully bringing the scriptures from India to China. Pigsy, Sandy, Monkey,
and Tripitaka each receive a spiritual promotion, since the success of the journey
and the achievement of enlightenment on the part of Tripitaka is contingent on
the social cohesion achieved by the entire group of pilgrims. Each pilgrim contributed individual gifts and sacrifices so that the collective journey would succeed, and the merits each pilgrim earns are tailored to his deeds. Monkey,
however, is singled out by Buddha for "turning [his] heart to the great faith and
[his] endeavor to the scourging of evil and the promotion of good" (303). His
self-cultivation complete, Monkey is promoted to "Buddha Victorious in Strife."

In the promotion ceremony that ends the novel, Wu Cheng'en brings together all three of the spiritual traditions that underlie popular religion and social
life in the Ming period. In joining Tripitaka on his journey and working together
to protect him from harm, each pilgrim undergoes the kind of self-cultivation
that the Confucian tradition sees as necessary to the proper ordering of the social
world. This is especially true in the case of Monkey. As an immortal being
schooled in the Taoist ways of internal alchemy, Monkey executes seventy-two
transformations in order to protect Tripitaka on their journey. The magical cap
teaches him to control his monkey mind until doing so becomes natural and the
cap is no longer needed. To borrow the language of the *Great Learning*, his
heart has been "rectified" and his thoughts "made sincere." Secondly, while
Monkey and the other pilgrims cultivate themselves in order to protect Tripitaka,

that self-cultivation occurs within the context of a web of relationships. Again, this correspondence is best exemplified in the moral and spiritual development of Monkey. Through his relationships with Tripitaka and the Bodhisattva Kwan-Yin, Monkey not only becomes schooled in the Buddhist doctrine of emptiness, but also in the way of compassion. This quality comes at last to permeate Monkey's nature, and by the end of the novel his impulsiveness has become infused with Buddhist concern for all beings. Finally, the successful retrieval of the Buddhist Scriptures from India allows the knowledge they contain to be "extended to the utmost" so that Buddhism can be reestablished in China. In this sense, the Confucian cultivation of "the root" and the ordering of the "branches" are thus seamlessly intertwined.

While the fictional world of *Journey to the West* provides many delights and its form invites comparisons to Homer's *Odyssey,* Dante's *Commedia,* and other western epics, the novel is grounded in the uniquely Chinese vision of the relationship between self-cultivation, enlightenment, and social harmony. Reading the epic in its broader context thus offers both professor and student a rich opportunity for untangling the complex matrix of Confucian, Taoist, and Buddhist values that delineate the spiritual quest of Tripitaka and his disciples. "O what an awakening," indeed.

Works Cited

Buddhist Scriptures. Trans. Edward Conze. New York: Penguin, 1959.

Cheng'en, Wu. *Monkey: Folk Tale of China.* Trans. Arthur Waley. New York: Grove Press, 1942.

Confucian Analects, The Great Learning, and the Doctrine of the Mean. Trans. James Legge. New York: Dover, 1971.

Lai, Whalen. "From Protean Ape to Handsome Saint: *The Monkey King.*" *Asian Folklore Studies* 53.1 (1994): 29-65.

Tao Te Ching. Trans. Jonathan Star. New York: Tarcher/Putnam, 2001.

Wong, Eva. *The Shambhala Guide to Taoism.* Boston: Shambhala, 1997.

The Morality of Makola in Conrad's *An Outpost of Progress*

Reena Thomas
University of Dallas

Conrad's other Congolese tale, *An Outpost of Progress*, much like *Heart of Darkness*, challenges the moral assumptions of a mainly Western audience by examining the effects of displacement and isolation within colonial Africa – in this case two French agents, Kayerts and Carlier, on a remote African trading post placed in their charge. But in many ways, *Outpost* hinges on the "third man on the station" (459), the African native Makola. With typical Conradian irony, the multi-lingual Makola possesses the leadership qualities expected in Kayerts and Carlier, who should be "pioneers of trade and progress" (466) but instead "did nothing, absolutely nothing" (465). Meanwhile, Makola "had charge of [the] storehouse" (459) and "bargained for hours…over an elephant tusk" (465); he handles the accounts, makes the trades, and in actuality (though not officially) manages the station. In this way, Makola functions as the story's true leader, the true agent of European colonialism, working more fruitfully than his white superiors, who "enjoyed the sense of idleness for which they were paid" (465). Conrad creates a clear contrast between the efficient Makola and his defunct white superiors, and he places onto the unofficial leader the moral weight of a difficult decision that is at the heart of this colonial tale. Without the agents' knowledge, Makola trades the station's ten tribal workers and nearby village men for a lucrative sum of six ivory tusks to a "knot of armed men" (469) who suddenly appear at the camp. The aloof Westerners react with disgust and righteous indignation, calling Makola a "fiend" (476); Makola, meanwhile, celebrates by "playing with his children" (477). Makola, especially in light of

Kayerts's and Carlier's disapproval, seems callous and amoral. However, Kayerts and Carlier never realize that through the seemingly inhumane slave trade Makola rescues the station from very real and imminent destruction. But Conrad neither commends nor condemns Makola, cloaking the character in dubious shades within the narrative. Rather, he grants the non-Christian African native a moral claim and uses the incident of the slave trade to explore how an individual's religious and political outlook shapes his or her response to human suffering and cruelty.

When seven armed men, "draped classically from neck to heel in blue fringed clothes" (469) mysteriously appear at the French trading post, the usually "impenetrable" (459) Makola reacts with a nervous anxiety, "[running] out of the storehouse" (469) and showing "signs of excitement" (469). Makola's behavior suggests he immediately recognizes the men as "perhaps bad men" (470). The leader, "powerful and determined looking...with bloodshot eyes" (470) agitates the typically cool-headed Makola, "who [now] seemed to be standing on hot bricks" (470). Makola stands defenseless against men who not only can destroy the entire station but, more personally, also can harm his family. Acting in self-defense, Makola consents to a slave trade in an attempt to protect his family and restore peace. However, Conrad never relates explicitly Makola's urgent fear of the armed men, and consequently, readers cannot empathize with the stoic Makola. After the trade, Makola retreats to the story's background unaffected, content, and unremorseful, to the "bosom of his family" (476) and to the daily errands of the station. Meanwhile, Kayerts and Carlier eventually consent to the trade in the name of profit, turning from a "couple of devoted friends" (481) into a "pair of accomplices" (481), and suffer from private guilt. They decline physically, mentally, and emotionally. For a Western audience, the striking contrast in reactions automatically raises questions about Makola's sense of right and wrong. During an intense confrontation, Kayerts and Makola "stood still, contemplating one another with intense eyes, as if they had been looking with effort across immense distances" (476). However, the distance between their reactions runs wider and deeper than the course of events that has transpired recently.

On one side of the crevasse is Makola: Conrad constructs Makola as a "civilized nigger" (475), making the African character relatable to a Western audience; yet Conrad includes quite casually a vital detail that instantly sets him apart ideologically. The narrative begins with a spotlight on Makola, making readers aware that Makola "spoke English and French with a warbling accent, wrote a beautiful hand, understood bookkeeping, and cherished in his innermost heart the worship of evil spirits" (459). Conrad instantly complicates Makola, the intermediary between West and non-West, in one brief sentence that starts out promising but ends alarmingly; this startling introduction sets Makola up to be evil and informs his character throughout the story. The use of the word *evil* is of course problematic and sets up one of the major differences between Makola and the Europeans. Readers expect Makola to be immoral or amoral, yet

Conrad burdens him, a man who worships evil spirits, with both the care of the station and, more important, a crucial moral crisis. Conrad uses the word *evil* for rhetorical effect, creating a huge distance between Makola and his readers, but he also uses the word with a sense of irony because for Makola the concept of evil differs greatly from his Western counterparts. Makola, the leader of the French trading post, the one most capable of opposing the vicious coastal men, possesses no grounding in a Judeo-Christian ethic.

The *worship* of evil spirits suggests that Makola conceives of evil inversely from his Western counterparts. A Christian understanding depicts evil personified in the devil as an adversary to God, a foe to be defeated, an enemy who can be defeated, one who through Christ has been defeated. But Makola does not imagine evil as an opponent to Christ or God. Makola has no reason to defeat evil and has no hope that he could; instead of defeating the evil spirit, he appeases it, highlighted sardonically by the narrator, who implies that Kayerts and Carlier arrived at the post as a way for Makola to "propitiate [the evil spirit] by a promise of more white men to play with" (460). Similarly, after the slave trade, the chief of the neighboring villages, Gobila, mourning the loss of his men in the exchange, "in his fear" (469) seeks to appease "all the Evil Spirits that had taken possession of his white friends" (469) with extra human sacrifices. The practice of human sacrifices is unquestionably barbaric. However, the narrative focuses not on the cruelty of the act but on the "fear, subtle, indestructible, and terrible" (479) that "lurks in [Gobila's] heart" (479). For the "mild old" (479) Gobila, his actions are placatory, not malicious. With these few references, Conrad infers an African relationship with evil that is wholly incompatible with Christian thinking. Instead of an immoral force to cast off, Makola views evil more generally, as a force that brings suffering, pain, and loss on earth. Makola engages in the realm of human suffering more intimately than the incompetent Kayerts and Carlier, who could not "grapple effectually with even purely material problems" (463). Makola respects and appeases evil, while those with a Judeo-Christian foundation, such as Kayerts and Carlier, want to conquer or ignore it.

On the other side of the crevasse are the Western trading agents Kayerts and Carlier. Conrad does not attribute any specific religious beliefs to the Frenchmen as he does to the pious Makola, yet Christianity is linked with imperialism throughout the story in the symbol of the cross. At the very start, the narrator mentions the grave of the first agent, who lay buried under a "tall cross much out of the perpendicular" (460) placed by the "ruthless and efficient" (460) director. The image of the misshapen cross, brought to the Congo trading post by the ruthless director, suggests that the Christianity imported to the outpost has been twisted and manipulated. When Kayerts and Carlier in their idleness pick up a copy of imperialist propaganda titled "Our Colonial Expansion," they pat themselves on the back as the "first civilized men to live in this very spot" (467) because the pamphlet described "the sacredness of the civilizing work and extolled the merits of those bringing light, and faith and commerce to the dark places of the earth" (467). The mingling of Christianity with imperialism fuels expansion with a divine purpose, and Carlier "replant[s] the cross firmly ...upright, [and] solid" (468). In their imperialist fantasy, colonial expansion in light of Christianity is a moral enterprise that should work against corruption and depravity. But Conrad relates the imperialist rhetoric ironically because, even if imperialism were superior and could defy the "Evil Spirit[s] that rul[ed] the lands under the equator" (460), Kayerts and Carlier, whom "society, not from any tenderness, but because of its strange needs, had taken care of" (463), are certainly not prepared to do so. After Makola's trade, the complacent agents lament slavery and suffering as an "awful thing" (477) and "frightful" (477), but the narrator discredits their trivial discussion, observing, "Everybody shows a respectful deference to certain sounds that he and his fellows can make. But about feelings people really know nothing. We talk with indignation or enthusiasm; we talk about oppression, cruelty, crime...and we know nothing real beyond the words. Nobody knows what suffering or sacrifice mean – except, perhaps the victims of the mysterious purpose of these illusions" (477-78). Conrad reveals a certain acknowledgement of or respect for those who have actively participated in suffering and grants moral authority "perhaps" (478) to the "victims" (478) of suffering and pain. Of the three characters, Makola is the closest to a moral authority on suffering because of his genuine grasp of it. The devout African native, who worships evil, is familiar with the "suggestion of things vague, uncontrollable, and [utterly] repulsive" (462) and decidedly more aware of the "unusual, which is dangerous" (462) than his white supervisors living in a morally deficient "fellowship of...stupidity and laziness" (465).

Yet, Conrad fails to endear the morally and intellectually superior Makola to his audience. Not only does Makola revere evil spirits, he keeps to himself, "despise[s] the two white men" (459), and "pretend[s] to keep a correct account of beads...and other trade goods" (459). Isolated, stoic, and deceitful, the character of Makola, painted in such harsh colors, simply is neither likeable nor trustworthy. Perhaps Makola's disregard is illustrated most fully when Kayerts shoots his former friend in a fit of paranoia. Makola displays no shock at the bloody suffering he witnesses; instead he "point[s] at the dead who lay there with his right eye blown out" (486) and says calmly, "I think he died of fever. Bury him tomorrow" (486). Conrad creates in Makola a non-Christian character more capable of handling intense suffering, yet his "I told you so" indifference disturbs readers. This ambivalent portrayal suggests Conrad neither praises nor vilifies Makola; rather, he hopes to unsettle his Western audience as they reconsider what qualities best prepare an individual to engage in evil and at what cost.

The matter of survival surfaces once again in *Heart of Darkness*. Conrad's most famous African tale also reveals the effects of the remote wilderness on the unaccustomed Western mind – in this case Kurtz. Many critics denounce Conrad for using a stereotypical image of Africa to further his own analysis of "one petty European mind" (Achebe). In his pivotal speech to Amherst in 1975, famed novelist Chinua Achebe remarks that "the West seems to suffer deep anxieties about the precariousness of its civilization and to have a need for constant reassurance by comparison with Africa.....Consequently Africa is something to be avoided." Achebe maintains that the downward spiral experienced by Kurtz is Conrad's warning to "keep away from Africa or else!" But Kurtz suffers not only as a result of succumbing to the "irresistible allure of the jungle" (Achebe) but also for mistakenly believing Africa has no moral ground by which he could be judged; consequently, Marlow concludes that "there was either nothing above or below [Kurtz]" (586) and he had "kicked himself loose of the earth" (586). The removal of a Western construct of societal norms misguides Kurtz as it does Kayerts and Carlier into believing that "anything can be done in this country" (534) because "nobody here…can endanger your position" (535). But, given the handling of Makola in *Outpost*, Conrad does not portray Africa as amoral; while *Heart of Darkness* does not possess a fully fleshed African character such as Makola to provoke readers, Marlow's commentary on the River Congo as he faces Africans in their homeland achieves a similar effect. In his discussion of the cannibals on board the steamer, Marlow admires their restraint in face of intense hunger. He looked upon them "with a curiosity of their impulses, motives, capacities, weaknesses, when brought to the test of an inexorable physical necessity" (548). Though Conrad uses a derogatory image of Africans as cannibals, Marlow must admit an undeniable fact – moral restraint is not only a Western claim.

In fact, much of Marlow's ruminations about Africa attempt to interpret (rather than judge) the motivations of a people shaped by concepts ultimately foreign to the passing visitor. He observes "the tremor of far-off drums, sinking, swelling…a sound weird…wild – and perhaps with as profound a meaning as the sound of bells in a Christian country" (515). Conrad's choice of adjectives – "weird, appealing, suggestive, and wild" (515) – could be viewed as denigrating, but Marlow's tone indicates his unfamiliarity with and curiosity about a country he is encountering for the first time. Rather, through Marlow's musing, Conrad hints at an African piety, reminding the audience that the country is not without its own spiritual foundation, a foundation that may not be Christian but perhaps possesses a comparable sense of moral relevance and reverence.

Conrad disturbs the moral inclinations of his Western readers through his depiction of Africa. In *Outpost*, the efficient Makola, a man who does not share the faith of the imperial West, must be read in conjunction with the inept Kayerts and Carlier. When the agents accept the blood-stained ivory, they believe they have become more like the barbaric Makola – lawless and unrestrained. Unfortunately, they misinterpret Makola. Makola "got on very well with his god" (460), and nothing in the text indicates otherwise. Makola, never tormented by his decision, is immune to the moral erosion that corrupts the two Frenchmen, who no longer view colonialism as pure endeavors but as criminal acts. The two men turn into the very savages they condemn because they fail either to adapt to the African wilderness or to subdue it with virtuous imperialism. Just as Kayerts and Carlier misinterpret Makola, Kurtz misinterprets his environment.

Kurtz turns into a brutish madman because he foolishly believes Africa is lawless and unrestrained. In each Congolese tale, Conrad urges readers to objectively and independently reassess their moral biases and assumptions about exactly which figure truly fits the definition of a savage.

Works Cited

Achebe, Chinua. "An Image of Africa: Racism in Conrad's *Heart of Darkness*."
    <<http://social.chass.ncsu.edu/wyrick/debclass/achcon.htm>> Accessed
    April 2, 2008.
Conrad, Joseph. *An Outpost of Progress*. In *The Portable Conrad*. Ed. M. Zabel.
    New York: Penguin, 1975.
---. *Heart of Darkness*. In *The Portable Conrad*. Ed. M. Zabel. New York: Pen-
    guin, 1975.

H.G. Wells on Being an Engineer

Christian Schumacher
Universidad Tecnológica de Bolívar
Cartagena de Indias, Colombia

This paper rises from the tension among three beliefs I have. First, I believe in the virtues of a humanistic and liberal education. Second, I believe that science is a crucial human endeavour and that engineering – science applied to the practical resolution of problems of human interest – is not only a respectable but also, in its core, a humanistic activity. Finally, I believe that we, the teachers, have a moral responsibility of being sympathetic with our students, that is, of taking their professional future seriously and of trying to encourage them to "make the best of it."

These three beliefs seem uncontroversial and simple; however, I found it extremely difficult to put them into curricular practice *simultaneously* when it comes to the education of future engineers. The common practice of liberal education is full of classics other than scientific, to the extent that some feel that there is a need of "bridging the gap," as for example a recent effort of the ACTC stated. However, there are scientific classics that are read: Euclid's *Elements*, Newton's *Principia*, Darwin's *Origins*, etc. They appear in many core curricula, and the reason for that is easy to see: these are texts that portray the human quest for truth and thus can be considered *philosophical* in nature, which makes them compatible with other, non-scientific philosophical texts that belong to the traditional canon.

However, engineers are oddly un-philosophical; their quest is not truth but practicality. It seems their main professional and disciplinary motivation is not to find out how it can be *known* but how it can be *done*. Alas, doing things is not a well respected life-goal amongst humanists. Aristotle and others have set the pace: a life dedicated to the production of goods, the provision of services, and the trades is an ignoble life, apt for the lower classes, slaves, and foreigners, while the quest for philosophical truth marks the final stage of the dignified life of a free and virtuous citizen.

The situation is further complicated by the wealth of modern literature that openly warns against the dangers of doing when based on scientific knowledge: *Frankenstein* is the generic name for what humanists expect as the outcome. Persons dedicated to physics are better locked away in the asylum, Dürrenmatt informs us; the *Homo Faber* who believes in rationality will end in a tragedy of Greek dimensions, Max Frisch warns us.

Thus, much if not most (or even all) of the reading in the humanist canon does not answer the fundamental question about the identity of the future engineer: How can I lead a dignified life dedicated to the resolution of practical problems? Even worse, some of the reading does carry a deeply unsympathetic message about the life-goal decisions of practical men and women. So, if we believe in the classics but also in the value of practicality, and if we are looking for culturally rich texts that express sympathy for engineers, what can we read?

A book that I think might work is H.G. Wells's *Tono Bungay*, and in the rest of this paper I want to argue for this position. What makes this book especially interesting is that it considers "modern" capitalism as both a condition for and a result of the activities of practical people, which provides a nuanced picture of the promises and the tensions of the profession.

The novel, written in 1909, has three layers. The first layer concerns the life of George Ponderevo and is semi-autobiographical. George, the son of a housemaid and a runaway father, is raised in a decaying manor, Bladesover House. Class is the determining social category, and the lives of everyone are channelled by its apparently timeless patterns. However, George is a bright lad; he has an inquisitive mind and a strong independent temper. He finds a room filled with forgotten books, belonging to the manor's better times, and starts to read the implicit canon of Victorian England: arts and history, political philosophy and social literature, etc. George recalls:

> And I found Langhorne's "Plutarch" too, I remember, on those shelves. It seems queer to me now to think that I acquired pride and self-respect, the idea of a state and the germ of public spirit, in such a furtive fashion; queer, too, that it should rest with an old Greek, dead these eighteen hundred years to teach that. (26)

However, books alone might free your mind but not your body. George, who has permission to play with the Hon. Beatrice Normandy, is attacked by her half-brother Archie Garvell. Archie insists that George can only play what he is, a servant but not a gentleman: "You can't be a gentleman, because you aren't. And you can't play Beatrice is your wife. It's – it's impertinent." And Archie explains further reasons to the protesting Beatrice: "He drops his aitches like anything" (40).

It comes as it must: George hits Archie, Beatrice takes Archie's side, and George is expelled from the manor. Thus, one of the themes of the novel is set: the relation of personal destiny to social class. This reminds us, in relation to our students, that a profession is not a simple and detached activity but a social fact. In George's particular case, the life of an engineer promises not only the liberation of the mind through knowledge, but also the liberation of the body from its social origins. At least in Cartagena and at my university, social mobility is still a strong motive for many of the engineering students (and of others, too), as it may also be elsewhere.

However, George's life is not simple and straightforward. He receives a degree in science, but to finally break his social bounds, he needs the assistance of his uncle, Edward Ponderevo, the inventor of Tono Bungay and visionary entrepreneur. Social prestige, which George feels is but a particular form of silliness, comes with "modern industry":

> So I made my peace with my uncle, and we set out upon this bright enterprise of selling slightly injurious rubbish at one-and-three-halfpence and two-and-nine a bottle, including the Government stamp. We made Tono-Bungay hum! It brought us wealth, influence, respect, the confidence of endless people. All that my uncle promised me proved truth and understatement; Tono-Bungay carried me to freedoms and powers that no life of scientific research, no passionate service of humanity could ever have given me.... (168)

However, due to his uncle's character and the nature of "modern industry," the business ultimately fails and Edward has to hide in France, where he dies. George flees from England in one of the battleships he designed for the highest bidder and writes the novel as a reflection on his life. Thus, the life of George Ponderevo is an open-ended affair, like the future life of our students. There are no straight paths, no clear and unequivocal answers to the question: What will be my life as an engineer? What the first layer of the novel clearly shows, however, is that this question cannot be asked in a social vacuum.

The second layer of the novel considers the historical circumstances of the birth of the engineering profession as well as "modern industry." *Tono Bungay* is a story of great social change, the end of what George calls the "Bladesover scheme." As George says,

> That all this fine appearance was already sapped, that there were forces at work that might presently carry all this elaborate social system in which my mother instructed me so carefully that I might understand my "place," to Limbo, had scarcely dawned upon me even by the time that Tono-Bungay was fairly launched upon the world. (10)

What is this change, and what are its driving forces? For H.G. Wells, the answer is clear. The change is the coming of the "mechanical and scientific age," the result of the industrial revolution. In another very interesting book, *Anticipations of the Reaction of Mechanical and Scientific Progress upon Human Life and Thought*, written in 1902, Wells detects (amongst others) two new "social elements" that this change brings about (73):

> The most striking of the new classes to emerge is certainly the shareholding class, the owners of a sort of property new in the world's history. (*Anticipations* 41)

However, it seems clear that Wells' sympathies are not with the shareholders, that he thinks capitalism needs a soul to be beneficial, and that this soul is not the money itself. Thus, he makes George consider what it might mean that financiers have bought Bladesover House and have thus "re-placed" the decaying aristocrats:

> It is nonsense to pretend that finance makes any better aristocrats than rent.... There was no effect of a beneficial replacement of passive unintelligent people by active intelligent ones. One felt that a smaller but more enterprising and intensely undignified variety of stupidity had replaced the large dullness of the old gentry, and that was all.... I do not believe in their intelligence or their power – they have nothing new about them at all, nothing creative nor rejuvenescent, no more than a disorderly instinct of acquisition; and the prevalence of them and their kind is but a phase in the broad slow decay of the great social organism of England. (72)

The second new social element is the new class of engineers! Again, in his *Anticipations*, Wells writes:

> And the point I would particularly insist upon here is, that throughout all its ranks and ramifications, from the organizing heads of great undertakings down to the assistant in the local repair shop, this new, great, and expanding body of mechanics and engineers will tend to become an educated and adaptable class in a sense that the craftsmen of former times were not educated and adaptable. (97)

Thus, George's personal history is more than just a biography: it is a reflection about the role of a new profession, of a new kind of human destiny, brought about by the dramatic changes of these "new times," changes which are still in effect today and which are operating vigorously on a worldwide scale.

Finally, the third layer of this novel concerns itself with the tensions among historical change, shareholder capitalism, and the engineering profession as a human destiny. The first is the tension between knowing one's place and at the same time contributing to change, a tension no one in the engineering profession can escape. The second tension springs from the fact that engineering needs finance, but shareholder capitalism is irresponsible and untruthful. Its aims are selfish, and its motive is greed. The third tension arises from personal vulnerability, from the many different ways in which a human individual can succumb to the temptations of prestige and wealth and forget his nobler, altruistic, even philosophical goals.

I invite you to trace these tensions in the book itself; if nothing else, it makes a good and enjoyable read. However, I will leave you with George Ponderevo's own concluding remarks:

> This is the note I have tried to emphasise, the note that sounds clear in my mind when I think of anything beyond the purely personal aspects of my story. It is a note of crumbling and confusion, of change and seemingly aimless swelling, of a bubbling up and medley of futile loves and sorrows. But through the confusion sounds another note. Through the confusion something drives, something that is at once human achievement and the most inhuman of all existing things.... It is something that calls upon such men as I with an irresistible appeal.... It is something we draw by pain and effort out of the heart of life, that we disentangle and make clear. Other men serve it, I know, in art, in literature, in social invention, and see it in a thousand different figures, under a hundred names. I see it always as austerity, as beauty. This thing we make clear is the heart of life. It is the one enduring thing. (458)

And because I think that H.G. Wells is right, that a dignified life consists in getting in touch with this "enduring thing" and that the engineering profession is but one specific way to grasp it, I think also that our engineering students can learn much about what it means to be an engineer from a critical assessment of this wonderful novel and of their own personal life-goal.

Works Cited

Wells, H.G. *Anticipations of the Reaction of Mechanical and Scientific Progress upon Human Life and Thought.* New York: Harper, 1902.

---. *Tono Bungay.* New York: Duffield & Co., 1916.

Who We Are and the Case for Economics in the Core Curriculum

David C. Rose
University of Missouri-St. Louis

Who are we? Aliens from outer space would likely conclude that there is something very different about the upright walking primates and all other forms of life. But what if they looked down on earth 25,000 years ago? The differences would not be so apparent. There would be no satellites, jet planes, skyscrapers, roads, or cities whose lights could even be seen from space. There would be no large firms, no organized law enforcement, no hospitals, and no high art or culture. So, why is there a difference between then and now? We are genetically indistinguishable from our ancestors going back at least 80,000 years, so genes cannot explain it.

The answer is that when we were stuck in the hunter-gatherer lifestyle, we lived in very small groups, but prosperity – especially general prosperity – is only possible with effective cooperation in large groups.[1] Humanity began to prosper and flourish when it began moving to ever larger scales of social organization. Without agriculture to produce city-states, for example, there would have been no Athens or Rome. So, the answer to the question "Who are we?" is this: We are a small-group species that has apparently found ways to transcend our small-group nature and to enjoy the benefits of being able to cooperate in very, very large groups.

Since the mechanisms required for effective cooperation in large groups are different from the mechanisms that evolved to facilitate cooperation in small groups, one thing we need to understand about ourselves is that we are essentially maladapted for large-group life. Our present lives should therefore be un-

derstood as something quite unnatural, like a Boeing 747 flying overhead in its
moment by moment struggle to overcome nature. . The good life comes from
large-group society, but our genes, like gravity, keep calling us back to our
small-group nature. Ten thousand years from now we will still have the genes of
a small-group species, so overcoming our small-group nature is a never-ending
struggle.

What does this have to do with the case for making undergraduates take
economics? Economics is largely an effort to understand the mechanisms that
make large-group society possible.[2] As such, economics is about what is required for humans to overcome their small-group nature so as to become prosperous enough to be able to flourish and to reach for the sublime. Since being
prosperous makes all other objectives easier to reach, this suggests that economics is an important discipline indeed.

Perhaps the most important lesson of economics, then, is that indulging our
small-group nature is very costly. Our small-group intuitions give rise to folk
wisdoms about economic behavior and free market societies. In many cases,
these intuitions give us exactly the wrong answers and contribute to an overly
mystical and pessimistic view of economic behavior in general and of how free
market economies function.

Consider the following example. Economic systems can be divided into
those in which economic activity is centrally planned and those in which it is not
(decentralized planning). Socialism, in a nutshell, is the central planning of economic activity toward a goal of maximal utility. There is nothing inherently
wrong with either central planning or maximal utility, so there is nothing inherently wrong with socialism. Indeed, it was evolutionarily inevitable that we
would all be born socialists because central planning to effectuate maximal utility turns out to be the most efficient way to run a hunter-gatherer band, so those
groups that did not evolve traits to support socialist group organization were
eliminated by those that did. Since your hardwired, moral intuitions and habits
of mind evolved in such small-group environments, it follows that socialism
necessarily sounds reasonable to you because you are hardwired to have it sound
reasonable to you.[3]

Socialism has its place (e.g., in running a household in modern society). But
when applied outside its place, we run into problems. The world we want – one
that is generally prosperous enough to allow human flourishing – is a world that
is impossible if efficient economic activity is limited to small groups because we
have adopted an ideology (socialism) that works well only when we limit our
cooperation to small groups. Humans are amazing because they are able to use
their abstract reasoning abilities to invent institutions that make the large-group
world possible. Economics is the study of many of those institutions.

In a very small group, the study of market economics is not relevant because there are no market prices, and there are none because there are not
enough buyers and sellers of any given thing at any given time. That is not a
problem in a small group because in such a case a single individual can know
everyone's talents and needs. But as we consider ever-larger groups and greater

degrees of specialization (which is the primary benefit of large groups), central planning becomes exponentially more difficult, whereas at the same time market pricing becomes easier and does an ever better job of effectuating economic cooperation.

The lesson is that a society that insists on central planning will find that it faces a terrible trade-off: it can be small and well managed (like a hunter-gatherer band 15,000 years ago or a nuclear family today), or it can be large and inefficient (like the Soviet Union circa 1975). Conversely, a society that effectuates decentralized planning through market pricing faces no such trade-off because the larger the society is, the better market pricing does in effectuating an efficient allocation of resources.

Because we are a small-group species, we have habits of mind associated with actively managing the (small) world around us, so allowing resources to flow according to self-regulating prices sounds completely ridiculous. Children of mothers who do not strive to actively manage their environment are not long for this world, and this sort of experience makes it hard for us to believe that an unmanaged economy is better than a managed one. So, unless we have been taught the lessons of economics, like moths drawn to a flame, we will be drawn to the active management of the economy associated with socialism.

Why do not socialists see this point? We naturally draw the wrong conclusions if we do not understand the mechanisms by which a small-group species is able to produce the benefits of having a large-group world, because our small-group approach is maladapted to the large-group world. The small groups in which we evolved produced moral intuitions, psychological mechanisms, and habits of mind that conflict with cooperation in large-group society. Economics matters because it is the study of those mechanisms that made (and make) large-group cooperation possible. How should we teach economics to make this point clearly?

First, we must begin by demonstrating the importance of large-group society. Prosperity makes nearly everything we value easier to achieve, but prosperity requires realizing the gains from specialization. In his classic *An Inquiry into the Wealth of Nations* (1776), Adam Smith demonstrated that the gains from specialization rise directly with group size. This means that prosperity is only possible with coordination mechanisms that work in large groups. To teach economics properly, we must teach students that they are hardwired to intuitively understand and embrace mechanisms that work in small groups, not the mechanisms that work in large groups, and that material prosperity is only possible through large-group society. Students are, therefore, effectively hardwired to find economics counterintuitive and therefore hard. The first step to overcoming this problem is for us to be aware of it and to explain it to our students.

Second, we must adopt a foundational approach to the teaching of economics that is based on the positive nature of voluntary transactions and that comports with our hardwired preference for cooperating with others. This is achieved by demonstrating early and often that all voluntary transactions are occasioned by one or two phenomena: the gains from cooperation or the gains from trade. The gains from cooperation are illustrated thusly: alone I make 10, alone you make 10, but working together we make 26 (not merely 20). The whole is greater than the sum of the parts. It follows that there are no losers, only winners. The gains from trade are illustrated thusly: what I have is worth $10 to me but is worth $13 to you. What you have is worth $13 to me but only $10 to you. By trading what I have to you and vice versa, it is as though each of us got a check for $3 in the mail – again, no losers, only winners. Free market economics is, therefore, about the nobler side of human existence.

What does any of this have to with core texts? It turns out that much of what was discussed above was addressed in some way by Adam Smith. Smith's *Theory of Moral Sentiments* provides a theory for the emergence of moral standards in a small-group context. No doubt Smith, sensing that this was only half the story, provided a theory in his *Wealth of Nations* for why large-group cooperation is necessary for general prosperity (gains from specialization through division of labor), as well as a theory of the mechanisms necessary for mediating cooperation in such groups (market pricing to facilitate decentralized production, which market pricing only requires the pursuit of self-interest within the bounds of moral propriety). For one man to have such insight into both the limitations and virtues of our small-group nature as well as the possibilities of our capacity for large-group cooperation was remarkable.

Large-group social behavior is so interesting to us precisely because it does not come naturally to us. Large-group social behavior has been aided by moral, philosophical, and scientific beliefs about the nature of the world around us. How we, as a small-group species genetically programmed to engage in small-group social behavior, were able to construct an entirely new world from nothing but our intelligence is the great story that all intellectuals are obliged to tell the world. That story cannot be told in the absence of economics, and it is best told at the beginning, through the voice of Adam Smith.

I submit that the classics are classics precisely because they are part of a larger narrative that exemplifies humankind's struggle to transcend small-group nature. This is why almost nothing written by the great thinkers of human history is of much relevance to tribal life. Their writings are all about achieving civilized life. We are on the happy side of the rise of civilized, that is, large-group, society. We are able to work together for a common cause in staggeringly large groups because we hold common beliefs that make it possible to trust each other for the most part. The problem is that the rise of civilization, or large-group society, took a very long time, so it is all too easy to take it for granted, to forget how we got here and the fundamental nature of the struggle to get here. It si our job to make sure the narrative is not lost.

Notes

1 This is hardly a controversial point. Economists from Adam Smith to *New York Times* columnist Paul Krugman have made important contributions to our understanding of the propositions that the key to prosperity is realizing the gains

from specialization and that the larger the groups within which the gains from specialization are realized, the greater are such gains. See also Buchanan and Yoon.

2 For example, the study of markets is central to the study of market economics. But the markets that work best for society – competitive markets – are possible only if there are very many buyers and very many sellers. In other words, markets work better the larger society is.

3 See Ken Binmore's *Natural Justice*.

Works Cited

Binmore, Ken. *Natural Justice*. New York: Oxford UP, 2005.

Buchanan, James M. and Yoon, Yong J., eds. *The Return of Increasing Returns*. Ann Arbor: U of Michigan Press, 1994.

Smith, Adam. *A Theory of Moral Sentiments*. Eds. D. D. Raphael and A. L. Macfie. Indianapolis: Liberty Fund, 1977.

Smith, Adam. *An Inquiry into the Nature and Causes of the Wealth of Nations*. Eds. R. H. Campbell and A. S. Skinner. Indianapolis: Liberty Fund, 1982.

Reading Texts and Liberal Education

Core Texts, Introspection, and the Recovery of the Renaissance Ideal in Twenty-First-Century Higher Education

Hugh R. Page, Jr.
University of Notre Dame

What is a core text? What role should introspection play in a liberal education? Should the choice of courses one takes as an undergraduate in college be determined by one's intended career path? Should coursework at the bachelor's, master's, or doctoral level be geared to develop in students an appreciation for the arts, sciences, and humanities – a transformed consciousness shaped by fourteenth to fifteenth-century Renaissance educational ideals that valued broad learning, classical texts, experimentation, and exploration?[1]

When I look back at more than fifteen years in academe, I realize that these questions have never been of peripheral concern to me. Although they were not directly addressed in graduate language classes or seminars on the Hebrew Bible, comparative Semitic grammar, or Northwest Semitic epigraphy, those who designed our doctoral program at Harvard had in fact their own answers to them. It was all too clear from the shape of the curriculum and the faculty selected to teach us.[2] Every now and then one could hear a concern with such meta-questions echoed in parenthetic remarks made by this or that professor. In the case of some of our more senior faculty, one could see clear evidence of a wrestling with epistemological issues if one looked closely at the bibliographic citations or footnotes in their major works. Thus, when I left graduate school and drove cross-country from Connecticut to California to assume my first academic position, I too pondered these questions – even as I wondered quietly whether there would be any way for me to engage them and gain tenure while so doing.

I started out as a newly minted PhD as an assistant professor of Humanities at California State University, Sacramento in 1991. Happy to have a paying job in a warm climate, I set aside worries about teaching outside of the strict parameters of biblical and cognate studies more or less normative for those trained, as I had been, in Near Eastern languages and civilizations. My *curriculum vitae* had caught the eye of the department chair at Sacramento State because my theological and linguistic training suggested that I might be a good fit for a service department that offered required introductory courses in the Humanities and electives in Religious Studies. This was a fortuitous match for me as well. Working at a teaching institution helped me to appreciate the challenge of developing effective student-centered pedagogical techniques when one has a heavy teaching load. Being a faculty member at a commuter university helped me to appreciate the urgency with which students holding full-time jobs are forced to approach undergraduate education. Teaching a syllabus that exposed students to art, architecture, literature, and ideas covering the period from roughly 35,000 BCE to the beginning of the Renaissance nudged me out of my intellectual comfort zone. Interestingly enough, it helped me to gain a new appreciation for my teachers and my teachers' teachers, most of whom were in fact broadly trained humanists. It also brought me a new appreciation for my parents, grandparents, aunts, and uncles, each of whom in some way passed on to me the tradition of *Black Diasporan Humanism*. It was, after all, under their tutelage that my interest in core texts, introspection, and the embrace of a holistic educational ideal first began to flower.

As a graduate student I found myself asking questions neither strictly philological nor theological about texts like the *Baal Cycle* from ancient Syria or the fragmentary Old Babylonian Version (OBV) of the *Gilgamesh Epic* – an oft-cited core text. This continued as I began teaching undergraduates in Sacramento. Larger issues – anthropological, cosmological, and ontological – animated my thinking. Being at a place where I could muse on these and juxtapose in reading and conversation a wide array of texts and other artifacts from several cultures and time periods was exciting. To my astonishment, I found that many of my students were interested in matters expressly religious. Some were, if memory serves, taking their first college courses. All were extraordinarily pressed for time and sorely tested by the required reading, which included Homer, Dante, etc. After losing no small amount of sleep plowing through the reading myself and wrestling with approaches to teaching it that would engage students who saw the class as a burden rather than an opportunity for personal growth, I decided that perhaps the best thing to do was to show them how to establish a *relationship* and have a *conversation* with a book, a painting, or any other human artifact. I found myself at the same time teaching basic skills like reading, listening, and interpretation with nuances derived from my own quest for meaning. I tried to let them know that we, as a class, were a kind of learning cohort each, in our own way, searching individually for answers to a huge number of questions, some of which had even perplexed our ancestors. The materials we covered in class would present us with a chance to see how others had dealt with these questions and give us a chance to haggle over them ourselves. I let them know that I too was perplexed, stressed, and in search of answers. I wanted them to know that their journey was, in part, my own. Texts, reading, and contemplation were for all of us basic survival skills, ways to make sense of life. A willingness to see the entirety of life as a field for intellectual engagement, even if such engagement had pragmatic aims, I saw as essential. I also saw value in their becoming late twentieth-century Renaissance Idealists who had a nuanced understanding of the past, an appreciation of beauty, and a willingness to be effective stewards capable of investing our intellectual and artistic legacy so as to guarantee a yield of justice and peace. Insofar as all of us were pondering imponderables and asking questions about ultimate reality, I saw this as a search for truth, a process I understood to have a profoundly spiritual dimension. So as to create an inclusive and non-sectarian atmosphere to contextualize the process, I stressed the interconnectedness of human experience and the communal nature of education as foundational for learning.

This formative teaching experience shaped my life as a researcher. When I later joined the Theology faculty at the University of Notre Dame, I did so having deeper insight into the role that texts of all kinds play in the generation of culture and ideas. As an instructor in, among other courses, our Foundations of Theology class, the one-to-one encounter with texts – broadly construed – remained the focus of my pedagogy. When sometime later I volunteered to teach in our College of Arts and Letters Core Course, it was a kind of homecoming. Within a Catholic context, matters of faith could be front and center in discussions about the search for truth. It was a most congenial atmosphere in which to ponder the relationship between authors, ideals, texts, society, nature, and the Divine.

My experience as a Theology professor these past sixteen years has only strengthened my conviction that core texts, cultivation of the inner life, and an education that has breadth and depth in the Arts, Humanities, and Sciences is absolutely essential to prepare the next generation of global citizens. Such an educational experience needs to begin when students set foot on campus, and the intellectual *ethos* of a college or university needs to be so enlivened by liberal learning that it is palpable in every aspect of undergraduate life. As an academic administrator responsible for the advising, mentoring, and intellectual development of more than 1900 first-year students each year, I see this as a job ideally shared by all campus educators, whether they are faculty, residence hall staff, or advisors. As a dean, the prospect of helping to ensure that this takes place is particularly daunting. Students entering colleges and universities today, and their parents, have to navigate some significant hurdles, not the least of which are college or university options, affordability, and vocational uncertainty. At some institutions, course availability is an additional concern. Many parents and students are understandably worried about the impact that the choice of major may have on post-baccalaureate opportunities in the job market. Others wonder about the practical value of certain requirements. Helping to allay the fears of students and those who are part of their primary support network at home, while at the same time being an advocate for a curriculum that is intellectually rich and rewarding is no mean feat. Doing so while generating additional programming that helps students to develop a synthetic understanding of liberal learning and to see how their courses facilitate epistemological reflection that, in turn, helps to shape their character is even more difficult. Anxieties about the completion of requirements, "credentialization" through majors, minors, and concentrations (where such exist), and time pressures provide little incentive to take a more comprehensive view of liberal education as a life changing experience, the first stage of which is the completion of an undergraduate degree. Increasingly, I see the job of an academic administrator, particularly one in a decanal position, as that of weaving the roles of scholarship, teaching, and institutional oversight into a seamless garment. By so doing, one can ennoble the search for truth commonly shared by faculty, students, and others served by the academy and thereby become a more effective spokesperson for the value of texts, contemplation, and a twenty-first-century re-appropriation of Renaissance Humanism.

This may be a tough sell in some settings. Few people begin their academic careers with the intent of becoming academic administrators. Even fewer consider themselves to be particularly well prepared to take on these roles. Fewer still, I dare say, called upon to take on an administrative role, would self-identify as scholar-teacher-administrators. The demands on one's time and energy are so substantial, and the duties so unlike those typically associated with research and teaching, that many view academic administration as the antithesis of scholarship. Since 1999, I have been a program director, an associate dean, and now a dean. Along the way, I have wrestled with questions of professional identity and fundamental objectives while at the same time trying to keep my e-mail inbox from overflowing and my calendar from crowding out time for the contemplation necessary to make informed decisions about policies and practices that effect peoples' lives. I have struggled to find solid ground on which to stand while balancing responsibilities as scholar, teacher, and steward of the University's resources. It has been a tremendous struggle. Like anyone involved in this kind of work, I have enjoyed successes and suffered a few failures. However, there are some interesting discoveries – some "aha" moments – that have made the process more than worthwhile. They have helped me to reaffirm my commitment to core texts, introspection, and the pragmatic and integrative focus one sees reflected in certain Renaissance notions of the *homo universalis* as constitutive of the stable center from which all endeavors within the academy – whether those involve service, administration, learning, teaching, or research – can proceed.[3]

The first of these discoveries is that in my role as administrator, I am at my best when I temper my reading of the ubiquitous "how to" books and articles in periodicals targeted toward novice administrators with a reengagement of those texts that form the core of the *world's* intellectual tradition.[4] The second is that I am most productive and at peace about the decisions I have to make when contemplation is a regular part of my daily routine. The third is that of all the skills I possess, three are most critical to survival and well being in my several distinct roles. These are the capacity to read, write, and quantify. The fourth realization is, perhaps, the most significant and jarring. It is that in many respects, the values embedded in today's consumer-oriented cultures of accountability and achievement, some of which have been taken on with little adaptation by institutions of higher learning, appear to conflict with those at the heart of the three aforementioned *maxims*.

These realizations served as a wake up call for me. Several years ago, I was a newly tenured associate professor with a fairly traditional profile, portfolio, and career trajectory. However, the teaching of our undergraduate Core Course, a few personal crises, and the opportunity to help build our African and African-American Studies Program changed all of that. I started seeing myself as a *human* and a *humanist* once again. I began to read new things, develop new and unusual academic interests, listen to new music, and conceive of my role as scholar in new ways. I started writing poetry again, joined a blues band, and taught myself to play the harmonica. I put all of the disparate pieces of my life on the table and reconfigured them in playful ways. I was certain about only one thing: I did not want to be involved in doing anything that did not *matter*. I had come through the tenure process with a couple of books, some articles, a guaranteed job, and not much else. At 43, I did not want to spend my remaining years thinking about or writing about issues that did not promise, in some way, to be potentially transformational for those I taught and with whom I worked.

Things were great for a while, but something started to happen. The academy seemed to change. My administrative responsibilities started to mount. My calendar filled with meetings. I was producing statistical charts, productivity reports, proposals for initiatives, and budget projections. I had to squeeze in time to read and write, two activities that fed me intellectually and spiritually. Conversations about ideas were contravened by strategic planning sessions. New positions were added to older ones, and new committee assignments replaced existing ones. Time to teach diminished. Moments to think about the big picture were supplanted by what some have rightly called "the tyranny of the urgent." The fear and distress of which I had rid myself after having survived the academy's greatest initiatory ordeal was once again a constant companion. I saw the stress etching itself on the *text* with which I had the most intimate of relationships, my body. Most distressingly, I noticed that my struggle was not unique. Faculty colleagues and students, even those just beginning their collegiate experience, appeared to share aspects of this same struggle.

Why, I have wondered, is this problem so acute for many of us? Why do we in academe simply mirror the life-ways and behavioral patterns prevalent in the rest of society? Why are we typically working 60 to 70 hour weeks, yet barely able to keep up? Why does it seem that the more diligently we work, the more there seems remaining to be done? Are we lacking in the drive needed to achieve at the highest levels in an increasingly competitive environment? Do we need to work longer, harder, or more effectively? Do we need to ask more of ourselves, our colleagues, and our students? I think not. When I look at the results of our collective and individual labor, I marvel at its quantity, but wonder at times about its quality and the pain out of which it often emerges. I am particularly concerned about our *stewardship of knowledge*. For those things we create, learn, and teach to endure and have their desired impact, sufficient time for close reading, conversation with colleagues, careful formulation and testing of theories, contemplation, and peer feedback are needed. There also needs to be some degree of genre experimentation on the part of those involved in the creation of new knowledge so that those discoveries and ideas can leaven our consciousness through personal correspondence, essays, and other media.

Perhaps this is absolute madness, given the time pressures we are under. Yet, is this not exactly the kind of thing that the global canon of core texts contains? The oral performance of an ancient epic, the wise sayings of a sage, a prophet's edited *logia*, a preacher's homilies, the *Bhagavad Gita*, Confucius' *Analects*, the Gospel of John, the *Pensées* of Pascal, Hahneman's *Organon of the Medical Art*, the *Maxims* of Goethe, the music and *materia medica* of Abbess Hildegarde of Bingen, the personal correspondence of George Washington Carver, and Zora Neale Hurston's *Mules and Men* have all contributed immeasurably to our intellectual advance. They are core texts that reflect, in some instances, records of chance encounters and in others a lifetime's contemplation. Would most of them qualify the authors for tenure in today's colleges or universities? One wonders. Do they illustrate the kind of broad and deep intellectual engagement we want most to see in our students today? Indeed, they do. Do we have in place the kinds of structures needed to encourage intellectual output of this kind on the part of faculty or students? I am less than certain. We award and praise derivative discourse that consists, in whole or part, of the critique or deconstruction of works valued because of their capacity to chart the unknown, propose new ways of seeing the world, or offer new insights into ourselves. Yet, one wonders if we have sufficient courage to support and reward truly pioneering thought that takes many years to refine, or to teach our students and muster within ourselves the abilities needed to generate it?

Are we providing sufficient opportunity and training in reading? Are students given the room in densely crowded undergraduate curricula to take courses that will teach them to write poems, produce freehand sketches, compose music, operate a camera, make a film, throw a pot, paint in acrylic, plant a garden, knit a scarf, crochet a hat, or even sew on a button? Graduates seem to be leaving our colleges and universities with an increasingly narrow set of basic proficiencies. The languages with which they can express themselves creatively seem quite modest when compared to the people whose classics form the basis of their education. The transmuting touch of Renaissance Humanism, experienced in its pure or various derived forms, is in danger of becoming an anachronism whose reality is less concrete for today's graduates than Neo's cinematic awakening in the *Matrix* trilogy.

We appear to be facing a systemic problem that touches faculty, students, staff, and administrators in higher education. Is there anything we can do about this? In my less sanguine moments, I think there is little hope. The internal machinery of academe and the external energies that fuel it *commodify* academic productivity and student success to such an extent that quantifiable measures such as books, articles, test scores, and grades take on greater value than less tangible outcomes such as values, transformed consciousness, and dreams. However, there are times when I am hopeful that there are ways that we as mentors to undergraduate and graduate students can, in fact, make a difference. It will take some creativity to bring core texts, contemplation, and the Renaissance Ideal from the periphery to the center of what we do in higher education. Above all, I think of the kind of guidance provided by Athena, in the guise of Mentor, to the youthful Telemachus in Homer's *Odyssey* – guidance that gives those about to undertake a new stage in their educational pilgrimage the capacity for contemplative thought, the courage to discover and use their own voice, and the drive to discover the unknown.

I propose three steps: (1) make the teaching of multi-dimensional reading and other basic skills at a higher level the backbone of an undergraduate curriculum, (2) empower students (and faculty) to make space in their schedules for introspection while at the same time promoting discussion about the place of silence and periodic *disengagement* in the life of the mind, and (3) begin the study of core texts with an examination of the self and the social world within which individual selves are situated.

Much of what I have in mind is not novel. Others have already suggested and implemented parts of it in venues within and outside of academe.[5] If there is anything really new about what I am proposing, it has more to do with the *teleological* objective of the plan, which is to produce people who self-identify as liberal artists, poets, and humanists. In sum, I am advocating an educational curriculum, particularly during the first year of college or university life, geared toward the production of *polymaths* rather than *specialists*. I think our aim should be to help students become intellectuals capable of producing works of art, scientific theorems, sculptures, physical edifices, and ideas that are *primary* rather than *secondary*. We need women and men who are passionate about learning and use the holistic engagement of multiple fields of knowledge to deepen their appreciation of the world and its peoples and to empower them to become responsible protectors thereof.

Our students are in need of higher order reading skills. These include: (1) the ability to classify a work by *genre*, (2) strategies appropriate for understanding and interpreting poetry, narrative, scientific writing, etc., and (3) the capacity to do the kind of multilayered reading advocated by Adler and Van Doren in their classic *How to Read a Book* (1972). They also need to grasp that genre assignments are imperfect constructs that often cannot classify works that are *transgressive*. They need to be given permission to do what many of us learned to do as children: to read oneself slowly into the narrative of a book and let its sights, sounds, smells, and tactile sensations come alive. To do so, they will need to behave in a manner that is completely counterintuitive and step away from the modes of seeing and thinking about the world that were common to the highly structured educational system in which they were embedded before their collegiate matriculation. Reflective reading, nuanced reading takes time. To make the most of this experience one needs not only a strategy for reading, but for personal annotation as well. The ability to mark a text is becoming a lost art. Moreover, the use of a journal to carry on a conversation with the books one reads appears to be, if my experience with students is an accurate indicator, the exception rather than the norm today. The compilation of *sententiae* or *maxims*, an exercise that allows one to reflect on the central ideas of core texts and to think about their larger meaning, is also anomalous. We also need to help students learn to read texts in their original languages so that they can enter directly into the thought world of authors. No student should feel comfortable if she or he cannot read a rudimentary musical score or understand basic mathematical symbols and notations. These too are languages. The ability to draw, express ideas using various poetic verse forms, or use basic principles of composition to set up and expose a basic photograph should be part of the repertoire of every student. We live in an information-rich environment. Words, visual images, and sounds constitute a currency of greater value than precious metals and money. Freedom, the alleviation of poverty, the healing of physical diseases, and the cure of social ills are dependent on a literate, multilingual, well-read populace fully conversant with global issues and knowledgeable of the artistic and intellectual heritage on which today's world rests. Twenty-first-century life will increasingly demand the ability to communicate persuasively in written and oral form.

We need to reclaim introspection as an indispensable component of the academic enterprise. In order to do so, we will have to rethink our relationship with calendars and electronic networking devices and machines – e.g., PDAs, cell phones, computers, and automobiles. Encounters with core texts, as we all know, cannot easily be scheduled in fifteen-minute appointment slots. Those we teach and mentor will need, at times, to be convinced of the value of unplugging themselves periodically from the networks that link them with family and friends. There is some evidence suggesting that today's so-called "Millennial" students are more comfortable than their "Generation X" predecessors with belonging to social aggregates and with parental involvement in decision making. Consequently, we may have a difficult job as teachers convincing them that liberal learning that involves reading – and being read by – core texts requires a considerable amount of *alone time* and silence and that there are some texts best engaged when not multi-tasking. It may be that the most prudent course of action here is to redouble our efforts to help students view everything as text and to *problematize* their reception, reading, and interpretation of such texts.

This leads to my third proposal, that we begin the encounter with core texts by reading self and society – two foci of the old Core experience at Notre Dame. Here one might make texts such as race, ethnicity, gender, and sexuality subject matter for close reading. Personal adornment – e.g., clothing, jewelry, and even hairstyle – could also be points of entry for more probing explorations of the human body as text. Language, emotions, the physical senses could then be taken up as discussion points. By beginning the core text experience with a study of what is perhaps our most basic text, we will send a subtle message that hermeneutical proficiency is an essential life skill for those hoping to thrive in a world saturated with texts. Sustained reflection on one's reception of texts can productively begin with a critical examination of one's mode of handling the body – i.e., with what anthropologist Marcel Mauss termed "body techniques" almost four decades ago (1968). By beginning with the self, one can then examine other texts for which the body has served, according to some, as primordial pattern. Here I refer to the social world in particular. Moving from here to a study of other texts might help to highlight the fact that what Umberto Eco has said about novels applies equally to humans. Eco suggests that a novel is "a machine for generating interpretations" (1984: 2). One could just as well say that humans are *texts* that generate *texts*.

I conclude with the questions with which I began. A core text: what is it? Introspection and liberal education: what do we make of them? Coursework: what is its purpose? Twenty-first-century Renaissance *polymaths*: should we aim to produce them? Faculty and administrators: what should our role be in promoting the reading of core texts? My proposed solutions are modest and will be seen, I trust, as a part of a *reflexive midrash* aimed at furthering our collective consideration of these difficult questions. My hope is that we will take them on, nonetheless, with some degree of urgency.

Globalization has made ours an increasingly complex world that generates scores of multifaceted and incredibly difficult texts each year. In spite of appearances to the contrary, the day-to-day world we occupy is filled with incongruities, asymmetries, and mysteries. Curricula that stress reading, introspection, and the cultivation of a diverse set of interpretive skills are much needed if we are to produce adults capable of reading a world whose *exoteric* and *esoteric* realities resist simple generalizations.

Those best equipped to take on the challenge of twenty-first-century life, to discern its hidden rhythms, to appreciate its beauty, and to root out its systemic evils, are likely to be those who possess multiple intelligences. As those who have chosen to help guide them, we too will need to cultivate some of the same proficiencies. It will not be easy, but it is a noble calling. As one who has chosen the path of the scholar-teacher-administrator, a decision that some see as alignment with what is referred to in the *Star Wars* epic as the "dark side of the force," my choice is to stretch to the extent possible beyond my own artistic and intellectual comfort zone. I do this because I think our greatest gift to the students we teach and the institutions we serve is to model the core text experience in all that we undertake. We each need to read, inscribe, and at times re-inscribe the texts that fall within our domain in ways that are *uniquely* our own.

That is why on weekdays you will find me pouring over budgets, attending meetings, teaching, advising students, and, when time allows, coaching tennis. When I can rise early enough, I work on my early Hebrew Poetry manuscript. On the occasional Sunday, I preach. I almost always carry a sketchbook or camera, though the quality of my creative output is that of neither Picasso nor

Gordon Parks. I do my own sewing. I talk to our dog and our houseplants. I write love poems to my wife. And at least once a month, you will likely find me late on a Friday or Saturday night, harmonica in hand, performing in a Michiana nightspot – reading and playing the Blues.

Notes

1 Taking the Italian Renaissance as an illustrative case in point, Nauert has noted that a shift in focus occurred during this period – i.e., away from the medieval universities' emphasis on logic, science, and speculation and toward those grammatical and rhetorical proficiencies deemed useful for informed decision making in public life (13-15). My (re)-conceptualization of this educational ideal for twenty-first-century education sees it as a *matrix* encompassing the pragmatic and humanistic focus of the fourteenth century, a dynamic and continually evolving disciplinary structure that is derived from, yet significantly expands, the older *trivium* and *quadrivium*, and a *telos* aimed at equipping *all* members of the global community for responsible citizenship. An interesting popular appropriation of Renaissance Humanism can be seen in the work of Gelb (see Works Cited).

2 See, for example, the curricular profile prepared by Cross and Wright in "The Study of the Old Testament at Harvard."

3 I find particularly salutary Leon Battista Alberti's assertion in the Prologue to his *De Pictura* (*On Painting*) that achievement in any artistic or scientific endeavor is more a function of diligence than of natural giftedness.

4 I was glad to see this affirmed in the recent work of Sample (55-70).

5 There are even popular writers who have espoused building adult continuing education programs around some of them.

Works Cited

Adler, Mortimer and Charles Van Doren. *How to Read a Book.* 1940 ed. New York: MJF Books, 1972.

Alberti, Leon Battista. *On Painting.* Trans. M. Kemp. New York: Penguin, 1991.

Cross, Frank Moore, Jr. and G. Ernest Wright. "The Study of the Old Testament at Harvard." *Harvard Divinity Bulletin* 25 (1961): 14-20.

Eco, Umberto. *Postscript to the Name of the Rose.* Trans. W. Weaver. New York: Harcourt, 1984.

Gelb, Michael J. *How to Think like Leonardo da Vinci.* New York: Delacorte, 1998.

---. *The How to Think Like Leonardo da Vinci Workbook.* New York: Dell, 1999.

Mauss, Marcel. "Les techniques du corps." In *Sociologie et Anthropologie.* Paris: Presses Universitaires de France, 1968.

Nauert, Charles G. *Humanism and the Culture of Renaissance Europe*. Cambridge: Cambridge UP, 2006.

Sample, Steven B. *The Contrarian's Guide to Leadership*. San Francisco: Jossey-Bass, 2002.

Adverbial Play in Plato's *Ion*

David Roochnik
Boston University

This paper explores Plato's use of a particular part of speech, the adverb, in a single dialogue, the *Ion*. With it I hope, first, simply to reinforce a conviction most readers of the dialogues already share: Plato is a consummate literary artist who uses his medium brilliantly. Second, and more important, this one case illustrates how Plato is able to utilize his literary skill in the service of his larger project, namely raising philosophical questions.

What follows focuses on the use of adverbs and adverbial constructions that (mainly) modify inflections of *legein* in the *Ion*, a dialogue which explores the "old quarrel" between philosophy and poetry.[1] I demonstrate that there is a consistent pattern to the way Plato has Socrates and Ion use their adverbs and how this pattern, once uncovered, draws the reader into the crucial question of the dialogue: Is it philosophical or poetic language that constitutes the perfection, the highest achievement, of the human capacity for *logos*?

Consider the following passages:

T1: 530b2. After Ion explains that he has won first prize at Epidaurus, Socrates says to him, *eu legeis*, literally "you speak well."[2] While this is an innocuous colloquialism, which can be translated as "congratulations," it also encapsulates the basic question of the dialogue: What exactly does it mean to speak well?[3] Is it when one recites the words of Homer in splendid, rhapsodic enchantment, or when one uses the plain words of philosophy in the attempt to articulate the truth?

T2: 530b10-c6. Socrates asserts, without argument, that it is incumbent upon the rhapsode to understand the "thought" (*dianoia*), and not only the words, of the poetry he sings. The rhapsode must be an interpreter (*hermênea*) of the poet's thought. This he cannot "do well" (*kalôs poien*: 530c5) unless he knows (*gignôskonta*) what the poet means (*legei*).

Socrates' assertions provoke a question: Has he, as many commentators have suggested, imposed an exaggerated and inappropriately epistemic demand upon the rhapsode?[4] In other words, why must the rhapsode know the meaning of the poet's words in order to perform his task "well?" Furthermore, what does the ever-flexible *kalôs* mean in this context? At first glance, no more than *eu*. But its meaning also tends towards the aesthetic. In order to recite "beautifully," why must the rhapsode understand what Homer means? Even further, what do "mean" and "know" and "understand" (*ekmanthanein*: 530c1) mean in this context?

T3: 530c7. In a master stroke of irony, Plato has Ion respond to Socrates by saying, *alêthê legeis*: "you speak truthfully."[5] Ion, the rhapsode, describes and so evaluates Socrates' statement on the basis of its truth content, while Socrates, the philosopher, demands of Ion that he speak *kalôs*. Again, Ion's response is colloquial, but through the adverbs, an issue is being articulated: How does the poet or the rhapsode speak "well?" How does he do his job "beautifully" (or "well" or "admirably" or "finely")? By speaking the truth? Or by giving a moving, convincing, electrifying performance whose connection to the truth is far more tenuous?

T4: 531a1-b9. Socrates asks Ion, "are you clever only about Homer, or about Hesiod and Archilochus as well?" Only Homer, answers Ion. What about those passages where Homer and Hesiod say the same things about the same subject? In that case, Ion would "expound them similarly."

Socrates continues this line of questioning. When Homer and Hesiod say different things about, for example, prophecy, who is able to expound what they say "more finely" (*kallion*: 531b5), Ion or one of the good prophets? One of the prophets, Ion answers. Socrates asks, "And if you were one of the prophets, and if you were able to expound the things they say similarly, wouldn't you know how to expound the things they say differently?" (531b7-9).

The point Socrates makes here is one he will later elaborate (see **T5, T9,** and **T13** below). If persons A and B speak about the same subject X, they can do so either similarly or differently. If they do so differently, then only the expert in subject X can successfully "expound" what A and B have to say. So, for example, if Homer and Hesiod both speak about prophecy, and do so differently, then it is only the trained prophet who can "expound" both their statements.

It is clear that by "similar" and "different" Socrates refers *only* to truth content. By his lights, what A and B say can be reduced to propositions that are either true or false. For example, Homer and Hesiod might both say that prophets read the paths of flying birds. This is true, and so they speak similarly. Homer might say that prophets read the livers of goats, while Hesiod might counter that they read the kidneys (which, let us assume, is false). In this case, the two statements are different, and only one of them is true. It is the trained prophet, and not Ion, who will be able to "expound" what they have to say. In this context, which has been thoroughly engineered by Socrates, "expound" means to tell whether a statement is true or false.

This is a strange way to approach the art of the poet. A poet might say, "prophets read kidneys," not simply in order to make a factually accurate statement about prophecy, but in order to say something fitting or beautiful in its context. Since it is possible in some cases that false statements, or errors, may well be fitting or beautiful, a good exposition or interpretation of the passage need not be restricted to determining whether its statements are true or false. Socrates, however, seems to insist that it be so restricted. In this sense, he imposes upon the discussion an excessively epistemic notion of poetry, for at the outset he seems to equate "speaking well" with "speaking truthfully." If this is in fact what he does, then he is precisely begging the question that the "old quarrel" demands to be debated.

T5: 531d12-e3. "Therefore, my dear friend Ion, whenever many men speak about number, and one man speaks best (*arista*), will someone be able to identify who it is that speaks well (*eu*)?" Yes, and this will be the person who can also identify who speaks badly (*kakôs*: 531e2), namely the person trained in arithmetic.

When A and B speak about number, and do so differently, it is only the person knowledgeable in arithmetic who can correctly identify who speaks well and who does not. Once again, Socrates equates "best" or "well" with "truthfully." The only job left to the rhapsode is identifying what is true and false in the poem. To reiterate: through stipulating the meaning of this series of related adverbs, Socrates establishes the rules of, and thereby dominates, his examination of Ion.

T6: 532c2. The refutation of poor Ion's claim to possess an "art" of, or "expertise" (*technê*) in, rhapsodizing – a claim Socrates puts into his hapless mouth (530b7) – continues. Only if one can identify and speak about both those who speak badly and those who speak well on a given subject, can one claim to understand or have mastered that subject. Ion claims to be able to speak only about Homer, and not about poets such as Hesiod and Archilochus. Indeed, says Ion, "I simply doze off" (*atechnôs nustazô*) whenever the discussion is about another poet. This is sure evidence, according to Socrates at least, that Ion has no real *technê*. "It is clear," he says, "that you are incapable of speaking about Homer with expertise and knowledge" (*technêi kai episêmêi*) (532c7). It is equally clear that Plato's use of *atechnôs* ("simply"), which without accentuation would be indistinguishable from *atechnôs* ("without expertise" or "artlessly"), is a pun.[6]

What Socrates has done is effectively rendered the adverbial construction *technêi kai episêmêi* equivalent to such positive adverbs as *eu* and *kalôs*. To speak well or beautifully is now equivalent to speaking with *technê*. To speak badly is to speak *atechnôs,* ("without *technê*"). At least according to the philosopher.

T7: 532d6. After Ion has described him as wise, Socrates responds, *bouloimên an se alêthê legein*: "if only you were speaking truthfully." Socrates' words echo Ion's earlier use of the same phrase (530c7, 531d3, 532a8). It seems likely, then, that Socrates is subtly rebuking Ion. From the perspective of the philosopher, the rhapsode is in no position to identify what is true or false. Ion has been overly ambitious in thinking he has the capacity correctly to attach the privileged adverb *alêthê* to the verb *legein*.

T8: 532d8. It is, says Socrates, Ion and the other rhapsodes and actors who are and say things that are really wise (532d6). By contrast, "I," says Socrates, "say nothing other than the truth." Here Socrates substitutes *t'alêthê* for *alêthê*, but the difference is inconsequential. He reserves the privileged adverb for himself. He maintains the equivalence he has imposed on the discussion: speaking well equals speaking truthfully.

Socrates finalizes his refutation of Ion's claim to having a *technê* with a series of examples. When someone is clever at determining and articulating whether a given painter paints well or not, he is capable of commenting on any painter whatsoever. It is similarly true when someone is clever at explaining whether a sculptor does well or not. The point, again, is this: when someone is truly knowledgeable about a given field, he should be able to comment on anyone who enters that field regardless of whether the work is good or bad.[7] Ion claims to be knowledgeable about poetry. But he can speak only about Homer, and not poets he takes to be inferior, like Hesiod. Therefore, Ion's description of himself as he listens to lesser poets, *atechnôs nustazô* (532c2), is (if we disregard the accents) exactly accurate.

T9: 533c5-7. How is it, the now puzzled Ion asks, that about Homer *kallist' anthrôpôn legô*, "I speak more finely than all men," and that everybody says that "I speak well" (*eu legein*)? In other words, now that he has been shown that he lacks expertise, Ion seems genuinely perplexed about the source of his own success.

T10: 533e6-534d1. Socrates responds to Ion's perplexity with a lengthy speech describing the inspiration of the poets. Good poets, he says, do not speak "by

533e6). They are full of god, out of their minds, possessed by the electrifying power of the Muse.[8] Socrates' evidence for this is the following: each poet is restricted to producing only works of a single genre. An epic poet produces only epics, a lyric only lyrics, and so on. If poets possessed a genuine *technê* in (or of) poetry, then, since a *technê* provides expertise in an entire field, they would be able to produce works in all the genres. Socrates states his principle: "if about one [subject] they know well (*kalôs*) how to speak with expertise (*technêi*), they would know about all the rest" (534c6-7).

Socrates' point here extends the one he has been making all along. When someone possesses "technical" knowledge, he gains mastery over the entirety of the field. This the poet, as well as the rhapsode, fails to do, for he is restricted to the individual genre in which he works. (Or, in Ion's case, to the individual poet with whom he is fluent.) This is sure evidence that they do not have technical knowledge, and their successful productions are therefore the result of non-epistemic inspiration.

What is astonishing about this passage is that Socrates gives the poets credit for a rather sophisticated understanding of themselves. They *admit* that they are inspired when they describe themselves as follows:

T11: 534b1-3. "Poets tell us that they gather songs at honey-flowing springs, from glades and gardens of the Muses, and that they bear songs to us as bees carry honey" (534b1-2). As such, they quite appropriately use a poetic simile to say who they are. For this reason, Socrates says of them, "they speak truthfully" (*alêthê legousi*: 534b3). The use of the adverb here is another stroke of brilliant irony. The poets speak truthfully, but only when they describe themselves poetically. They speak truthfully, but only in tacitly confessing their incapacity to speak the plain truth and admitting that they are not philosophers.

T12: 534d8. Sure proof that poets are inspired and do not produce their work by means of a *technê* is provided by the case of Tynnichos. He had never produced a poem worth mentioning until one day he came up with the paean that is now on everyone's lips. Such a spontaneous and unexpected act of creativity must, just as he himself says, "simply" or "artlessly" (*atechnôs*) "be an invention of the Muses." Again, the adverbial pun is unmistakable: Tynnichos' unreproduced work was the result of the Muses' inspiration and so was produced without technical expertise.

According to Ion, Socrates speaks "well" (*eu*) in describing the poets' inspiration. But he does not speak so well that Ion would agree with him that he is "out of his mind" when it comes to speaking beautifully of Homer. And so Socrates is forced to refute Ion once again, and here Plato's adverbial play becomes most pronounced.

T13: 537c3. First, Socrates asks, "which of the subjects that Homer speaks about do you speak about well (*eu*)? Surely not all of them?" (536e1-2). Yes, says Ion, he can speak well about them all. What about the passage in which Nestor offers some fine points about chariot-driving to his son Antilochus? "Who knows better, Ion, whether Homer speaks these lines correctly (*orthôs*), the doctor or the chariot driver?" (537c1-3). The chariot driver, obviously, for he has the *technê* of chariot-driving.

This is the most critical, and potentially objectionable, substitution of adverbs. Ion claims to speak "well" about all passages in Homer. Socrates takes "speak well" to mean to "speak correctly," that is, to decide if Homer speaks correctly. And the person who can do this, the master of correctness, is the man with the proper *technê*, for he can judge the truth of Homer's assertions about chariot-driving. But of course the same question raised above must be asked again: is the ability to determine what is correct equivalent to "speaking well" about Homer? Is speaking well equivalent to speaking with technical expertise? According to Socrates, it seems to be.

T14. 538b1-3. Who knows better (*kallion*) whether Homer "speaks finely" (*kalôs legei*) or not about chariot-driving? The chariot-driver, of course. Yet again, the meaning of *kalôs* has drawn extremely close to that of *orthôs*: the chariot-driver knows whether Homer speaks with technical accuracy about his subject.

T15. 538c4-5. The doctor, and not the rhapsode, is able to "determine finely" (*diagnônai kalôs*) whether Homer "speaks correctly" (*orthôs legei*) about medical matters.

T16. 538d5. The fisherman, and not the rhapsode, is better able to judge whether Homer "speaks finely" (*legei...kalôs*) about fishing.

Through the examples above, Socrates' principle becomes plain: he who possesses technical knowledge about a specific field can judge whether Homer speaks well or badly, *eu* or *kakôs* (538e4). This is a result of the equivalence Socrates has foisted upon the discussion, namely "finely" equals "correctly," *kalôs* equals *orthôs*. Since the obligation of the rhapsode is to speak *kalôs* about his poet, he fails. Indeed, it is implied by the passage that the poet himself does not speak "finely," for he does not speak "correctly," with technical accuracy.

These adverbs have told a little story. Through his character Socrates, Plato exhibits his preference for philosophy over poetry. This is hardly surprising. But what is worth noting is how Socrates manages to state and insinuate his preference. Through Socrates' repeated substitution of adverbs, Ion unwittingly plays with a stacked deck. If speaking well is speaking correctly, if interpreting a poem well is determining which of its propositions are true and which false, if poetry can be reduced to an encyclopedia of technical information, then the rhapsode is in no position to speak finely about the poet, and the poet himself is relegated to a status decidedly inferior to the philosopher. But it is precisely these assumptions that need to be questioned in order to adjudicate the "old quarrel" between philosophy and poetry, to determine what is ultimately the finest form of human *logos,* and this neither Socrates nor Ion explicitly does. Perhaps the only excuse for Socrates' shameless manipulation of Ion is that through his playful treatment of the adverbs, Plato invites the reader to ask the very questions that the participants in the dialogue seem to ignore.

Notes

1 This phrase comes from *Republic* 607b.
2 My Greek text is Burnet. Translations are my own.
3 Andrew Miller suggests "congratulations" (2).
4 W. C. Guthrie (205) makes just this charge. To some extent, it is answered by T.F. Morris.
5 I consistently treat this phrase as an adverbial accusative.
6 David Roochnik discusses this pun at length.
7 Rosamond Kent Sprague effectively explains this theme in the *Ion.*
8 E.N. Tigerstedt presents the most thorough discussion of this passage.

Works Cited

Bloom, Allan. *The Republic of Plato.* New York: Basic Books, 1968.
Burnet, John. *Platonis Opera* III. Oxford: Oxford UP, 1903.
Guthrie, W.C. *A History of Greek Philosophy* IV. Cambridge: Cambridge UP, 1975.
Miller, Andrew. *Plato's Ion.* Bryn Mawr: Bryn Mawr Commentaries, 1984.
Morris, T.F. "Plato's *Ion* on What Poetry is About," *Ancient Philosophy* 13 (1993): 265-272.
Roochnik, David. "Plato's Use of ATEXNVS." *Phoenix* 41 (1987): 255-63.
Sprague, Rosamond Kent. *Plato's Philosopher-King.* Columbia: University of South Carolina Press, 1976.
Tigerstedt, E.N. *Plato's Idea of Poetical Inspiration.* Helsinki: Societas Scientarum Fennica, 1969.

Remembering Ancient Truths: The Four Roots of Plato's Recollection

Max J. Latona
Saint Anselm College

Plato's Doctrine of Recollection (*anamnesis*), as presented in the *Meno* (as well as the *Phaedo* and *Phaedrus*), claims that all knowledge is contained in the soul prior to birth, that it is forgotten at birth, and that all learning in this lifetime is a matter of recollecting what one already knows. This theory appears to run up against common experience in several ways, not the least of which is that it appears to deny that knowledge can be transmitted from one individual to the next. Indeed, it is perhaps partly out of adherence to this transmission-model of learning that many interpreters of Plato, from Aristotle to the present, have viewed the Doctrine of Recollection as outlandish and have struggled to understand Plato's intentions in developing the doctrine. In fact, a survey of recent literature reveals at least three theories about the origins and meaning of the Doctrine of Recollection – in turn Socratic, metaphysical, and Pythagorean – all of which interpret the doctrine exclusively as an internal process of reminiscence. In the following analysis of Plato's *Meno*, after briefly reviewing these three versions of recollection, as well as an obvious inconsistency for Plato in each, I will argue for a fourth reading of the doctrine as a necessary supplement to the first three. This interpretation reads recollection as emerging from the mythological tradition and as tacitly reinforcing remembrance as a collective, public act (in addition to any internal, private character it might have). In other words, Plato's Doctrine of Recollection should be understood at least in part as an argument for the importance of preserving tradition, understood precisely as the transmission of knowledge from one individual or generation to the next.

According to one prominent school of interpretation, one that arguably traces its origins back to Aristotle himself, the theory of recollection emerges from the Socratic manner of pursuing philosophy and, specifically, as a Platonic response to a problem accompanying the Socratic examination (*elenchus*) and its search for definitions. This is apparent in the *Meno*, in which the Socratic *elenchus* fails to make much progress at all, as Meno (a typical Socratic interlocutor) provides definition after definition and Socrates reveals the flaws in each, the most common of which are that the definitions lack sufficient universality or beg the question in some important way. Meno then becomes perplexed, begins to call Socrates names (specifically, a "torpedo fish," insofar as he is guilty of numbing Meno's mind), and poses the following problem in exasperation:

> How will you look for [virtue], Socrates, when you do not know at all
> what it is? How will you aim to search for something that you do not
> know at all? If you should meet with it, how will you know that this
> is the thing that you did not know? (80d)[1]

In other words, the problem with any inquiry (*dizesis*) about anything is that in order to grasp an answer to any question, one must first possess all the relevant criteria that will enable the inquirer to recognize the correct answer *as* the correct answer. On the one hand, if all the relevant criteria are already known, then one knows everything important that is to be known, and there is no need to search for an answer; on the other hand, if the object of inquiry is not known, then one lacks the sufficient criteria by which to judge any possible answer correct. Plato was arguably aware of this problem with the Socratic method (after all, as the method is presented in the early, "Socratic" dialogues, Socrates and his interlocutor typically fail to arrive at a satisfactory definition). Thus, according to this view of recollection's origins, Plato saw the need for a constructive theory of knowledge to remedy the deficiencies of the Socratic method and posed the Doctrine of Recollection precisely as such a remedy. The reasoning is this: if persistent questioning is to work as a method of teaching, then the knowledge of the truth must already be contained in some latent fashion within the mind of the questioned (if not the questioner), and the role of the teacher here is merely to act as a midwife and assist in its birthing to memory.

This theory of recollection's origins suggests that recollection is an internal process that happens only through the type of rigorous inquiry exemplified in the Socratic *elenchus*, a type of rigorous inquiry in which the ordinary run of men do not participate on an everyday basis (otherwise, there would have been no need for a Socrates!). By the same token, it suggests that most people rarely, if ever, engage in this internal act of recollection (and therefore rarely engage in genuine learning); for as argued by Scott in *Recollection and Experience: Plato's Theory of Learning and Its Successors*, the knowledge that is subject to

Plato's Theory of Learning and Its Successors, the knowledge that is subject to recollection (i.e., the only kind of knowledge there is) is the kind of specialized knowledge achieved by structured, perhaps even disciplinary, investigations into a given subject matter. This is borne out by the text of the *Meno*, where Socrates attempts to illustrate the process of recollection in Meno's slave using the discipline of geometry as the subject matter for inquiry.

Now what is ironic about the demonstration that Socrates employs is that the principle Socrates hopes to help midwife in the slave is one that was cultivated in an intellectual discipline with archaic roots. Regardless of how recollection of a geometrical principle might happen as an ahistorical process internal to the individual, it would not be denied by Plato that geometry, as a discipline, had a history of development and transmission over succeeding generations and cultures. Although its history prior to the time of Socrates is sketchy, we are fairly certain that it originated in near Eastern civilizations (in fact, the Greeks themselves attributed the origins of mathematics to the Egyptians) and was cultivated and further developed by the Ionians and later by the Pythagoreans. Indeed, the principle to be established with the slave-boy in the *Meno* is one that, in antiquity, was strongly associated with the Pythagoreans, a fact of which Plato was doubtless aware.[2] Indeed, Plato makes no attempt to hide the fact (it would have been fruitless to do so) that there existed in the fourth century a tradition of geometers and mathematicians: at *Meno* 85b, Socrates specifically refers to the masters (*sophistai*) of the craft of geometry. All of this raises an important puzzle for Plato's doctrine: if Plato argues that all learning is merely a matter of an internal process of recollection, what role, if any, do disciplines play as they are developed over time? How does Plato make sense of the apparent incongruity between, on the one hand, arguing that knowledge is not passed on from one individual to the next and, on the other hand, demonstrating his point with a theoretical discipline that the Greeks themselves acknowledged as having been inherited from previous generations and cultures?

A second theory about recollection's origins looks to Plato's metaphysics for an explanation. According to this view, supported by Cornford, Bostock, and others, Plato developed the theory in order to satisfy the epistemological demands of his Theory of Forms.[3] As it happens, some support for this reading also lies within the *Meno*, particularly where Socrates implores Meno:

> Even if virtues are many and various, all of them have one and the same form which makes them virtues, and it is right to look to this when asked to make clear what virtue is. (72c)

According to Socrates here, knowledge of virtue is to be found by looking to the one common form (*eidos*) shared by all instances of virtue. In these remarks we find latent the problem of the *one and the many*, which lies at the heart of Plato's metaphysics, as it is articulated in other dialogues. According to Plato's developed Theory of Forms, it is impossible to arrive at knowledge of the *one* on the basis of experience of particular instances of the one. First, no amount of experience of particular instances will amount to a true universal insofar as the universal arrived at will always be limited to the imperfect and incomplete set of particulars experienced.[4] Comparison of like instances is also of no help inasmuch as one must already know what the universal is, or what is essential to it, in order to select instances of a like kind to compare with one another. Recollection is posited as an answer to this problem insofar as it suggests that knowledge of the particulars in experience is made possible by knowledge of the one Form, and not the reverse. It is because I already know what virtue is, in some important way, that I am able to recognize individual virtuous things and to call them virtuous. Thus, in contrast to the previous theory of recollection's origins, this theory claims that recollection was developed by Plato in order to explain ordinary concept formation and language use: we cannot experience or speak about things like equality, beauty, virtue, etc. without first understanding what these things are, i.e., the universal, ideal Form that is only imperfectly reflected in sense experience. That universal Form must be known in some way prior to experience and linguistic acquisition, since it is a condition for the possibility of such experience and language in the first place.

Although this theory of recollection's origins avoids the burden of explaining the development of disciplines over time, it encounters its own puzzling juxtaposition of the ahistorical and the historical. Here, recollection is offered as an internal process to explain how we acquire ordinary language, and yet the doctrine is itself articulated by Socrates through a language, Attic Greek, that possesses a diachrony, passed on as it was from one generation to the next. Plato himself, we know, is attentive to the etymological history of his own language, as attested by the dialogue *Cratylus*. In that text, he argues that although the words we use to designate things developed and changed over time, these words are not arbitrary but have a "natural correctness" in that they originated as an expression of the very essence of the thing named. This means that to learn the name of a thing is to learn its essence or Form, and to learn its essence or Form is to learn its name. The question is this: if words and their meanings are known through an internal process of reminiscence, how do we explain the obvious phenomenon that the Athenians of Plato's day learned Attic Greek (not Ionic Greek, not Persian), precisely because it was handed down by the previous generation of Athenians? If language is ahistorically recollected, how do we explain the history of linguistic transmission?[5]

Yet another theory of recollection's origins is supported by the *Meno*. When Socrates first introduces the theory, he quotes the following lines from Pindar:

> Persephone will return to the sun above in the ninth year the souls of those from whom she will exact punishment for old miseries, and from these come noble kings, mighty in strength and greatest in wisdom, and for the rest of time men will call them sacred heroes.
> (81b-c)

These lines suggest that soul is immortal and that after death it ascends into the aetheric heavens whereupon it receives postmortem punishment, only to be reborn again in human form. Immortality, ascent, and transmigration of souls – these are telltale signs of Pythagoreanism, the ancient philosophical and religious school that is accordingly cited by Cameron, Burnet, Taylor, and Gulley to have been the inspiration for Plato's Doctrine of Recollection.[6] The Pythagoreans thought that just as forgetfulness of the soul's divinity was tied up with its fallen status, so too the practice of remembering was important for its ascent once again into the heavens.[7] They reportedly developed memory practices intended to help purify the soul and enable it to escape the cycle of birth and death. Plato too, as indicated in this poetic introduction to his theory, as well as in the *Phaedo* and the *Phaedrus,* thought that recollection is important for the soul's purification (*katharsis*) and ascent to the Plain of Truth.

Once more, we might pause and reflect on what is yet another puzzle. According to this theory of its origins and significance, recollection takes on the esoteric character of a spiritual practice undertaken by the philosopher for the sake of purification of the soul. However, if, as Socrates declares in the *Meno*, all learning is recollection, then recollection must be something more, for how would Plato account for his own acknowledged dependence on the Pythagoreans for the learning of this important spiritual discipline? In other words, if all learning is recollection, what role do we assign to the historical transmission of religious practices and rituals?

Plato's solution to this now familiar problem gives us a fourth root for his Doctrine of Recollection. Again, regardless of whether we adopt the Socratic, metaphysical, or Pythagorean view of the origin and nature of the Doctrine of Recollection, or some combination of those theories, the same question has emerged: how does Plato account for the obvious role of tradition in handing down the conceptual knowledge, language, or practices that facilitate recollection as an internal process of remembrance? The key to understanding Plato's answer here can be found in Plato's view of myth. In the *Meno*, the Pythagorean myth about Persephone and the transmigration of souls at the outset of Plato's Doctrine of Recollection is emblematic of many of Plato's middle dialogues, namely, that Plato resorts to myth quite frequently in many of his most important dialogues and in some of the most important philosophical passages of these important dialogues. These tales are presented to the reader as traditional ones, as tales that have been handed down from remote antiquity through oral transmission. In the *Meno*, for example, the Doctrine of Recollection itself is traced to a myth that Socrates traces back to the words of "some wise priests and priestesses."[8] More often than not, however, the speaker in Plato's dialogue prefaces a myth by citing rather vaguely, "wise men" or "ancient legends" or simply "what has been said." These remarks overwhelmingly suggest that Plato wishes to impress upon the reader that these tales were not fashioned by him or by any identifiable individual; they are simply traditional. As for whether they truly are traditional, it appears that they were. According to Frutiger's research

If these myths were superfluous additions to the dialogues, then the matter would be of little importance. However, in most cases, the myth contains a thesis that is central to Plato's philosophical arguments.[10] Given this fact, what is remarkable is that the previous three theories have overlooked the evidence from the dialogues themselves as to Plato's view of the origins of human knowledge. Agonizing over whether recollection happens exclusively through Socratic method, ordinary experience, or a spiritual practice, interpreters have overlooked the testimony of Plato himself about a parallel process of remembrance that is just as crucial to learning as any internal process. After all, as Plato tells us, the Doctrine of Recollection is itself passed on to him from ancient myth and tradition. In other words, for Plato (as well as for those of us now reading Plato), whatever recollection may mean as an individual process, it clearly has a collective side: human knowledge is cultivated in society in large part by recollecting and reiterating the insights of the ancient thinkers. These insights are accordingly preserved in what is handed down from parent to child, teacher to student, bard to audience, priest to initiate, and, in short, generation to generation. While they do not relieve us of the duty to investigate and discover the truth for ourselves, it is these traditional tales and practices that serve as the vehicles for any such internal process of discovery. As Socrates remarks prior to retelling an old tale in the *Phaedrus* at 274c: "I can tell what I have heard from the ancients, who themselves knew the truth. If we could but discover it ourselves, why would we be concerned with the opinions of men?" (translation mine).

Notes

1 As Socrates rephrases it, "a man cannot search either for what he knows or for what he does not know. He cannot search for what he knows – since he knows it, there is no need to search – nor for what he does not know, for he does not know what to look for" (*Meno* 80e).

2 The principle in question is that the area of square A that is drawn on the diagonal of square B will be twice the magnitude of the area of square B.

3 See Cornford's *Plato's Theory of Knowledge: The Theaetetus and the Sophist of Plato* and Bostock's *Plato's Phaedo*.

4 Put differently, there will always remain the possibility of other, yet-to-be experienced realities that contribute different data to the universal.

5 For example, at *Meno* 85b Socrates acknowledges that the name (if not the significance) of the diagonal is learned from the *sophistai* of the day. It is a curious acknowledgment to make in the course of an argument that all learning is recollection.

6 See Cameron's *The Pythagorean Background of the Theory of Recollection*, Burnet's *Greek Philosophy. Part I, Thales to Plato*, Taylor's *Plato: The Man and His Work*, and Gulley's *Plato's Theory of Knowledge*.

7 See Jean Pierre Vernant. *Myth and Thought Among the Greeks*, 113-115.

7 See Jean Pierre Vernant. *Myth and Thought Among the Greeks*, 113-115.

8 At *Republic* X 614b, the Myth of Er is traced to Er the Pamphylian; at *Phaedrus* 244a, Socrates' entire second speech is attributed to Stesichorus of Himera; at *Symposium* 201d, Diotima's Ladder is said to have been heard at one time from "a Manitean woman named Diotima"; and at *Republic* III 414c, the Myth of the Metals is said to be "something Phoenician."

9 He concludes: "Quiconque se donne la peine de rechercher les sources des mythes platoniciens ne peut manquer de convenir que la part d'invention proprement dite y est minime" (266). The two myths that he concedes may – for lack of pre-Platonic precedent – be original to Plato are the Myth of the Cicadas (*Phaedrus* 259b-d) and the Myth of Theuth (*Phaedrus* 274c-5b), though Plato himself suggests there that the stories were already in currency.

10 For example, the *Republic's* Myth of the Metals provides Plato with the tripartite structure of human society that pervades his entire analysis of individual and social justice; and the *Symposium's* Myth of Diotima's Ladder presents the striated structure of beauty. In short, the Platonic myths infuse the dialogues with core philosophical claims, and it is precisely these claims that Plato claims to have received from tradition.

Works Cited

Bostock, David. *Plato's Phaedo*. Oxford: Clarendon, 1986.

Burnet, John. *Greek Philosophy. Part I, Thales to Plato*. London: Macmillan, 1914.

Cameron, Alister. *The Pythagorean Background of the Theory of Recollection*. Menasha: George Banta, 1938.

Cornford, Francis Macdonald. *Plato's Theory of Knowledge: The Theaetetus and the Sophist of Plato*. New York: Liberal Arts, 1957.

Frutiger, Perceval. *Les Mythes de Platon: Étude philosophique et littéraire*. Paris: Librairie Félix Alcan, 1930.

Gulley, Norman. *Plato's Theory of Knowledge*. London: Methuen, 1962.

Plato. *Meno*. Trans. G.M.A. Grube. In *Plato: Five Dialogues*. Indianapolis: Hackett, 1981.

Scott, Dominic. *Recollection and Experience: Plato's Theory of Learning and Its Successors*. Cambridge: Cambridge UP, 1995.

Taylor, A.E. *Plato: The Man and His Work*. London: Methuen, 1960.

Vernant, Jean Pierre. *Myth and Thought Among the Greeks*. London: Routledge & Kegan Paul, 1983.

Dante Is from Mars

Marc A. LePain
Assumption College

Dante, the pilgrim of the poet's *Comedy*, enters the heaven of Mars in Canto 14 of *Paradiso* and remains there until he ascends to the heaven of Jupiter midway through Canto 18. In these central cantos of *Paradiso*, the pilgrim meets his ancestor Cacciaguida, who reveals to him his fortune and his mission as poet. Dante's time in Mars is thus the most explicitly self-reflexive portion of his *Comedy*. Just what do these cantos teach us about who Dante is and who we are as readers of his *Comedy*?

As Dante enters the heaven of Mars, he hears a hymn sung by the warriors who first appear as lights streaming from the cross and whose singing holds him rapt. Dante states that, although he "could not tell what hymn it was, I knew it sang high praise since I heard "'Rise' and 'Conquer,' but I was as one who hears but cannot seize the sense" (*Par.* 14.123-126). [Sanza intender inno./ Ben m'accors' io ch'elli era d'alte lode/ però ch'a me venìa 'Resurgi' e 'Vinci'/ come a colui che non intende e ode]. The hymn is, as most commentators hold, a hymn to Christ celebrating his resurrection from the dead and his victory over sin. A mortal man still in the flesh would be incapable of grasping the rest of such a heavenly song.

There is, however, no known hymn to Christ that includes these two words. Moreover, the words can be understood either in the imperative or in the indicative second person singular. Without a context, either form is possible. The difference may matter little, however, for, just as the angel that Dante hears sing a beatitude on the terrace of Envy in *Purgatorio* 15, "Beati misericordes"; he adds in Italian the words, "Rejoice, you who conquer" (*Purg.* 15.39), [Godi, tu que vinci!], so the warriors in *Paradiso* may be singing to Dante himself and not to Christ, either urging him to "rise and conquer" or acclaiming him as you who "rise and conquer." The earlier beatitude's confirmation in the heaven of Mars would be, as Dante says he knew, "high praise" for Dante himself.

In light of what Dante states elsewhere about the art of speaking and writing, it is entirely possible and even plausible that the hymn might be addressed both to Christ and to Dante. That the same passage would hold two different and quite divergent meanings is in keeping with what in the *Convivio* Dante speaks of as *dissimulatio*, "a rhetorical figure [that is] highly praiseworthy and even necessary, namely when the words are addressed to one person and the meaning to another" (III.10.6).[1] As we shall see, Dante's account in the *Convivio* has a bearing on how one understands not only his present encounter with Cacciaguida but as well his *Comedy* as a whole.

As Dante advances in the heaven of Mars, he beholds in the canto that follows a fire like a star come forward from the cross to greet him in words more solemn because they are exclusively in Latin and they echo Virgil's account of Anchises' words to his son Aeneas in Elysium as well as St. Paul's brief account of an experience of rapture:

> O sanguis meus, o superinfusa
> gratia Dei, sicut tibi cui
> bis unquam celi ianua recluse?[2] (Par. 15.28-30)

Dante reports that the light added to his first words "things that were too deep to meet my understanding" (*Par.* 15.38-39). [cose, ch'io non lo 'ntesi, sì parlò profondo]. Yet soon enough he is able to hear what the light is saying once it descends to the level of his capacity to understand.

The first words he can grasp are a blessing to "you, three and one, that shows such favor to [my] seed" (*Par.* 15.47-48). The voice then declares that the one he calls his "son" has "at last appeased" his "long and happy hungering [he] drew from reading the great volume where both black and white are never changed" (*Par.* 15.49-52):

> "Benedetto sia tu," fu, "trino e uno,
> che nel mio seme se' tanto cortese!"
> E seguì: "Grato e lontano digiuno,
> tratto leggendo del magno volume,
> du' non si muta mai bianco né bruno"

The ancestor's blessing is quite patently addressed to the Blessed Trinity, God in three Persons – Father, Son, and Holy Spirit – who has shown favor to Dante. It is likewise manifest that the "great volume" he has been reading is a metaphor for the immutable decrees of Divine Providence, a metaphor based on the Book of Life spoken of in Revelation 12.1.

As with the voices singing "'resurgi' e 'vinci'" upon Dante's entering Mars, his ancestor's first intelligible words may hold another meaning. After Dante reports hearing things too deep for him to understand, the "three and one" his ancestor blesses and the "great volume" he has read may refer not only to the Trinity and to God's Book of Life but also to Dante's *Comedy* itself. Dante's poem, one work divided into three canticles, is indeed "three and one," and it shows favor to Dante in bringing him from the dark wood thus far to the heaven of Mars. The "great volume" his ancestor has been reading is the book that traces the journey up to this point, the book wherein the author has ordered everything aright, where "black and white are never changed."

Dante's as yet unnamed ancestor is thus a character within the very book he has been reading who plays his own part in his descendant's "great volume...three and one." Who is this person, and what does he have to tell Dante? At his ancestor's invitation to Dante to "proclaim his will and longing" that he desires to satisfy, Dante makes three requests, each one briefly formulated and in turn answered at some length.

Dante first wishes to know the name of his ancestor. The answer occupies the remaining 61 lines of Canto 15, lines 88 to 148. The reply opens with a further greeting in which there are echoes of biblical passages associating Dante with no less a figure than Christ himself: "O you, my branch, in whom I took delight even awaiting you, I am your root" (*Par.* 15.88-89). ["O fronda mia in che io compiacemmi pur aspettando, io fui la tua radice"]. The greeting incorporates words first found in Isaiah 42.1 and spoken by the heavenly voice at the Baptism of Christ. Only much later, at line 135, does he answer Dante's question. He is, he says, Dante's great-great-grandfather, Cacciaguida.

Why Dante chose to meet this particular ancestor of his, about whom so little is otherwise known, may become clear from Dante's second request: to learn of his family's history and of Florence in earlier times. Cacciaguida's reply, which he gives "not in modern speech," occupies the greater part of Canto 16, from lines 34 to 154, and is delivered without interruption. After a convoluted account of the date of his birth couched in astronomical calculations (assumed to be A.D. 1091), Cacciaguida goes on to speak of his life as a warrior in the Crusades and to give a glowing account of the good old days of Florence by contrast with the bad days of Dante's own time. There is just enough time elapsed between the two kin to make the contrast stand out to good effect for Dante's purpose.

At the beginning of Canto 17, Beatrice encourages Dante to make known "the flame of [your] desire" (*Par.* 17.7-8). [la vampa/ del tuo disio]. Dante thereupon voices his third request: to know of his fortune in days to come. Cacciaguida, "hidden yet revealed" (*Par.* 17.36) [chiuso e parvente] replies "in clear and precise words" (*Par.* 17.34) [per chiare parole e con preciso] what Dante will undergo in the course of his exile from Florence, urging him to be "a party unto himself." Before Cacciaguida has finished telling of Dante's fortune, Dante interrupts his discourse to tell the reader of his *Comedy* that Cacciaguida "told things beyond belief even for those who will yet see them" (*Par.* 17.93-94). [e disse cose/ incredibili a quei che fier presente].

Dante then tells his forebear of his fear that, if he loses Florence, "the place most dear" [se loco m'è tolto più caro], he may "also lose the rest through what

[my] poems say" (Par. 17.110-111). [io non perdessi li altri per miei carmi"].
Dante adds that he fears that "if [he] is a timid friend of truth," he may "lose
[his] life among those who will call this present, ancient times" (Par. 17.118-
120). [e s'io al vero son timido amico,/ temo de perder viver tra coloro/ che
questtempo chiameranno antico].

In the remaining lines of Canto 17, Cacciaguida answers Dante's fear with
precise instructions on what Dante ought to do in his poem and what effect it
will have (*Par.* 17.130-135). In part, he tells him,

> For if, at the first taste, your words molest,
> they will, when they have been digested, end
> as living nourishment. As does the wind,
> so shall your outcry do – the wind that sends its roughest blows
> against the highest peaks;
> that is no little cause for claiming honor.[3]

Given what Cacciaguida has told Dante to do and what Dante does in his *Comedy*, the ancestor Dante chose to reveal his offspring's destiny is not only well
chosen but is indeed rightly named, for he is literally the "guide of the hunt."

As I have argued elsewhere, the Greyhound that will come to hunt the she-
wolf back into hell, according to Virgil's prophecy in *Inferno* 1.100-111, may be
Dante's poem itself.[4] Cacciaguida, who reveals to Dante his poetic mission at
the heart of *Paradiso*, is the guide to that hunt that is accomplished within and
by Dante's poem. He is as well a reader of the volume that is hunting down the
she-wolf and thereby saving low-lying Italy.

In this poetic achievement may lie the true cause for Dante himself being
hailed in the two words of the hymn he heard upon entering Mars, "'Resurgi' e
'Vinci'." Perhaps this is one of the "things beyond belief even for those who
will yet see them" that Dante heard Cacciaguida tell of.

Such a conception of himself and of his poem makes Dante appear bold. He
himself hints at his boldness when he says, just after telling of the words he
heard the warriors sing, "My words may seem presumptuous" (Par. 14.130).
[Forse la mia parola par troppo osà] because, he says, he dared to hold the words
he heard more dear than the smile of Beatrice. But, as we have seen, Dante's
true boldness goes further than the explanation he gives here.

I end by noting that the Italian addition to the beatitude the pilgrim hears in
Purgatorio 15.39 – "Godi, tu que vinci!" – is an abridgement in the singular of
what Jesus states in the Sermon on the Mount as the confirmation of all the beatitudes: "Blessed are you when men revile you and persecute you and utter all
kinds of evil against you falsely on my account. Rejoice and be glad, for your
reward in heaven is great" (Matthew 5.11-12).

Christ's blessing of the persecuted is absent from the beatitudes Dante hears
on the terraces of *Purgatorio*. Though he will suffer exile from Florence, the
poet of the *Comedy* will escape persecution of another, more profound kind. No
one will speak ill of him, persecute him, or lie about him on account of Christ.

Rather, Dante's position as supreme Christian poet is recognized by many among his readers, "never perhaps...as it is today."[5]

Notes

1 "E questa cotale figura in rettorica è molto laudabile, e anco necessaria, cioè quando le parole sono a una persona e la 'ntenzione è a un'altra" (184).
2 "O blood of mine – o the celestial grace/ bestowed beyond all measure – unto whom/ as unto you was Heaven's gate twice opened?"
3 "Ché se la voce tua sarà molesta
    nel primo gusto, vital nodrimento
    lascerà poi, quando sarà digesta.
    Questo tuo grido farà come vento,
    che le più alte cime più percuote;
    e ciò non fa d'onor poco argomento."
4 See Marc A. LePain, "'Tra feltro e feltro': Whence Dante's Greyhound?"
5 Pope Benedict XV, *In Praeclara Summorum*, par. 1.

Works Cited

The New Oxford Annotated Bible with the Apocrypha (RSV). New York: Oxford UP, 1977.

Dante Alighieri. *Divine Comedy*. Trans. Allen Mandelbaum with Italian text. New York: Bantam, 1982-1986.

---. *Convivio*. Milano: Garzanti Editore, 1987. English trans. Richard Lansing. 1998. <<http://dante.ilt.columbia.edu/books/convivi/>> Accessed Feb. 20, 2010.

LePain, Marc A. "'Tra feltro e feltro': Whence Dante's Greyhound?" In *Gladly to Learn And Gladly to Teach: Essays on Religion and Political Philosophy in Honor of Ernest L. Fortin and A.A. Lanham*. Eds. Michael Foley and Douglas Kries. MD: Lexington, 2002: 71-81.

Pope Benedict XV. *In Praeclara Summorum: Encyclical of Pope Benedict XV on Dante to Professors and Students of Literature and Learning in the Catholic World*. April 30, 1921. <<www.vatican.va/holy_father/ benedict_xv/encyclicals/documents/hf_ben_xv_enc_30041921_in _pracelara_summorum_en.html. >> Accessed Feb. 20, 2010.

Art and Revolution in the Images of Francisco Goya

Diana Wylie
Boston University

Francisco Goya refused to answer the question "who are we?" in a partisan or politically correct way. The way in which he refused is a measure of his greatness. His most probing paintings set our imaginations free. They challenge us to let go of conventional ideas about "who we *think* we are" and "who we *ought* to be."

This argument – that while Goya was revolutionary in his technique and in his ability to get people to look at themselves in new ways, he was not a partisan political artist – flies in the face of a lot of received wisdom. People often see contempt, for example, in the way he painted the less than beautiful faces of King Carlos IV's family. They suggest, wrongly, I think, that Goya intended to lampoon a monarch who was, in fact, his friend and whose patronage he was delighted to receive. Even his own words sometimes foster the impression that his purposes were didactic. Underneath his etching *The Sleep of Reason,* he wrote, "The author dreaming. His only purpose is to *banish harmful ideas commonly believed....*" It is true that he did produce some images critiquing ideas – like faith in witchcraft or respect for the Inquisition – that he considered "harmful." But the great body of his work reflected his *Ilustrado* or Enlightenment sympathies without forcing them on the viewer.

We have only to look at his *Colossus* (c. 1810) and compare it with Boris Kustodiev's 1920 painting *Bolshevik* to see how much liberty he allowed the viewer's imagination. Kustodiev's colossus strides through the streets of Moscow waving a colossal red banner above the masses at his feet. He projects a heroic image of the common man; the painting lauds the erasure of individuality. In contrast, Goya's giant wades through a landscape where refugees and cattle are fleeing every which way. Goya does not bother to specify whether this huge man embodies the valiant spirit of the victims or the human beast whose slow thighs are churning up all their trouble. The painting laments those moments in history when panic-stricken people have to flee.

Beyond expressing compassion for the creatures struggling toward safety, Goya has left the viewer's imagination free. We know only from the date that the refugees were victims of battles set off by Napoleon's invasion of Spain in 1808. Even his most famous war painting – *The Third of May, 1808* – avoids being overly explicit about the identity of the shooters and their victims. The faceless men with guns wear uniforms, and the men about to die do not. But the painting's power does not rest on knowing that the killers are French.

Did Goya never rant? Or does he belong in the ranks of many of our core authors, even the satirists among them, who indulged occasionally in partisan attacks, letting their tone of ironic distance drop briefly in order to hammer a worldly enemy? Jonathan Swift, for example, dropped his satirical tone at the end of *Gulliver's Travels* in order to rant against the "execrable Crew of Butchers" that set up *"modern Colon[ies]"* (Swift 269). Some of Goya's *Los Caprichos* etchings do share in the savagely satirical spirit of Swift or Rabelais, as when he depicts cannibalistic monks, their faces a repulsive cross between death's heads and pigs' heads. Most of his anti-Inquisition paintings, though, were illustrations of practices – judging heretics, flagellating believers – and not a condemnation of individuals. Goya rarely ranted in paint. He mainly painted predicaments.

Why was Goya's vision so lacking in explicit partisanship? The answer to this question may lie partly in his situation as court painter in revolutionary times. He was torn between, on the one hand, the demands of patronage and his personal liking for some of those patrons, especially the monarchs Carlos III and IV, and, on the other hand, the ideals, which he evidently shared, of his *ilustrado* friends. Crosscutting this tension was Spanish patriotism, intensified by the French invasion. That France had given birth to many *ilustrado* ideals complicated Spain's political drama beyond any easy partisan reading of the stakes and the actors. It was Goya's good fortune as an artist, and his misfortune as a citizen, to be living at a time when simple or doctrinaire political stands were belied by the sheer complexity of the political landscape.

Goya's own temperament probably contributed to his failure to produce partisan art. His images suggest that he was interested above all in human nature. He recognized that people can be vastly more than the social roles they play. He was able to paint with compassion the various moods of the Countess of Chinchon – wistful, amused, frail, grand – as she sat pregnant with her detested husband's child. He captured the playful light in the eyes of Carlos IV's small son as he stood with the rest of the royal family, utterly uninterested in their glitter. He was even able to paint probing and appreciative portraits of some members of the clergy.

How is Goya's art likely to affect our students? I suspect his early art – his cartoons, like *The Parasol*, drawn for royal tapestries – meld very well with their preoccupations and our culture. Many of his portraits – the Duchess of Alba and whoever the naked and clothed Maja was – are analogous to contemporary celebrity portraits. They are flattering pictures of beautiful and desirable people. *The Parasol* could pass muster as an advertisement for...parasols.

To move to twenty-first-century political terrain: how is Goya's refusal to paint ideologically revolutionary art likely to affect our students, that is, young people growing up in a less politicized age than the Cold War that produced us, their professors? We have not seen combat on our soil since the Civil War, and there has not been a draft since 1973. Do Goya's war pictures mean anything at all to our students? What do they really make of the terrifying *Disasters of War* etchings? During a recent core lecture, trying to make the point that Goya was a precursor of brutally honest war photography, I asked students to name an image of war that had stuck in their mind's eye. I had expected people would mention the photograph of a napalmed child in Vietnam, and one did. Another student surprised me. She mentioned a scene from *Forrest Gump*.

This answer provoked me to ask myself a lot of questions. Was it a sign of her great distance from scenes of extreme social disorder, like ones Goya depicted, that are going on daily elsewhere in the world? Does her recourse to a Hollywood film to name a war image suggest that she is at some level detached or even unaware of the nature of our actual national involvement or complicity in such scenes? Why is there no great Iraqi war photography? Has a highly technological and censored war made it difficult for her and her peers to acknowledge our capacity to commit atrocities, if the conditions are right? Do many Americans – like Britons in the late nineteenth century – need to believe that they are "not only a superpower, but also a virtuous, striving and devoted people," and so our minds reflexively block perceptions of contrary messages? (Colley 303).

I do not propose to answer these troubling questions here, but rather to ask whether studying Goya's images might help such students see "who we are" or "can be" as a species and as a nation. Does Goya have the capacity to provoke revolutionary thinking in our students, not in the sense of partisanship but in the sense of broadening their conceptions of war and human nature? I will give two possible answers, one dark and one light. A pessimistic response would suggest that painted or etched images no longer have the power to create or break down ideas about human nature because our students' eyes and sensibilities have been captured by photography, whether documentary or fictional. The power of visual images to revolutionize thinking seems to have been taken over by photography and, apparently, by Hollywood. Perhaps our students are, in addition, so inundated with both images and tasks that no single picture merits much attention in their world. Individual images have been devalued by their sheer quantity. Their world encourages them to multi-task rather than to linger. It requires more time and imagination to absorb the messages of a painting than those of a photograph.

A more optimistic view would argue that the act of lingering over core texts, in this case Goya's paintings, does indeed have revolutionary potential in two ways. First, Goya's work, because of its non-doctrinaire empathy, can stimulate acts of imagination that transcend the present and connect us with familiarity to events in the past. He can help create a sense of compassionate sympathy across time.

Secondly, he can instill a complex vision of what we are. If we linger over his images and actually concentrate on them, we may begin to recognize ourselves and our capacities for self-delusion (his portrait of Manuel Godoy, *Prince of Peace*), dissipation (his portrait of his son Javier), brutality (*Disasters of War*), as well as fear (*The Third of May, 1808*), intelligence and intellectual integrity (the portraits of Gaspar de Jovellanos and Sebastian Martinez), bravery (the *Disasters* again), the values and pride of both privileged and under-classes (the paintings of the royal family and blacksmiths). Goya had a gargantuan repertoire. Along with his marked empathy came his fearlessness in confronting the dark side of our species. His fearlessness in encountering darkness and in giving it an unusual immediacy can still move us, if we linger long enough in front of his images.

How does Goya help our students answer the question "who are we"? The revolution to which Goya can give rise is not a political one but one of perspective. He can help us see that we are beings who can be made to imagine that we may not be who we think we are.

Works Cited

Colley, Linda. *Captives: The Story of Britain's Pursuit of Empire and How its Soldiers and Civilians Were Held Captive by the Dream of Global Supremacy, 1600-1850.* New York: Pantheon, 2002.

Swift, Jonathan. *Gulliver's Travels.* London: Penguin, 2003.

Incorporating Eastern Texts into a Western Core: Teaching the *Tao Te Ching* in Conversation with Wallace Stevens

Julie Steward
Samford University

In 1997, Samford University established a freshman-year interdisciplinary humanities course called Cultural Perspectives. In the first semester of the course, instructors teach a list of common texts, including "The Allegory of the Cave," *Antigone*, *The Prince*, and *King Lear*. However, we have also built enough flexibility into the course that faculty can weave in texts that reflect their own specializations and interests. Personally, I build CP 101 around the theme of knowledge and enlightenment. Like most faculty, I begin the semester with Plato, introducing students to Greek origins of Western thought by setting up questions such as: What is the nature of reality? What is truth and how do we arrive at it? I spend a week on "The Allegory of the Cave," but then I move from the West immediately to the East and spend the next week on the *Tao Te Ching* in order to compare more effectively Western and Eastern ways of looking at the world.

Oftentimes the *Tao Te Ching* is taught in core courses as a political text. For example, in Lee A. Jacobus's anthology *A World of Ideas*, Lao-tzu is grouped with Machiavelli, Jefferson, and Thoreau as a thinker who addresses the issue of social order versus individual liberty. For my course, however, the *Tao Te Ching* works best as a philosophical text that not only offers a different perspective on the fundamental nature of reality, but also serves as an instruction manual for what Taoists call "following the natural order."

While there are many excellent renditions of the *Tao Te Ching*, the specific translation I assign is by Taoist Master John Bright-Fey. I have chosen this translation because it most clearly communicates the fact that the *Tao Te Ching* is a *living* text. As Bright-Fey explains in his introduction:

> [No previous translations of the *Tao Te Ching*] reflect the perspective of a practicing Taoist initiated into the mystic tradition – that is, until now. The *Tao Te Ching* you are about to read comes from the secret oral tradition of the *T'ien-Shih* or "Celestial Masters" sect of Taoism that combines elements of both the philosophic and religious schools. Also known as the *Wu-tou-mi-Tao* ("Five Pecks of Rice School"), this sect maintains a private body of arcane Taoist rituals, meditation techniques, and mystic literature. Initiates in this school are charged with maintaining a continuous link with Lao-tzu himself in order that the authentic Taoist wisdom of the past will always be available in the present. (6)

I explain to the students that Bright-Fey inherited the text via an oral tradition, yet his memorization and subsequent translation of the text is secondary to the fact that the *Tao Te Ching* is as alive today as it was during its composition roughly 2,600 years ago. This is crucial because one of our tasks in core classes is to impress upon students the relevance of ancient texts to our contemporary moment. If we can get students to view a text like the *Tao Te Ching* as something other than hopelessly alien to their own experience, then we can sharpen their ability to think critically across historical eras and deepen their understanding of themselves and the world. To this end, when I begin the course with Plato, I pair "The Allegory of the Cave" with the film *The Truman Show*. Then, to illuminate and illustrate Lao-tzu, I pair selected chapters from the *Tao Te Ching* with poems by Wallace Stevens. Yes, Wallace Stevens is a far cry from Jim Carrey, and while it might seem that modern poetry would only muddy the waters even further, especially for the poetry-phobic in the class, my aim is to show students that these ancient Chinese ideas have been taken up again and again throughout the centuries and across the globe.

With only a week to spend on this unit, the central idea I try to get across is that the ancient Taoists saw the world as alive, as a play of energetic forces constantly in flux. The previous week in class, we discuss Plato's unchanging, essential Forms. Now we shift our focus to a world constantly renewing itself, but instead of reaching for a perfection found elsewhere or striving to control dynamism and change, Taoists try to live in harmony with the environment. The key is to discover and cultivate an authenticity that enables us to live within the rhythms of life, not against them, to behold the external world with our whole being so that it becomes part of us and we of it. Ultimately, to understand without, we have to look within.

I ask the students to read the entirety of the text, but the chapters I focus on in class are 13-16, 33, 37, 47, 57, and 71. I choose these because they speak to the idea, as Chapter 13 puts it, that "if you view the unlimited world as the self/

then you can be trusted with it/ because only people who sees the world as themselves/ and their self as the world/ will take care of it" (23). Chapter 33 states simply, "Learn to understand the outside world by looking inward/ and you will access true and authentic wisdom" (65). Chapter 37 elaborates further: "this is how you transform yourself/ by anchoring yourself amid the flow/of a sea of life force/ by tranquilly sitting between heaven and earth/ by turning around and listening to your soul" (76). Chapter 71 affirms, "all the knowledge of the universe can be sensed at the corner of your senses/ locked away inside each and every cell of your bodymind" (132). In Chapter 47, the ancient child defines knowledge in a way far different from what the students encountered with Plato: "to know the world is not to think into it by reason/ reason is not revelation/ to know the world is to allow the world to think into you" (94). Contrary to pure reason, the *Tao Te Ching* offers guidelines for cultivation. Chapter 16 provides instruction for standing meditation, and Chapter 57 speaks to the importance of *doing,* although "action" and "doing" are paradoxically defined by "doing nothing."

The paradoxical, even mystical, nature of the *Tao Te Ching* calls perhaps most urgently for some kind of further illustration, and this is where Wallace Stevens enters the course. When we discuss Chapter 14, we focus specifically on the description of awakening: "look all around yourself deliberately and attempt to see the nothing that is/ deliberately all around yourself" (24). At this point, we turn to one of Stevens's most famous poems, "The Snow Man," which concludes with the lines: "For the listener, who listens in the snow,/ And, nothing himself, beholds/ Nothing that is not there and the nothing that is" (ll. 13-15). In Chapter 15, Lao-tzu describes wise men as seeming "distant and removed yet present and intrigued as they gave their fullest attention to observe the smallest of happenings" (l. 26). This description parallels the creative consciousness Stevens describes in the opening lines: "One must have a mind of winter/ to regard the frost and the boughs/ of the pine-trees crusted with snow" (l. 1-3). The mind must be able to apprehend its environment without controlling or embellishing: "not to think/ Of any misery in the sound of the wind" (ll. 7-8). As the poem moves from the specificity of such images as "junipers shagged with ice" (l. 5) to broader descriptions of a "bare place" (l. 12), Stevens allows for a changing world larger than the one we can anthropomorphize, one both filled and empty – what Lao-tzu calls a formless form, what Stevens calls "the nothing that is" (l. 15). Ultimately, the mind becomes one with the scene it perceives.

Stevens is a poet chiefly concerned with how the mind interacts with the external world. "The Snow Man" dramatizes Lao-tzu's wise man in Chapter 15, one who beholds the world with his own being so that it becomes part of him and vice versa. Then, in order to emphasize the importance of connecting with the natural world even further, I have the students read "Arrival at the Waldorf." If Chapter 57 urges, "mindfully chip away at your life to see what is inside," then the addressee in Stevens's poem is precisely the person who needs this advice. Stevens is speaking to one "home from Guatemala back at the Waldorf" (l. 1). Once separated from the natural world, words supersede lived experience:

"the wild poem is a substitute/ For the woman one loves or ought to love/ One wild rhapsody a fake for another" (ll. 3-6). Disconnected from the Tao, the man at the Waldorf tries to limit and control his world through proclamation. He says, "The world in a verse/ A generation sealed, men remoter than mountains,/ Women invisible in music and motion and color" (ll. 9-11). He does not have a "mind of winter." He cannot behold what *is* there, and he certainly has no ability to apprehend "the nothing that is." Stevens's scorn comes in the last line as though he were shaking his head at a man who once was connected to the universe: "After that alien, point-blank, green, and actual Guatemala" (l. 12). This is the world the *Tao Te Ching* describes, one that is alien, point-blank, green, and actual. Guatemala becomes a metaphor for the possibility of connection with the Tao and the cost of refusal.

In many ways, these two poems by Stevens illustrate Taoist principles and, at the same time, present students with similar challenges in reading and comprehension. Entering poetry through poetry might, paradoxically, be the clearest way to understand what is by nature perfectly knowable…and largely unknowable at the same time.

Works Cited

Lao-tzu. *Tao Te Ching*. Trans. John Bright-Fey. Birmingham: Sweetwater, 2004.

Stevens, Wallace. *The Palm at the End of the Mind: Selected Poems and a Play*. New York: Vintage, 1972.